Just a Few
LINES

LETTERS HOME FROM WORLD WAR 2

ARTHUR L. JOHNSON

Copyright © 2021 by Arthur L Johnson

Just a Few Lines: Letters Home from World War 2

All rights reserved. No part of this publication may be reproduced, distributed, or transmitted in any form or by any means, including photocopying, recording, or other electronic or mechanical methods, without the prior written permission of the publisher, except in the case of brief quotations embodied in critical reviews and certain other noncommercial uses permitted by copyright law.

Although the author and publisher have made every effort to ensure that the information in this book was correct at press time, the author and publisher do not assume and hereby disclaim any liability to any party for any loss, damage, or disruption caused by errors or omissions, whether such errors or omissions result from negligence, accident, or any other cause.

Neither the author nor the publisher assumes any responsibility or liability whatsoever on behalf of the consumer or reader of this material. Any perceived slight of any individual or organization is purely unintentional.

Cover Design by 100Covers.com
Interior Design by FormattedBooks.com

CONTENTS

CHAPTER 1 — A BOX OF LETTERS 1
    Pulling a letter from the box 1
    Family Tree 2
    The US enters the war 5
    V-Mail 6
    The Letters 7
    A final note before we begin 9

CHAPTER 2 — 1942 11
    December 1941 11
    March 1942 11
    April - May 1942 12
    June 1942 20
    July 1942 26
    August 36
    September 47
    October 60
    November 79
    December 89

CHAPTER 3 — 1943 99

    January 99

    February 105

    March 108

    April 112

    May 116

    June 118

    July 122

    August 125

    September 130

    October 136

    November 142

    December 150

CHAPTER 4 — 1944 159

    January 159

    February 164

    March 175

    April 185

    May 193

    June 201

    July 208

    August 215

    September 226

    October 228

    November 235

    December 240

CHAPTER 5 — 1945 249

    January 249

    February 257

    March 261

    April 271

    May 280

    June 288

    July 297

    August 304

    September 309

CHAPTER 6 — CLOSING THE BOX OF LETTERS 313

    Photos 316

    Author's Note 326

CHAPTER 1

A BOX OF LETTERS

PULLING A LETTER FROM THE BOX

> Postcard Postmark November 25, 1940, Arlington
> Mr. Henry Franklin
> Gretna, Virginia
>
> Dear Pa,
>
> Got home Sunday, 5:30. Made the trip fine. Had a fine time. Will write you a letter.
>
> Gilbert

The above was written on a picture postcard of the Masonic Temple in Alexandria, Virginia, sent by my granduncle Gilbert to my great-grandfather, the Monday after Thanksgiving, 1940. Gilbert had just returned to his home in Arlington, Virginia, after spending Thanksgiving weekend at his parents' home in Gretna, Virginia. World War II had been raging in Europe for over a year now, but the US had not yet entered. It would be a full year until the attacks on Pearl Harbor. I came into possession of this and roughly six hundred other letters after my maternal grandmother passed in 1997.

While cleaning out her house, we found a box of letters among her possessions. I began pulling out random letters, as they were not in any order, and discovered they were letters from all three of her brothers sent home during WWII. Uncle Herman was the oldest and stayed stateside. Next was Uncle Gilbert, who was in the European Theater, while the youngest uncle, Ernest, was in the Pacific. Mom did not know why Uncle Herman stayed in the states, but I eventually found the answer in the letters.

You can learn a lot from letters—including the answer to long-standing family stories and rumors. I hear stories of friends and coworkers helping clean out their grandparents' or parents' houses after death and throwing out boxes of communications—letters, cards, notes, journals. What history was just lost?

While reaching in for another letter, I came across two scraps of paper from 1944. They were drafts of telegrams. The first was to Uncle Gilbert, stating that letters were forthcoming and to wait until he received my grandmother's letter before doing anything. The second was to the chaplain of Uncle Gilbert's unit, asking that he reach out to Gilbert, as he was not a religious man and would not reach out to the chaplain on his own. There was a story in these letters, and though it was still fuzzy to me at the time, I could tell it was a story that needed telling.

I sorted and scanned the letters. During this process, my mother informed me that her cousin had another batch, the letters that were sent to my great-grandparents. I contacted her, and she sent them to me, bringing the total to roughly the six hundred mentioned. I then scanned those letters, which added to the story. The picture became clearer, letter by letter, line by line.

Still later, my mother gave me more of Gilbert's possessions, among which was the letter that the telegram above foretold. I now had all the pieces of the puzzle, and it was time to put them together and let the letters tell their story.

FAMILY TREE

Before we begin, we first need to make clear the cast of characters. Below is an abbreviated family tree that includes all the family members mentioned in the letters, starting from my great-grandparents.

Henry and Virginia Franklin lived in southwestern Virginia in a town called Gretna. They had six children: Herman Blake was the oldest, then, Gilbert Charlie, Bessie Virginia, Gladys Lucy, Elizabeth Susan, and Ernest

Harris. Herman and Bessie, my maternal grandmother, were the only two married at the time of the war, and Bessie was the only one with children: my mother, Cynthia Ann Conlon, and my uncle, Frederick Michael Conlon—though we always called him Uncle Michael. Below is an abbreviated family tree with their birth year and age in June 1942 if available.

Henry B. Franklin (b.1876 age 66) m. Virginia M Shelton (Jennie) (b.1885 age 57)

Children of Henry and Virginia
- Herman B. Franklin (b.1906 age 36) m. Calendra (Cleo) Pachuilo (b.1907 age 35)
- Gilbert C. Franklin (b.1907 age 35) m. Mary Elizabeth Simmons (Jimmie)
- Bessie V. Franklin (b.1911 age 31) m. Frederick J. Conlon (Fred) (b.1908 age 34)
    Children of Bessie and Fred
    - Cynthia Ann Conlon (b.1935 age 6) m. Arthur L. Johnson (b.1935)
        Children of Cynthia and Arthur
        - Arthur L. Johnson, Jr. (author) (b.1960)
    - Frederick Michael Conlon (Mikey) (b.1940 age 2)
- Gladys L. Franklin (b.1913 age 29)
- Elizabeth S. Franklin (b.1916 age 26) m. James Walter Mayhew (b.1915 age 27)
- Ernest H. Franklin (Ebo) (b.1920 age 22)

ARTHUR L. JOHNSON

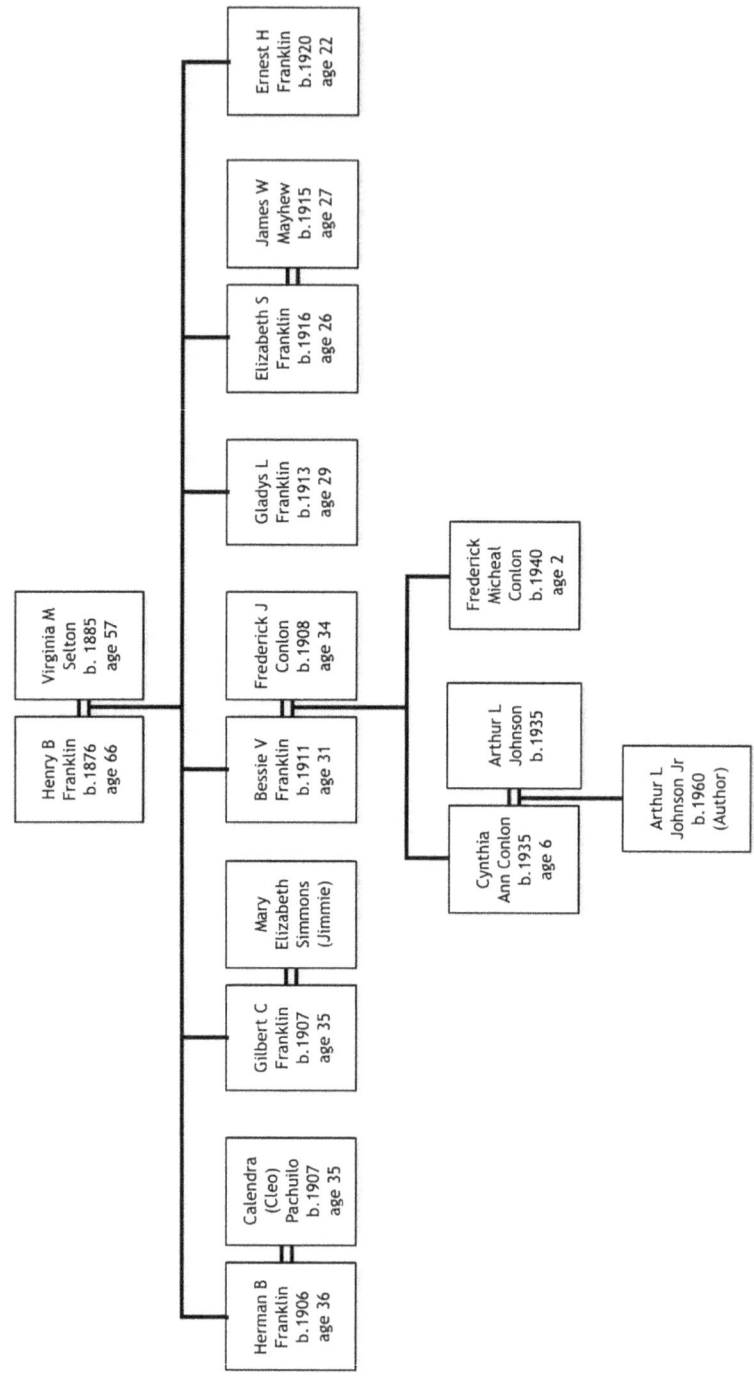

There will be others mentioned in the letters. Warren Franklin is the nephew of my great-grandfather, Henry. Anyone mentioned in the letters with the last names of Franklin or Shelton are extended family of some sort. Pete Conlon is Fred Conlon's nephew. The rest of the people mentioned, if a relationship is not stated in the narrative, are family friends or neighbors.

Just before the war started, Uncle Herman was living in East Reading, Pennsylvania. Uncle Gilbert was living in Arlington County, Virginia, though I don't know where. He was working as a plumber/steamfitter.

Because of the Depression, my grandparents rented out their house in Clarendon, Virginia, and were living in Miller School, Virginia, where my grandfather had a job as a steamfitter. By the end of 1942, they would be back in Clarendon, as the need for steamfitters in the Washington D.C. area were in demand with everyone off to war.

The rest of the Franklins lived in either Gretna or Danville, Virginia.

THE US ENTERS THE WAR

The Second World War officially began when Germany invaded Poland on September 1, 1939. Most Americans were not interested in another European war, but after France fell in 1940, many believed it was just a matter of time before the US entered the war. Congress passed the Selective Training and Service Act on September 16, 1940. If the US had not entered the war by October 1941, they would release the men they had recruited. They required men ages twenty-one to thirty-six to register.

With the Depression still ongoing, life in the Army with a guaranteed paycheck was better than civilian life. In 1941, however, Congress barely passed an extension to eighteen months of service before being released. The attack on Pearl Harbor on December 7, 1941, changed that. Congress altered the enlistment period for the duration of the war.

Herman was the first of the brothers to enter the Army when he enlisted on March 15, 1941. The enlistment record shows he joined in Harrisburg, Pennsylvania, where he was living with his wife and was a salesperson. He had attended three years of high school. Herman was thirty-four at the time of his enlistment. As the war broke out before his year or eighteen months were up, he was in for the duration.

Ernest could not register in 1940, as he was only twenty and not required. However, he registered in 1941 and was drafted shortly after that. His enlistment date was April 24, 1942 in Fort Meade, Maryland. He was listed as a single with no dependents.

Gilbert registered in 1940 as well, but he was not drafted until May 22, 1942, at Fort Myers, Virginia. He, too, was listed as a single with no dependents.

Although my grandfather was the same age as Gilber, he was given a deferral several times from the draft. He lost the tip of his thumb and two fingers at the first knuckle on his left hand as a child, playing with blasting caps in an unattended construction site. This deemed him unfit for service.

V-MAIL

"The Post Office, War, and Navy Departments realize fully that frequent and rapid communication with parents, associates, and other loved ones strengthens fortitude, enlivens patriotism, makes loneliness endurable, and inspires to even greater devotion the men and women who are carrying on our fight far from home and friends. We know that the good effect of expeditious mail service on those of us at home is immeasurable" (Annual Report to the Postmaster-General, 1942).

Even before the war—as early as 1938—the postal service started preparations for emergency mail service. After four years of planning, on June 15, 1942, the Post Office official announced the service with the War and Navy Departments. They called it V-Mail, or Victory-Mail, and it followed Great Britain's Airgraph (airmail) service and integrated microfilm technology.

You would write your letter on an eight-and-one-half-inch by eleven-inch paper that was both stationary and envelope in one. If the soldier was in the European theater, it went to New York. The letter was sent to San Francisco if the soldier was in the Pacific. A censor opened the letter, reviewed it to ensure no vital information was disclosed, then microfilmed it. One hundred fifty thousand standard pieces of mail would take thirty-two sacks and weigh over two thousand pounds. One hundred fifty thousand one-page V-Mail letters microfilmed would be on several rolls of film in one mail sack, weighing only forty-five pounds. Converting the mail in this way saved room for war supplies and equipment going over. Once there, they would print the letters on a smaller sheet of paper and distribute them. The process was the same for the return from the soldier home. The soldiers also had pre-printed greeting cards available with cartoons and an area for the soldier to add a personal message.

Because the end document was small, you were to write legibly, and they discouraged small lettering as it was illegible when printed. V-Mail was not mandatory, but they encouraged it. In the batch of letters I have, some are standard, and others are the printed V-Mail.

THE LETTERS

I had the documents transcribed for ease of reading the best as could be deciphered. The letters span the full length of the war. They have misspellings, grammatical errors, and run-on sentences. I have left these mostly intact, but have added some punctuation to help make them a little more readable. All the original letters are in the Library of Congress' Veterans History Project.

The letters were first scanned and named by date, who from, and who to. The file naming convention allowed for ease in ordering the letters, but not all the letters were dated. Some would say only, "Sunday Night." If the envelope with a readable postmark was available, I referred to a calendar for the year and chose the Sunday before the postmark.

However, some letters did not have envelopes. For these, I had to do some detective work. I would use the content and compare it with similar letters, and a possible date was determined through these contextual clues. If a letter was not dated and based on postmark or some contents of the letter (i.e., "Thanksgiving Night,") the date is in parentheses like so: (Nov 26, 1942). If an exact date cannot be determined, it is placed in the best location that could be identified, and noted as such.

There are places in the letter where words could not be deciphered. The men in the field did not always have a desk or table to write on. This led to some illegible handwriting. Some letters were damaged, either by mice or water over seventy-odd years in storage. If a word could be recognized but was in doubt, it is in brackets with question marks [?in-doubt word/phrase?] If it could not be read at all, it is [ILLEGIBLE]. In one case, it is marked by a dash for each letter unable to decipher. The reason is with the letter.

As mentioned, the letters contain long, run-on sentences with bad grammar and spelling, making the letters hard to read. It was as if the punctuation had faded over the years. Or, because of their mindset at the time, they did not think about it. Although this does show the mental state of the writer—a tired, worried, homesick soldier—I felt the content was more important than strict adherence to original punctuation. Therefore, I performed some minor edits for readability. Some sentences had a capitalized word in the middle, so I hypothesized that they meant a sentence break. I also ran the documents through a grammar checker to help with other long sentences.

I did not correct all the grammar errors, as this gives the letters a touch of humanity—the letters are written how they spoke. I did the same with the spelling. However, if a word was consistently misspelled but phonetically correct, I used the correct spelling. I also corrected words that would be spelled correctly in one letter and incorrectly in another, or within the same letter. Others, I left because it was the way they spoke. They were just good old boys from southwestern Virginia.

Uncle Ernest was "relly" [really] hot in the south Pacific. He also used the most slang and colloquialisms. Uncle Gilbert's spelling improved over time for the most part—though he had trouble with the word "cigarette." With him being a supply sergeant, he eventually got it correct. I left the earlier misspellings so you can see this change. He also liked to put a "t" before the letters "ch." It was as if that was how he spoke, so I left them: "mutch" and "sutch."

None of the grammar checkers knew what to do with Uncle Herman's 1940s slang. Everything was "swell" with him. They all said it was a misspelling and wanted to either drop the "s" in the beginning or add one at the end. Chuckling, I chose to ignore those suggestions.

Not all the letters made it into this version of the book. Because mail could be held going either way as the room was needed for supplies, there were times when one would write every three days, saying the same thing. Although it shows how much their morale depended on the letters from home, this type of repetition does not add to the narrative. In a similar vein, when reading the letters, you feel that some did not get saved or were lost over time. Unfortunately, while I do have six hundred letters, many more remain missing, and so these gaps in the story remain.

With few exceptions, the letters are only one side of the conversation. The brothers did not keep the letters sent to them. With the constant moving around and all the people writing, it would be hard for a soldier to save what could be a couple of books worth of letters. It makes for interesting interpretations at times.

I have also included some letters that are not from or to one of the brothers. They do, however, contain information about one of the brothers or other family members. Some just give another glimpse into the war. These were in the box of letters from my grandmother or among Uncle Gilbert's possessions.

Although the soldiers were not to give their whereabouts, Uncle Gilbert would, on occasion, state what country he was in. This usually occurred in the first letter from the new place, and only occasionally after. Uncle Ernest was more careful. His letters only told of where he had been, usually not where he was writing from at the moment.

I believe one can clearly see the change between 1942 and 1945. The letters showcase little details between training life and life in the battle zones, as well as the effects of emotional stress. To put the letters in context, I have put a paragraph or two explaining what was happening in the world at the time. A timeline, if you will.

A FINAL NOTE BEFORE WE BEGIN

In 1941, the country did not want to go to war—but after Pearl Harbor, we did. Men were drafted, became soldiers, and went off to war. Most were fighting more than one battle: the first being the enemy, the second being the issues of family and life back home.

The movies only show the battles, the decisions made, the men's struggles in the battlefield, maybe a secondary love story. They do not show everything the men were dealing with mentally.

These letters show the other side of the war.

Men faced problems at home, and though these problems may not qualify as a hardship that could exempt them from serving, they were still genuine. The health of a parent, sibling, or dependent, for example. During these family issues, the soldiers could not be there to provide comfort or handle the problems for their family. This weighed on them heavily, as you will soon discover.

Read on, and you will learn something about life in the army during the war.

CHAPTER 2

1942

DECEMBER 1941

The Japanese bomb Pearl Harbor and the US declares war on Japan. The rest of the month includes the countries from the Axis and the US declaring war on each other.

MARCH 1942

American troops land in Nouméa, New Caledonia, an island in the Southwest Pacific. It will become an important staging base for the eventual invasion of Guadalcanal.

ARTHUR L. JOHNSON

POSTCARD POSTMARK MARCH 18, 1942
WASHINGTON, D.C.

Dear Ma,

    Jimmy and I are leaving here Tuesday night and will be down there sometime but don't wait up for us because we might change our minds and come Wednesday morning.

Gilbert

LETTER NO ENVELOPE, NO DATE
(Based on the letter it is before May and Gilbert is still in Arlington, Virginia)

Dear Bessie & Fred,

    I want to write and tell both of you how enjoyed myself and I know Jimmie did. I wish you wasn't so far so we could see each other more too. Made the trip back fine. We didn't get in any rain, but they had a bad storm up here before we got here. Ernest came back yesterday until they could place him. I was glad he came back. Well Bessie, all of you come up to see us. Well, I will tell you again I enjoyed myself.

Gilbert

APRIL – MAY 1942

April sees the Japanese continuing their advance in the Pacific, starting to attack the Philippines and Burma. Both will fall before the month's end. In May, the first big naval battle occurs: the Battle of the Coral Sea. It is a tactical win for the Japanese in the total number of ships sunk, but it is a strategic win for the US, as two Japanese aircraft carriers were forced to return to Japan and would not take part in the Battle of Midway.

Having been in the army a year already, Herman is a Staff Sergeant. Ernest, having been drafted and enlisted on April 24, is at Keesler Field in Mississippi. For Army Air Corp and today's Air Force, a basic tactical unit is called a Flight. A Flight consists of thirty-five to sixty Airmen. Earnest is in Flight 268E and the 400th Technical School Squadron (400TH TCH SCH SQD). As he moves through the years, these will change. Gilbert will enter the Army on May 22.

PVT ERNEST H. FRANKLIN FIGHT 268E 400TH
TCH SCH SQD KEESLER FIELD, MISS.
(May 2, 1942)

Dear Bessie,

Did you ever think I would ever be here in Miss, well I didn't. It is some hot here. I can't say I like it here too well. Will write you a letter soon.

Love Ernest

S/SGT H.B. FRANKLIN, CO. B 51ST MED BN,
CAMP BLANDING, FLA.
Sunday Night, 10 p.m. (May 3, 1942)

Dear Bessie & Fred,

I guess you think I am a fine guy for not writing sooner. But I have had four of my cooks on Furlough at one time and I have been working in the kitchen and believe me it's some hot.

Bessie, I want to thank you for the present again. And the pictures of the kids was swell. Only wish I had two that size and maybe uncle Sam would not have wanted me.

I guess you know I was made Staff Sgt last month. Not doing as bad for the short time I have been in.

The weather is swell down here. I was in swimming all afternoon, and the water was fine.

I had a long letter from Gladys today and one from Cleo. I hope to go to see Cleo this month sometime. But she does not know it. I want to surprise her.

So, I will close for this time.

Love Herman

PVT ERNEST H. FRANKLIN FIGHT 268E 400TH TCH SCH SQD KEESLER FIELD, MISS.
May 6, 1942

Dear Bessie & Fred,

How are you all getting along fine, I hope? This leaves me feeling just fine. Well, I am way down here in Miss. in the Air Core. Given it will be a long time before I can go home again. But I will get back there some day. So far, we have had only about three days drilling we won't get but a very few weeks drilling we won't even have rifle drilling. When we leave here, we don't know where we will go but we will go to some other air base, there we will be assigned some special duty. We will not be in field battle. We get about three weeks drilling here and that all we get. Our duty will be to work around the air base.

Bessie, it is as hot here now as it is at home in July and August. Well, I have gotten my uniform & two shots so far. I just got a letter from home, they told me you were down there Sunday. I guess you carried C. A. home. If so, tell her and Micky I said hello. Bessie, I didn't mean to slight you by not telling you I enjoyed being down to your house when I left but there was so much excitement I just forgot it. But relly [really] I enjoyed being down there even if you didn't have any <u>hot dogs ha ha</u>. Well, what do you think of Gilbert being married? Well, I guess the both of them are better off.

Well, Bessie, they told me you were going to move soon. Be sure and answer this letter before you move, I afraid of that after you get up there, you might forget to wright, ha ha. But laying jokes aside, I hope you like it up there when you get moved, which I am sure you will. Well, Bessie as I haven't much news this time, I will close so the best of luck until I hear from you all.

Love Ernest

My Address Pvt Ernest H. Franklin, Flight 268E, 400th Tech Sch Sqd, Keesler Field. Miss.

PVT ERNEST H. FRANKLIN, FIGHT 268E, 400TH TCH SCH SQD, KEESLER FIELD, MISS.
May 15

Dear Bessie,

I received your letter was more than glad to hear from you. That's all us boys look forward to is getting mail. Bessie I am glad you got moved and hope you like it up there which I know you will.

You asked me if I asked for Mechanic, yes I did but it is no good to ask for anything because they give you just what they want you to have. I haven't been assigned to anything yet. We haft to take our basic training, then we are shipped out to some permanent station. I sure will be glad when this training and the shots are over. Then we won't have it very hard. I just took another shot today, and it sure is sore now. We have about four more to take then we will be through. You asked me about my cap and belt, no I haven't gotten them yet. They will not let us keep them down here. I had to send my hand bag home. They wouldn't even let me keep it. But when we get station, we can have those things, then I am going to get them. You ask if I stayed with Gilbert, no they had only one bed so he and Jimmie had to sleep in it so I stayed down at the lady's house where I used to board. Well, I guess they are really married. As you said she has to put up with a lot. I wrote to you all, and I have heard from everyone but him. But he will soon find out how it helps to get a letter, or I got a letter from home and they said he had to go the 22nd of the month.

Well, Bessie, our company got our first KP duty yesterday. We had to get up at three (3) o'clock in the morning and we didn't get off until eight (8) o'clock at night. 18 hours without stopping and it like to get the best of me. I don't know when we will get it again, but I guess we will get it again next week. It has rained down here just about every day this week. I have never seen it rain so hard. Bessie, I got the money and sure thank you for it. You shouldn't have sent me that much, but I relly appreciate it, and maybe someday I can return it.

Did you go to Washington? I don't guess it will be much traveling this summer as they have cut down on the gas. Do you all expect to take a vacation this summer?

I got a letter from home, and they all seemed to be getting along just fine. Well, Bessie as it is just about time for the whistle to blow, I guess I had better close. This leaves me feeling just fine and hope it finds you all fine. Tell CA, Micky & Fred Hello. So, the best of luck until I hear from you all.

Love Ernest

PVT ERNEST H. FRANKLIN, FIGHT 268E, 400TH TCH SCH SQD, KEESLER FIELD, MISS.
(May 23, 1942)

Dear Bessie,

I just got off guard duty, I had 24 hours of it on 2 off 4. I received the candy. Thanks a lot. I also got your card. Say Bessie since you got moved, were you getting your house fixed? You don't want to get fixed up too much. You might not know me when you see me. I will write you a letter soon.

Love Ernest

PVT ERNEST H. FRANKLIN, FIGHT 268E, 400TH TCH SCH SQD, KEESLER FIELD MISS.
May 28

Dear Bessie & all,

 I will drop you a few lines, would have written before now, but I just haven't had the time. Hope this letter will find you all feeling fine. It leaves me feeling fine, the only thing it sure is hot down here. You should see me. I am beginning to look like a negro. Well, Bessie, I think I told you about being on guard duty. I was on for 24 hours straight. We worked in shifts. We were on 2 hr, and off 4 hr. It wasn't so bad. I received the candy, thanks a lot. I sure did enjoy it. Did you have a nice time in D.C.? Did you get your permanent move?

 Well Bessie, I got a letter from home and they said Gilbert was down there and was leaving for the army. I guess he sure did hate to go. I also guess Jimmie hated to see him go. Bessie, I guess it worry Mamma & papa about all of us being in the army. If it wasn't for the worrying about us being in, I wouldn't mind the army.

 Bessie when you write them, try and always write them a cheerful letter, which I know you will. I always try and write them good news whether there is good news or not. Well Bessie, I am doing a lot of walking now I have war [wore] out one pair of shoes already. We are supposed to finish our drilling tomorrow. I sure will be glad when it is over. I guess we will be leaving from down here pretty soon. I do not know where we will go from here, they never tell you where you are going

 Bessie, I have seen two boys down here from home. A Simpson boy and a Shelton boy. I don't think you know either one of them.

 How are you liking your new home? I know you are liking fine. I hope in the near future I can come to see you all. But right now, as I am so far away, and it is so hard to get a pass I guess it will be quite a while yet. I got a letter from Herman this week. He is back in camp he said he had a nice time while he was at home. Tell C.A. & Micky & Fred I said hello. How is C.A. & H.V. getting along? Tell her not to get married while I am away. Well, Bessie as I do not know much news, I guess I had better close for this time so the best of luck until I hear from you all.

Love Ernest

P.S. I am sending you a snapshot. It's not any good, but rather than throw it away I will send it to you.

Pvt. Ernest Franklin, Keeling Air Base, Mississippi, May 1942.

POSTCARD POSTMARK MAY 28, 1942
CAMP LEE, VA

Dear Ma & Pa,

I will leave tomorrow to some place I don't know so don't write until you here from me. I don't have time to do anything. I got your letter. Will write as soon as I can.

PVT Gilbert Franklin, 1303rd S U Co C T28,
Camp Lee Va

PVT GILBERT FRANKLIN, 6TH TRAINING CO
36TH DIV TR REGT, APO#36 CAMP BLANDING,
VA (Florida actually)
(May 29, 1942)

Dear Ma & Pa,

    Just arrived here today. I guess I will be here for eight weeks. Will write you a letter later. Lots a love.

Gilbert Franklin

PVT GILBERT FRANKLIN 33190550, 6TH
TRAINING CO 36 DIV TR REGT, APO#36, CAMP
BLANDING, FLA.
(May 30,1942)

Dear Ma,

    Just a few lines to let you know that I just don't like up here, it is the worst place I have ever been in my life. I don't believe I can stand it, but there is nothing I can do. They treat you just like a dog and the ones that are back there don't know what they will have to go through. We have to stay in for two weeks. We can't ever go get nothing, not even cigarettes.
    We are living in tents. We only have two blankets and a pillow, no sheets no place to put your clothes, and I had rather be in the prison but as I say it is nothing I can do. Do you ever hear from Jimmy? I get a letter every day. I show [sure] did hate to leave her and it like to kill her when I was in Camp Lee. She would call me up every night. Ma, you said something about my clothes. Well I have so much to think about in my car just leave it there

or do anything with it the way I feel I won't need it. Well, I feel so bad I guess I will close. I haven't eat anything since I've been up here. I got up sick this morning but feel better.

Gilbert Franklin

My address is:
Pvt Gilbert Franklin, 6th Training Co 36 Div TR Regt, APO#36, Camp Blanding, Fla.

JUNE 1942

June opens with German General Rommel starting a push in North Africa toward Cairo. The Japanese are defeated at Midway, losing four aircraft carriers, while the Americans only lose one: the Yorktown. The Japanese then attack the Aleutian Islands, off the coast of Alaska.

PVT GILBERT FRANKLIN, 6TH TRAINING
CO 36 DIV TR REGT APO 36, CAMP
BLANDING, FLA.
(June 6, 1942)

Dear Bessie,

I received your card and was glad to hear from you. Well, I am in the army and I show [sure] do hate it. This is the worst place I ever been in my life. It so hard on us because we were supposed to have thirteen weeks training, and they have cut it down to eight weeks and might cut it to six so we have the same amount of training. We are confined for two weeks. We can't go anywhere nowhere in the camp. Just stay in our tents unless we are drilling, so that makes it hard on us. I can't even see Herman, so you see how the army is they need the men. This camp is about 15 miles square and about 30 thousand men. They are coming every day and leaving every day.

It like to kill Jimmie when I left. Bessie will you write her a letter if you please and make her understand that I had to go, and I would be back soon. Her sister said that she won't eat and can't sleep. She has lost about 9 pounds so that worries me. So, if you would write, it might cheer her up. Bessie, if it wasn't for Jimmie, I don't think I would mind it so bad, but she was so good to me and we were always together. Bessie it has rained every day since I been down here, but we have to drill just the same. The people on the outside don't know the half of what we have to go through and the ones that volunteer has no more chance than the other. They treat you so you don't care if you are dead or not. That is to make you want to fight. Bessie, I know I will like the cookies because you eat what you get and like it.

Gilbert

PVT GILBERT FRANKLIN, 6TH TRAINING CO 36 DIV TR REGT, APO#36, CAMP BLANDING, FLA.
(June 6, 1942)

Dear Pa and Ma,

I got your letter but haven't had time to write. Well, this is the worst place I ever been in my life. I wouldn't want my dog in a place like this. I get a letter every day from Jimmy. She told me that she got a letter from you. You write to her as often as you can. Her sister wrote me and told me that she won't eat and can't sleep. She has lost a lot of weight. Mom, do you think she will get over it? I guess she love me, but it worries me. I got a telegram from her today and she was coming up to see me and I wrote back to her and told her that I could not see her until the 16th of the month. So, I guess that will hurt her. Mama Jimmy went to her home last week in [weekend] but she wasn't satisfied. Ma tell Papa to fix that little cedar chest and send it to Jimmy that all she talks about so tell him to send it to her. Pa, I had two payments to be made on my car and before I left, I sent one of them and told them that Jimmy would send the other. That I was in the army and they sent me the money order back and sent me the title and told her that the car was paid for. Wonder why they did it. Pa will you find out if I have to make payments on my income taxes. My payment is due 12th of this month and I don't know what to do so if I don't have to pay it now I won't. I have the money, but I don't want to spend now. I got a letter from Bessie. Pa, if you want to you can put the car in the old stable or do anything. Will write later.

Gilbert

PVT ERNEST H. FRANKLIN, FIGHT 268E, 400TH TCH SCH SQD, KEESLER FIELD, MISS.
Monday (June 8, 1942)

Dear Bessie & Fred,

I guess you all think I am not going to write to you all anymore, but I have been a little busy lately. I have been on night K.P. again and I think I have got it again tonight. I am not quite sure yet. It is not so bad, as you have the next day off. Well, Bessie, most all of our flight has been shipped out. There was about two hundred and now there is only about sixty left. All but two of us that came down from Arlington has left. I sure did hate to see them leave because we all ran around together. There was only one boy that I know when I came down. But I had made quite a number of friends and now most all of them have gone. I guess I will be leaving most any time now. I hope that I can get back close to home. Well Bessie, since we have finished our drilling, we have it pretty easy. We just work around the campground. Did you all go down home over the week in? If so, did Gladys and Bay come with you all back? I had a letter from home, and they said Gladys was there for a while. Well Bessie I received the cookies today, and they sure was good. There is nothing that tastes better than homemade cooking. And I sure do thank you for them.

Fred, I received your letter and I couldn't believe it came from you. I relly enjoyed receiving it. So, you think that you are going to take it easy during the summer? Well, don't take it too easy, I am like you Fred. Why should Gilbert write such things home? It is hard enough on mamma & papa now, and things like he writes makes it much harder for them. There is nothing they or anyone else can do about it. I or no one else really likes but you just as well be contented because it will make it a lot easy on you. He will soon find out who is boss & will be allright. Bessie I will wait awhile before I send you your box back as I want to get a few more extra ones together and send you (ha ha) _ I was just called out and I am on K.P. tonight so I will haft to wait until tomorrow to finish this letter. Well, here I go again. I am just about half asleep. Talking about potatoes. I have never seen so many. We had thirty-five bags to peel. I think I have seen enough potatoes for a while. Well, Bessie, some more boys have been called out today for shipping and I do not know when they will leave. I haven't been called as yet. Well as there is not much news, I guess I had better close. Tell C.A. and Micky hello so they best of luck until I hear from you all.

Love Ernest

ARTHUR L. JOHNSON

PVT GILBERT FRANKLIN, 6TH TRAINING CO
36 DIV TR REGT, APO#36
Saturday (June 13, 1942)

Dear Pa and Ma,

I received your letter was glad to hear from you. Well, I don't like much better, but I am still here. I have seen Herman twice since I've been here. Pa I want to let you know if anything happens such as sick or death and I would have to come home you will have to go to the nearest Red Cross and tell them that you want me to come so don't send a telegram to me. The Red Cross will send it for you. That because they will look into see if it is true that is the reason. I think Jimmy is coming next Friday. I know she should not come, but I can't tell her not to come. They have a guest home here that she can come, and I can be with her all the time. It only costs $.50 a day and night and it is a swell place a little way from our tent. Mama tell Elizabeth that Jimmy wrote and told me how nice the dress was, and she showed [sure] did think Elizabeth could fix nice things. Jimmy show [sure] do like all of you. She says something about all of you every time she writes. Well, I got my first pay that was the last part of last month. $6.30. I ought to frame it, but I guess I will need it. I think some of you asked what Regt. means. That means regiment which is the no. of men. I have been original to Company C, 141st division 36th Regt, but I will still stay here until I get my training. I think that is the worst part of the Army there is, but that would be my luck. Well, I think I will take dinner with Herman tomorrow. I got a nice letter from Bessie this week she said if they could that they were coming down there and Fred would fix my car don't worry about the old car because it won't do me any good so just forget it that the least thing I can think about.

Gilbert

S/SGT H.B. FRANKLIN, CO. B 51ST MED B.N., CAMP BLANDING, FLA.
(June 14, 1942)

Dear Bessie,

 I guess you think I have forgotten you. But I am like you don't find much time to write to anyone. We are very busy down here. Getting ready to go maneuvers again up in N.C. and S.C. Oh well, such as the army life.

 Bessie, I want to thank you for the taffy you sent me from Washington, D.C. It was very good and did not last long. I got the cakes yesterday, and they were swell. Thanks again.

 Bessie, I did not know Gilbert was here until Yesterday. I got a card from him, and I went over to see him, he is about 1/2 mile from me. He is getting along very good. But he is very homesick, I feel sorry for him. I hope he makes the best of it. His wife is worrying the hell out of him she wants to come down to see him. He was talking with me yesterday and crying.

 So, I wrote her a few lines and told her not to come down until he is better stationed. I think he will make a good soldier. I am going and keep him in a good mood all I can. And take him around all I can. So don't write and tell him what I told you. He will be all right in a few days.

 So, I will close.

With love to all.
Your Bro.
Herman

ARTHUR L. JOHNSON

POSTCARD POSTMARK FORT BRAGG NC
JUN 24, 1942.
PVT ERNEST H. FRANKLIN, 13 TRANSPORT
SQD., POPE FIELD, FORT BRAGG, NC

Hi Bessie

Hope this finds you all well. I am in N.C. It is pretty nice. We are living in tents. Hope I can get to go home while I am down here. Wright to me soon.

Love Ernest

JULY 1942

The Germans march into Stalingrad. The Allies repel Rommel at El Alamein. The Japanese land in New Guinea.

PVT. GILBERT FRANKLIN, 6TH TRAINING CO
36 DIV T. R. REGT. APO#36
(July 5, 1942)

Dear Bessie,

I know you think I never will write. Well, I don't have time to write to Jimmie. The only time I write to her is while I am waiting to eat. We are on rifle range now. We have to get up and leave the camp at five o'clock and we have to walk fifteen miles with a full pack and our rifle, and it is nine to ten o'clock when we get in. You know the letter I got from you well I had to wait until the next day to read it. I am so tired when I get in, I can't sleep at night. Well, Jimmie was down to see me, and she is the worst-looking thing I ever seen. She won't weight 90 pounds it made me cry when I seen her, but I was so glad to see her she means the world to me. She would do anything for me, she thinks, the world of you. Bessie papa wrote me and told me what Fred did to my car, but Bessie I didn't forget it, I just haven't had time to write you and Fred. Now don't think hard of me because you know he couldn't do anything any better than that so I will pay him back sometime. I am in here to help to protect the ones that not in here, but it is good to know I am able to be here, but I had rather be out. Bessie it show [sure] is lonesome. Since Jimmie had gone back and Herman has left well, I don't have time to be with anyone now. Bessie, I guess I will be here about a month then I don't know where I will go. Herman is in N.C. I guess he will see Ernest, but there are not in the same camp. Bessie, Elizabeth sent me a package, and I show [sure] was glad to get it. Even a letter helps. Then I know someone is thinking of me. Well Bessie, I show [sure] do get lonesome to be back this is the worst place in the world. we are on six days a week and might have to work a Sunday. we were out until about nine o'clock fourth a July. Bessie it's nothing but a thank you I can do for what Fred did for my car so if you need the tires or anything just go and get it. It all paid for. Until I get a chance to write you and Fred be good Bessie. Write to me if I don't answer, will you? Tell Sythan [Cynthia Ann] and the Boy [Mikey] I said hello and be good.

With love to all
Gilbert

S/SGT H.B. FRANKLIN, APO 306, CO. B 51ST MED BN, DILWORTH, NC
(July 5, 1942)

Dearest Bessie,

I will answer your most welcome letter which I received to-day glad indeed to hear from you.

Well Bessie, you will notice that I am in N.C. on maneuvers. But the second day we got here I was sent to the hospital. I have got yellow jaundice. They say it came from the yellow fever shots they gave us in Feb.

Bessie I am a funny-looking sight. I am as yellow as a pumpkin. I don't feel bad, but I must stay in bed. I am put on a diet and I get one quart of Dextrose with Thiamin Chloride every day. They put in my arm through the vein and they give us all kinds of vitamins. I will be in the hospital about 6 or 8 weeks. We have about 70 of our men in the hospital with the same thing. I was told to-day that they are going to move us to Fort Jackson S.C. Our men are all over Fla., Ga., S.C. & N.C. hospital. I am now in the station hospital at Camp Sutton N.C. Bessie, you should see this place here. It looks like it was built overnight and they don't give us nothing to eat.

Tonight, they gave us some skimmed milk, toast, cottage cheese and 1/2pear and the other meals are just as bad.

But there is nothing to worry about.

I have not written home about it as yet but I am going to write to-morrow.

Bessie will you send me Earnest address. No one has sent it as yet. I left Fla. one day before Gilbert's wife came down. Too bad I did not see her. I got a letter from Gilbert today and one from his wife. His wife wrote me a very nice letter telling me all about her trip down.

Gilbert worries a lot and his wife worries the hell out of him. He was very good when I would be with him. You ask me what he was in. He has got the toughest job in the army. He is in the infantry. But he seems to like it.

Yes, Bessie, I am still in charge of the mess. And under this new way I will make $131.50 a month. Not so bad is it. I will send you some pictures as soon as I get out of the hospital. How is Fred and the rest of the family getting along? Fine, I hope.

Bessie, if I get home, I will let you know. I would give most anything to see all of my people. So, I will close with all my love.

> Your Bro,
> Herman

$131.50 would be about $2,096.88 in 2020 dollars, or just over $25,000 a year. This amount is for a married Staff Sergeant. Today a Staff Sergeant could make anywhere from $32,324 - $50,065.

PVT ERNEST H. FRANKLIN, 13 TRANSPORT SQD, POPE FIELD, FORT BRAGG, NC
Tuesday (July 7, 1942)

Dear Bessie,

I received your letter some time ago, was glad to hear from you. I am in N.C., but I do not like it much here. We haft to work seven days a week here. Bessie you said that you were going to send me a box. Bessie, if you haven't sent it, do not send it because I might not be here. Not that I do not want it, but I am afraid we will be gone, and I will not receive it. I do not know, but when we leave here, I think we are going a long ways from here. I sure would like to go home and see them all before I left but I do not think there will be a chance to do so as we cannot get off. It is about fifteen miles from town to camp. I haven't been to town yet and don't guess I will get to go. I sure would have loved to have been down there when you all was at home. I bet you all had a nice time. So, you have gone into the paper business now. Keep in mind whenever this war is over, and I ever come back and get married. Will give you the job of papering my house. I got a letter from Buz and Gladys. They sure did like your new place. Bessie, I have been assigned to AM. That is airplain macanic [Airplane Mechanic] so now you can buy you an airplain and I will keep it running for you. Well Bessie as it is just about time to go to work I will haft to stop.

Love Ernest

PRIVATE GILBERT FRANKLIN, 6TH TRAINING CO. 36 DIV T.R. REGT, REAR DETACHMENT, CAMP BLANDING
Sunday evening (July 19, 1942)

Dear Ma and Pa,

I just haven't had time to write I don't get a chance to write to Jimmy they are working the he-- out of us and it is so hot down here you think you will pass out anytime. We drill from sunup to sundown. Then we have to clean the rifles until 10 o'clock. Sometime when I get mail, it the next day when I get to read it. So, you see what time I have to do anything. I haven't been a hundred yards from the tent in almost 2 months except when Jimmy was down here. I don't care when they send me across, it can't be any worst then here. It looks like we won't be here long, and then we don't know what they will do. We have finished on the rifle range. I show [sure] am glad it. I show [sure] did do some good shooting. I made one of the highest scores and that will go down on record. We had one of our boys to drown this week. There were three boys on an old boat, and it turned over, and one that got drowned couldn't swim. He drowned Friday and it was Sunday at 10 o'clock when they found him. He came to the top. You couldn't tell who he was, it show [sure] was a sad thing. You know we all have to learn to swim. We have to go in two or three times a week. But don't worry about me because things will be changed now. I heard from Herman today and he is feeling a little better but still in the hospital. I will close right soon.

I have wrote to everyone to send Ernest address and I haven't got it yet I guess I will have to write to the war Department

Lot of love
Gilbert

Tell Elizabeth I got her letter and that I will write to her and I want to thank her for making Jimmie the dress and for her to go up and see Jimmie.

PVT ERNEST H. FRANKLIN, 13TH TROOP CARRIER SQ., 61ST TROOP CARRIER GROUP, POPE FIELD, FORT BRAGG NC
(July 22, 1942)

Dear Bessie,

I received your letter was very glad to hear from you. No, Bessie, we haven't left yet. We were supposed to leave last week. We had everything packed and had all of our material loaded on a freight car ready to go. We were going across the pond. We had took our shots for foreign service and turned in our summer clothes.

We had one more truck load to put in the freight car. When a message came in not to leave and continue normal operations. I am telling you there was the hot words I have ever heard since I have been in the army. You should have seen the beer party we had in our mess hall after the good news came in. Just about everybody got tight.

So now I do not know how long I will be here. It would suit me to stay here. You said in your letter that I sounded somewhat discouraged. Well I tell you Bessie, I haven't been feeling good at all since I have been here.

My stomach has been giving me a lot of trouble and I have been having the injections so bad I can hardly stand it. I have been on sick call three times, but they only give you a little mineral oil or a pill of some kind that doesn't do any good.

I think it is their greasy food that we have here. I can hardly eat any meat at all. But I am gaining weight all of the time. I weigh 152 now.

I had to send my watch & rings and all personal property home. I even had to send my slippers. I wrote & told them at home I thought we were going across. I sure hated to write them, but it was all I could do. I guess it upset them a lot. Bessie, you asked if I had a girld [girl] yet. Well, I have been to town a number of times and I found me a little redhead over there. She works in a resident. She pretty nice looking, but as we work seven days a week. It pretty hard to get in town much as it is about 20 miles to town.

I can go in at night, that is about the only time, but we can stay out until six o'clock in the morning. Well, Bessie, I have been taking a few rides in planes. I was up in one for 1-1/2 hr. Saturday. I am assigned to one plane to work on, and whenever it goes up, I can take a ride on it. I can go up anytime I am not working. Well, as there is not much news, I guess I will close for this time. Tell C.A., Micky and Fred all hello so until I hear from you the best of luck.

Love Ernest

P.S. Bessie two of the boys in my tent got married about a week ago. So, I have two papering jobs for you when we all get out.

My address: 13th troop carrier sqd, 61st troop carrier group, Pope Field, Fort Bragg, N.C.

The postscript is referring to a "papering job" for my grandmother. Bessie wallpapered her house herself. My uncle was referring to her doing the same for his friends. I am not sure how she would take that.

PVT. GILBERT FRANKLIN 33190550, 6TH TRAINING CO 36 DIV T. R. REGT. APO#36, REAR DETACHMENT.
(July 26, 1942)

Dear Bessie and Fred,

I received your letter I don't have mutch time to write except Sunday. Well, I have been laying around all day. I get so lonesome I don't know what to do. It has been so hot down here you can't hardly live. It has been 117 in the shade and you know how hot it is drilling all day long. I got a letter from Ernest and he told me that they were ready to go across and then they were sent back to their work. I know he was some glad. I also got a letter from Herman and he is still in the hospital and said he was sitting up a little but will be there for a month or more. Well Bessie, I guess we will be leaving in a week or two. I think we will be going to N.C. on maneuvers. Bessie, I made good on the rifle range. I made expert now I am instructing a bunch of men on the rifle, but I not like the army and never will. Bessie, I heard from home and everyone is well. I owe Gladys a letter. How is Fred getting along with his plumbing? I guess he has a plenty of work. Tell the kids I said hello hope to see them before they get grown. Bessie be show [sure] to go over to see Jimmie when you go up to Washington. I know she will be glad to see you. She went to her home this weekend with her sister. Well, I guess I will close.

Gilbert F

Bessie put Rear Detachment instead of APO 36 on my address. You will see the front of my letter.

ARTHUR L. JOHNSON

PVT GILBERT FRANKLIN, 6TH TRAINING CO 36DIV TR REGT, REAR DETACHMENT.
Monday Night (July 27, 1942)

Dear Bessie & Fred,

    I just wrote you a letter yesterday but receiving a nice pack like you sent me I just had to write and tell you that I received it. Bessie, I tell you the truth I just had to cry when I open it. Because all of you are so nice to send me nice things to make me feel good and I am so lonesome I don't know what to do. Bessie it isn't that I don't want to do my part, but I hate so bad to be away from Jimmie because I have never been away from her since I met her, and she is so good to me. Bessie, I wish I was there to tell you and Fred how mutch I enjoyed the things you have sent me but someday I might return it. Elizabeth sent me a nice package last week. She had some home-made cake in it. Boy, when you open a box here do it go. Everyone know when a package come in. Bessie we will be leaving from down here around the first so I will write. When I leave, I don't know for sure? Bessie, I taken out insurance on myself for Jimmie, do you think I should? I also made an allotment of $22 a month and gov will make it $50. Well Bessie, I have the headache so bad I don't know what to do. So, Bessie again, I will say that you show [sure] have been sweet to me and I will never forget what you and Fred did for me and tell Fred I hope to see all of you. And hope he will never have to go.

                                                     Gilbert

JUST A FEW LINES

PVT ERNEST H. FRANKLIN, 13TH TROOP
CARRIER SQ., 61ST TROOP CARRIER GROUP,
POPE FIELD, FORT BRAGG, NC
(July 29, 1942)

Dear Bessie,

Hope these few lines finds you all feeling just fine. Bessie, I received the package. I don't know how I can ever thank you for it. Bessie one of the boys in the tent is leaving, so we took some of the things you sent and got some beer and a few more things and I had a little party in our tent.

We have one guy in our tent that is very conseated [conceited]. He thought we were making too much noise and started to raise a little hell, so we just took him, his bed and all and threw him out of the tent and keep right on with our party. We relly had a good time. Bessie, we got another notice to move but only about half of us are leaving now. I am among those that are not leaving, but we do not know how long we will be here, after the others leave. Just when they are leaving and where they are going, we do not know. I do not know what we will do when they leave as they are taking all of our planes with them.

Bessie I just got a letter from Herman. He is still in the hospital. Said he was a little better. Gladys is down there with him. I also got a letter from Gilbert this week. He seems to be getting along all right. How is the weather up there, it sure is some hot here now! We have had about three storms this week. I was out in one of them all night. I was on guard duty, but I got up in one of the planes and keep dry. Bessie our outfit has the big twin motor planes. Like the ones that Eastern Air Lines uses. Maybe Fred will know what kind they are. They are B-47 [actually C-47]. They are relly large in size.

Bessie I was in [ILLEGIBLE possible "Leeser"] Saturday night and I ran into bout six boys that I knew in Miss. We got together and really put the dog on. I sure was glad to see them.

Well Bessie, as I do not know any news of interest, I guess I will close. Thanks again for the box you sent me. Tell C.A., Micky and Fred all hello. So, the best of luck until I hear from you.

Love Ernest

AUGUST

In August 1942, we see the first B-17 bombing raid in Europe, targeting the Sotteville railroad yard at Rouen, France. The US suffers heavy naval losses in the Battle of Savo Island near Guadalcanal. American forces establish bases in the New Hebrides islands.

S/SGT H.B. FRANKLIN, STATION HOSPITAL, WARD 16, FORT JACKSON, SC
(August 2, 1942)

Dearest Bessie,

Just a few lines to let you know I am getting much better. But I am still in bed and this hot weather is getting me down.

Bessie, Gladys came down last Sunday to see me. And she just left here Friday Morning. I sure did enjoy her stay here.

She has a girlfriend that she nursed with in Danville. She is stationed down here, and Gladys stayed with her. Eat and slept here at the Hospital. I think she had a grand time while she was here. She told me that she thought she was going to join the army. I guess papa would have a fit if she joined the army.

Bessie, while I was here my outfit was called out of the maneuver area and they were sent down here at Fort Jackson S.C. After they arrived here, they got orders to pack up. So, they left here Friday for overseas service. I don't know if I was lucky or not being in the hospital.

If I had to go overseas, I had rather go with my company than have to go with some other outfit.

But I will be in the hospital another month. That is what the Dr told me this week. I don't know where I will go after I get out of here.

The Dr. has promised me a sick leave. I hope I can get it. I want to go home for a few days. I am only about 300 miles from home.

I had a letter this week from Ernest and he was telling me that about half of the company has left for an unknown destination. And that he was lucky he was left with the other half of his company. He said that he did not know what they were going to do because they had taken most of their planes away. I have not heard from Gilbert in about two weeks. Said that they were going on maneuvers up in N.C.

Bessie I sure would like to see your new home. Gladys was telling me how nice it was.

I sure could use some of those vegetables you was telling me about. They feed us very good here. But no fats at all. I have lost about 10 pounds of weight since I have been sick, that is not so bad.

When you get time drop me a few lines.

Tell at home I said hello.

                                          Love your Bro.
                                          Herman

My address is: Station Hospital, Ward 16, Fort Jackson, S.C.

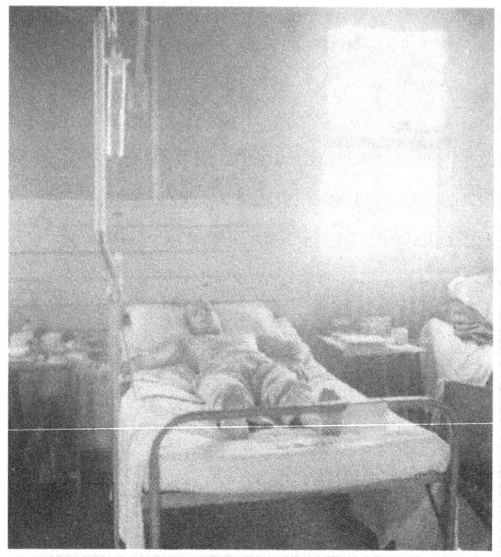

Herman Franklin in Station Hospital.

PVT ERNEST H. FRANKLIN, 13TH TROOP CARRIER SQ, 61ST TROOP CARRIER GROUP, POPE FIELD FORT BRAGG, NC
(August 5, 1942)

Dear Bessie,

    I received your letter was way glad to hear from you. well Bessie there is not much news now. No, Bessie, I did not receive the letter you sent from N.Y. I hope you do get it back. Let me know if you get it. Well, Bessie, I took a little trip yesterday. The plane I work on went to Langley Field VA, and I went along it was relly a nice trip. That is where Leo S. is, but I didn't get to see him.

    Bessie they are giving us all a week drilling with rifles and a gas mask. They take so many each week. I am not in it this week but guess I will get it next week. Bessie you know I told you that part of us was supposed to leave, well all of the planes were packed and already to go, and about a couple of hours we got word that they were not to go. So, we are now unpacking. You never know the dope around here anymore. Bessie as I have got to go back to work I will close and write you a long letter when I have the time. Tell all hello.

Lots of Love, Ernest

PVT GILBERT FRANKLIN, CO C 141ST INF, APO36 DIV DILWORTH, NC
(August 5, 1942)

Dear Ma,

I forgot to send the pictures, so I have a little time to send them. We leave here at 4 o'clock. Will write to you when I get there.

Gilbert

Gilbert Franklin, Camp Blanding, Florida.

Gilbert Franklin on the ropes, Camp Blanding, Florida.

Gilbert Franklin and fellow privates, Camp Blanding, FL.

Privates lining up for the mess.

PVT GILBERT FRANKLIN, CO C 141ST INF,
APO36 DIV DILWORTH, NC
Monday Noon (August 10, 1942)

Dear Ma & Pa,

I am down in N.C. I haven't had my clothes off but once [since] I [have] been here. We are fifteen miles from a town. We only have a blanket and a tent. I'm not far from Herman and Ernest, but I can't get to see them. They say that we will only be here this week but I don't know and don't know where we will go. So, don't expect much mail. I have to carry the paper in my pocket that why so dirty. It hot in the day but cool at night. I am eat up with chiggers. We sleep on the grown, have no lights, sometimes we have to move during the night as many times as 3 times a night. They walked 130 miles in two days. Some walking. I haven't heard from you since I left Fla. You write to me until I let you know. I will try and write every chance. My address is PVT Gilbert Franklin, Co. C. 141st Regt, APO36 Div Dilworth NC.

POSTCARD POSTMARK COLUMBUS OHIO
AUG 14, 1942
PVT ERNEST H. FRANKLIN, 13TH TROOP
CARRIER SQ, LOCKBOURNE AIR BASE,
COLUMBUS, OHIO

Hi Bessie,

I am in Columbus, Ohio. I like it just fine. It is a new camp and a swell place. Will write soon.

Love Ernest

POSTCARD POSTMARK CHERAW, S.C.
AUGUST 15, 1942
GILBERT FRANKLIN, CO. C 141ST INF, CAMP EDWARDS, MA

Dear Ma & Pa,

Just a few lines to let you know I got your letter. Well, I haven't had time to write. It has been raining down here. I don't like down here. Well, we will leave here sometime Sunday so when you write to me again my address is. Gilbert Franklin, Co. C 141st Inf., Camp Edwards MA

PVT ERNEST H. FRANKLIN, 13TH TROOP CARRIER SQ, LOCKBOURNE AIR BASE, COLUMBUS, OHIO
(August 16, 1942)

Dear Bessie,

Well, I guess you think I travel a lot. I am in Columbus, Ohio now. So far, I like it up here just fine. This is a new camp there is only about two thousand soldier here and the town has a population of about 125 thousand so you see it is a good soldier town. We have all new barracks, a big theater, a large P.X. and best of all we have a large beer palace and dance hall. For some reason I just can't stay away from that beer joint. We relly have swell food here. So far, I like this camp better than any I have been to yet. Hope we can stay here for a while. I am getting to see quite a bit of the country. I have been in 14 different states so far. We flew up to Michigan the other day. Yesterday we flew to Toledo, Ohio. From there we went to Cleveland, Ohio. I think this is the prettiest state I have been in yet. I don't haft to go on every trip the plane makes. But I go on most every trip as I want to see all of the country that I can as long as it doesn't cost me anything. We are supposed to train glider planes while we are here, but so far, we haven't started yet. I guess we will start as soon as they get theirs in.

I got a letter from home yesterday. They are getting along all right. Well, Bessie as I want to write some more letters, I will close and write more the next time. Tell all hello. So, the best of luck until I hear from you all.

Lots of Love
Ernest

My Address Pvt Ernest H Franklin, 13th troop Carrier Sq., Lockbourne Air Base, Columbus, Ohio

PVT GILBERT FRANKLIN, CO. C 141ST INF REGT, APO36, CAMP EDWARDS, MA
(August 20, 1942)

Dear Ma & Pa,

I will write to you as I have a little time. Well, we got here Wednesday. That was some trip. There were two men got kill. They fell off the train. Well, I thought we would be in camp, but when we go here, the camp was so full that we had to put tents outside the camp. So, we are still sleeping on the grown there is some life. We don't know now how long we will be here. We go out on a ten-day Problem which is learning loading and unloading boats then we don't know where we will go or do but I hope we will move closer to Washington.

I got the cakes Gladys sent me. They show [sure] was nice. I also got a letter from her too and got a letter from Herman and he said that he was getting on fine and don't know when he would get out. Ma, don't send me anything but mail because I don't have anywhere to take care of it. But write to me as mutch as you can. I got three letters from Jimmie and she show [sure] did like down there and she said that all of you're so nice to her. She thinks the world of you and Pa that all we talk about. Ma I think she is a nice girl don't you and I know she will make me a nice wife. I show [sure] do miss her. Well, I will have to close.

Gilbert

PVT ERNEST H. FRANKLIN, 13TH TROOP CARRIER SQ, LOCKBOURNE AIR BASE, COLUMBUS, OHIO
(August 26, 1942)

Hello Fred & Bessie,

 I received your letter was glad to hear from you, well this leaves me O.K. hope it finds you all the same. Well, it has been pretty cold up here for the past few days but it is somewhat warmer now. I started the first of this week Monday taking a week drill. All in our outfit has to have it. After this is over, I am going to school for a couple of weeks taking up airplane mechanics. Well, we can get off the post overnight now from 5 o'clock until 12 o'clock except Saturday, then we can stay out until 2A.M.
 I have had quite a lot of fun since I have been here. I like it fine here. I got a letter from Herman & Gilbert this week. Gilbert doesn't like where he is much. Herman is getting along OK and hopes to be out of the hospital by Sept. 1. I guess you all had a nice trip on your vacation. I tried to get a furlough, but I couldn't get one. They said I had to be in 6 months before I can get one. I hope I can get one then.
 Bessie, I have me a right nice little babe up here. Her home is in WVa. but she works here. It seems like we have the W.Va. leaner. You know you haft to have a sidekick wherever you go. There isn't any trouble at all to get a girld [girl] here. So don't be surprised if when I come

home I have something tied to my arm (ha). Well, I don't know much news of interest so I will close hope to hear from ya'll again soon. Tell C.A. & Mickey hello. So, the best of luck until I hear from you all.

Lots of Love,
Bro, Ernest

S/SGT H.B. FRANKLIN, STATION HOSPITAL, WARD-16, FORT JACKSON, SC, US ARMY (August 26, 1942)

Dearest Bessie,

Just a few lines to let you know I am getting along very well now but still in the hospital. I hope to get out next month sometime.

Bessie I just one of your letters mailed July 31. It went to Staten Island, NY. There is lots of mail I don't get that is mailed to me.

I think I wrote and told you Gladys was down to see me.

I had some pictures I wanted to send you. But the nurses took them all. When I get some more, I will send you some.

You ask me if I could have anything to eat. Just now I can eat anything.

Ernest and Gilbert sure are moving around. I had a letter from both of them this week. Earnest seems to like where he is at fine.

Bessie since I have been in the hospital my company has gone overseas. If I have to go I had rather went with my company. But I know I will have to go sometime soon.

I hear from Cleo most every day and she is getting alone very good. Drop her a card sometimes.

Bessie, you seem to be canning lots of food stuff this year. The war should not affect you this year about eats. How about sugar, do you get enough?

I will close for this time, tell all hello

I remain Your Bro,
Herman

SEPTEMBER

In September 1942, the Americans built a landing strip on Guadalcanal, readying for a lengthy battle. The Battle of Stalingrad begins. The US prevents the Japanese from taking Henderson Field on Guadalcanal.

PVT GILBERT FRANKLIN, CO. C 141ST INF REGT, APO36, CAMP EDWARDS, MA
Wednesday Night (September 2, 1942)

Dear Ma & Pa,

I got your letter today. Well, I am still up here and don't like and never will. I had rather be shot than be in here. We still staying out in these old woods. I haven't had any clean clothes clean since about a week before I left Camp Blanding. We shave when we can get water. I haven't had a haircut since I left Blanding. I am afraid I will get lice on me. It so cold when we get up, we almost freeze. Have to eat out old tin pans on the grown. We have to go to bed at dark because we have no lights. I haven't been any where since I been up here.

I haven't had any envelopes for a week. You can't keep things because they all stick together because it so damp. Well, we don't know how long we will be here, but we got word that we were going to be sent across soon. They are issuing us all new equipment so I guess we will be going across soon because they told us to take in all we can because we had just a little time. They won't let us out for nothing now. I didn't tell Jimmie so don't let her know. Well I just as soon be over there as be here because it couldn't be any worse.

Well, I heard from Herman the other day and he said that he would be out Sep 1st. I wrote to him today, but I don't know whether he will get it or not. Mama will you tell all of them to not think hard if I don't write because I only have a few minutes to state because when we get in it so late then it gets dark, we have no way to write. I worked all day Sunday making me a bed. It help a lot, at least I am off the damp grown. But it has been frost every morning up here.

Ma, I am not telling you to worry any of you, but I just wish you could see what we have to go through. They don't think any more of you that if you didn't live. Well, I guess you are getting tired reading this. Well I show [sure] has been disgusted for the past week? Sometimes I just can't sleep. you know it wouldn't be so bad if we were where we could get some clean clothes and clean up sometime. There are men that leave every day, but I feel sorrow those because that death now. Well Ma, I guess I will close I have so many letters to write. I don't know when I will ever get through.

Love Frankie

POSTCARD SEPT 8, 1942
PVT ERNEST H. FRANKLIN, 13TH TROOP CARRIER SQ, LOCKBOURNE AIR BASE, COLUMBUS, OHIO

Hi C.A. (Cynthia Ann)

How are you liking school? Do you have you many boyfriends now at school? When you learn to write, drop me a line.

Love Ernest

PVT GILBERT FRANKLIN, CO. C 141ST INF REGT, APO36, CAMP EDWARDS, MA
(September 11, 1942)

Dear Ma & Pa,

I received your letter and was glad to hear from you. Well, we are still in this da— place and it has been raining and the mud around the tents is about ankle deep and today it so cold you don't know what to do. I don't see how we are going to make it if we have to stay here mutch longer and I don't get a chance to write to no one because when we get in it almost dark and then when we eat it is dark and we have no light at all we have to go to bed.

Well, Ma & Pa, I received the sigaretts [cigarettes] and also the birthday card with the dollar in it. I was so glad that tears came in my eyes. You know it show do make one feel good to get anything from home. I owe a letter I know I don't write often, but I think I would write more often if I had the chance.

They give us the afternoon off to rest up because we start on a twenty-mile hike tonight. Start at 5 o'clock we have to march by a compass so that the reason I am writing.

Well ma, I got the nicest birthday cake from Jimmie. It was about I be the prettiest thing you ever seen. She had it baked at the bakery and on top it was Frankie love Jimmie. You just ought to seen it and on top of that she sent me a box of candy and in the middle of the candy she had me a wedding band. I show did like it. May you know she the sweetest thing to me. I don't think there is nothing she wouldn't do for me and she like all of you and when she don't get letters from all of you she writes me to know how all of you are. Ma, when you write her again you tell her that I show did like the cake and the ring. Ma, she is coming up here in Boston, Mass. to see me this weekend. The camp is taken part us men in Boston for the weekend and she is going to meet me there. She wants to come so bad and that might be my last chance to see her.

Ma, I think I told you before to tell of them that I just can't write. I just don't have time and at night I have to go to bed at 6:30 o'clock. Ma, I show did get a nice letter from Mr. Jack Adams and you tell him that I show did appreciate it and as soon as I get a chance, I show was going to answer it. Tell him I just don't get a chance to write. I counted up today and I owe nine letters I had to work all day last Saturday and Sunday. Ma, I show am glad you have rejoined the church and I hope it will help us to get out this army. Ma Jimmie goes every Sunday and she like it. Well I will close,

Love to all
Gilbert

I want to thank you again for the things you all sent me.

S/SGT H. B. FRANKLIN, STATION HOSPITAL, WARD-16, FORT JACKSON, SC
(September 15, 1942)

Dear Bessie,

Just a few lines to let you know I received your letter and glad to hear from you and to know you had a swell vacation.

Wish I could talk about vacations, but those days for me are over for a while.

Bess, I got out of the hospital last Wednesday (September 9). Have not did a thing as yet. I am waiting for an order to go to Charleston S.C. then from there I don't know where I will go. But I'll just have to wait and see Bessie you was talking about sending me a cake, I would like it very much but wait until I see where I am going. I will let you know at once.

I had a letter from Gladys this week, and she is getting along very good. I sure did like her being down here with me.

Thanks a lot for the pictures of the kids. They sure do look swell. If I had two like that maybe Uncle Sam would not have got me. But a guy never knows. I am glad Cynthia Ann likes school. She looks like she will make a good pupil.

I have not heard from Gilbert this week. He owes me a letter. I guess he is so busy that he cannot write. You say his wife is still having a fit because he is in the army. Well, that is that way life is.

No Bessie, I have not heard from anyone from my company. I have written but did not receive no answer as yet.

The weather sure has been hot down here for the last two weeks. Its look rain just now. Hope it hold off for a few days.

Had a letter from Cleo this week and she is getting alone very good and working every day. And all up home are good. I will close for this time, hoping to hear from you soon. If I move, I will write you at once.

Love to all,
Your Bro Herman

ARTHUR L. JOHNSON

POSTCARD OF HOTEL STATLER, BOSTON
PARK SQUARE AT ARLINGTON STREET
POSTMARK CAMP EDWARDS, MA SEP 16, 1942.

Dear Bessie and Fed,

Frankie and I are on the 6th floor of this hotel and we're having a time. [ILLEGIBLE] wonderful and [ILLEGIBLE] could stay.

Love, Jimmie

(From Mary Elizabeth Simmons, aka, Jimmie)
Thursday afternoon (September 17, 1942)

Dear Mother, Dad and Elizabeth,

I guess you thought I was never going to answer your letter, but I spent most all of my time last week getting ready to go see Frankie so I'm quite sure you will understand.

Frankie sent me a telegram Thursday to come and believe me it didn't take me long to get ready then. I left here Friday night at 11:00 and got into Boston Saturday morning about 9:15. I went to the hotel and got a room and tried to rest until time to go meet Frankie. If you can imagine how anxious I was to see Frankie, you may know I didn't rest much. I met him at the depot at 2:30pm and what a happy time that was. I was so glad to see him that I was speechless. Frankie surely does look good and has gained 15 pounds. Mother, we certainly were happy for those two days but when we had to leave each other, one go one way and one the other, it just broke both of our hearts. Mother, we did have such a good time, and I enjoyed every minute with Franke more than words can say. I do wish we could get together more often, but I guess in a way we are lucky to see each other as often as we do compared to some who are across. I do thank God for being able to go see Frankie and to know he is well.

Mother, I guess Frankie told you I sent him a five-pound birthday cake, so he brought me a piece of it and he was so tickled over it. He told me what you all sent him, and he certainly did appreciate it too.

I do hope this finds you all feeling fine and I do wish I could come down again real soon, but I just don't know. Frankie and I are hoping and praying he will get a furlough so we can come down there, but as yet he doesn't know. He was suppose to go today on an island I think about twelve miles from Camp Edwards on a problem for about two weeks then when he comes back he hopes to get his furlough.

Mother, I did have such a good time with Frankie and God only knows how glad I was to see him. I love him so much and I will always love him. Mother, I still say I have the best husband in the world and when he comes home, I know we will be so happy.

Mother, answer soon and tell Mr. Franklin and Elizabeth, "Hello" for me.

Love to you all,
Jimmie

Gilbert Franklin and wife "Jimmie" Mary Elizabeth Simmons.

Gilbert Franklin, on leave in Boston.

PVT ERNEST H. FRANKLIN, 13TH TROOP CARRIER SQ, LOCKBOURNE AIR BASE, COLUMBUS, OHIO
Sunday (September 20, 1942)

Dear Bessie,

I received your letter a short while ago. I was sure glad to hear from you. Well, Bessie, I was at home last weekend I sure had a nice time. I only had those days off, so you see I only had a short time at home. I sure wish I could have gotten to see you all. But I did know that I was coming until the last minute. Ma and them didn't know I was coming either. I went to see Gladys while I was there. I got a letter from Gilbert this week. He said that Jimmie was up to see him on the weekend and that they relly had a nice time. Bessie, I don't think we will be here long. Just when and where we are going, I do not know, but I think arrangements are being made for us to move pretty soon. I wish we would stay up here. I like it up here altho it is pretty cold up here now. we haft to have a fire now. Well, Bessie, if I get hungry I will know where to send and get something to eat. Since you have been doing so much canning. Bessie, I guess you miss C.A. a lot since she started school, how does she like going to school. Well Bessie as I don't know any news of interest I guess I will close. So the best of luck until I hear from you all, write again soon.

Love Ernest

ARTHUR L. JOHNSON

Uncle Ernest sent one of his patch insignias in the letter.

PVT GILBERT FRANKLIN, CO. C 141ST INF REGT, APO36, CAMP EDWARDS, MA
Sunday evening (September 20, 1942)

Dear Ma & Pa,

    I know I wrote you the last letter but I just got time for a few words. Well, we have moved over on an island about ten miles from camp, but my address is the same. We are still in the tents. We are taking up boxing and swimming. We have to go in swimming every day for three hours a day and we almost freeze. We went on a twenty-mile hike yesterday and then had to go swimming the rest of the day. They show are giving us plenty of exercise. Ma, Jimmie came up to Boston Mass. to see me over the weekend and we show did have a good time. She show did look better than she did when she came down to Florida I think she weighs more. I would give anything if I could get to stay somewhere closer so I could get to see her more often. I had a letter from Ernest, and he seems to like fine, but I show don't and never will.

I don't know how long we will be here, but I show do hope we can get in a camp some place, but I am afraid we will be going over. Well, I have several more letter to answer so I will have to close. We have to work on Saturday since we came over here on the island.

Yours Truly, Gilbert Franklin

FROM MARY ELIZABETH SIMMONS,
AKA, JIMMIE
Sunday night (assuming September, after the Boston Trip)

Dear Mother and all,

Will try to answer your most welcomed letter. I do hope it isn't as cold and rainy down there as it is up here. It has rained most all day here and been such a long lonesome day.

I still hear from Frankie every day and he is still out on the island and will be until the 29 or 30th of October. He says he may get a furlough then, but he is not sure. I do hope he does as I want him to come home so bad, and he is so anxious to come home. Mother, we did have the best time when I went down to see him. I shall never forget it as we had such a good time and seeing him meant all the world to me. I do love him so much and I miss him so much. Last Sunday I cried all afternoon and all night. I got so blue and lonesome that I just couldn't stand it. I wanted to call Frankie and talk to him, but I know he was out on the island, so I called mother and talked to her. Even after I called her it didn't help any, I still wanted Frankie. I do miss him more than anything in the world and I will never be happy until the day he comes home and what a happy day that will be too.

Frankie said he hadn't heard from you all in a long time and he seemed rather worried but said he guessed you had so many to write to that you just hadn't got to him as yet.

Poor Frankie, it just worries me to death to think of him being in the Army and he hates it so bad. One of these days he will be home and if anyone will happy, I sure am going to see that he is. If Frankie doesn't get to come home, I am going to see him in about two weeks.

Mother, I do hope this finds you all feeling fine and give my regards to Mr. Franklin and Elizabeth and tell them to write to me.

Our office moved up on the tenth floor of the building and as there are enough desks for all us in the daytime, they have cut out the night work so I start on days tomorrow. I sure do hate to start too as I know I will miss Frankie so much at night as I was always used to him being here when I came in from work. I guess I will have to make the best of it though, but I know it is going to be very hard.

> Well, mother answer soon and
> Lots of love to you all
> Jimmie

PVT GILBERT FRANKLIN, CO. C 141ST INF REGT, APO36, CAMP EDWARDS, MA
Sunday Morning (September 27, 1942)

Dear Bessie & Fred,

I guess you thought that I had forgotten you, well I haven't. I just don't have the time. I never write to no one but Ma & Jimmie. When we get in from work, it almost dark and we don't have any light at all, we have to go to bed or sit up in the dark. We're on an island (island) out from the camp.

We have been here for one week and will be here until about the 5th of next month. It show is cold up here and we are still in these old tents. I haven't had but one bath in about two months. We never get to wash our face in the morning, sleep with all our clothes on, my clothes has been washed one time since I left Florida. Now you can see how good the arm is. It a dam lie when they say we eat the best.

We are learning to load and unload on boats. We go out in the ocean about ten miles and then land on the shore and we have to start running just as it land and run until we give out and we are soaking wet every time. It a shame what we have to go through. I show will be glad when we go across because we will never get there and all this hell will be over with. This is the dumbest outfit I ever seen. I know as mutch as anyone.

Bessie, I show did have a nice time in Boston with Jimmie, but I show did hate to leave her. That the only time I have been out of the camp. I have to go on guard at 4:30 this evening so I don't have mutch time off. We have to work all day on Saturday so until I get time to be good and a lot of luck.

My address
Gilbert Franklin Co. C 141st Inf Regt APO#36 Camp Edwards Mass.

PVT ERNEST H. FRANKLIN, 13TH TROOP CARRIER SQ, LOCKBOURNE AIR BASE, COLUMBUS, OHIO
(September 29, 1942)

Dear Bessie,

I received your letter today was very glad to hear from you, I sure wish I could have been home while you all was there but as you know it is impossible. Bessie, I guess by the time you receive this letter I will be gone. Where we are going, I do not know. About 150 of our men left last week with our planes, we are to catch up with them.

Bessie I am sure we are going to ride the waves this time. We took out one seat ex (extra?) today.

Bessie, don't tell Ma & pa that I am going across it will just worry them. It don't worry me about going across. You know the old saying your time is not up until you hear the horn blow. We got a little job to do and we know how to do it. You watch and see if we don't come back with flying colors. Bessie our Sq. sure have been having a good time the last gone week. We have been having parties, dances, going to shows, football games, everything free, and we had plenty during and girlds. I guess they are showing us a good time before we leave. The 13th sq sure has got a reputation in Columbus. All of the other outfits up here is jealous of our Sq. because we have so many parties & things.

Bessie I never received the letter you sent me containing the money and if you don't get it soon let me know and I will report it to our orderly room and maybe they can trace it up. Bessie right now I haven't much I can send you but I am sending you a sign that we were on our clothes. If I can ever get a chance to have any picture made, I will send you one. Well, Bessie, I haven't any news now so I will close. Bessie, if you write before you hear from me send it to this same address as it will probably be forwarded to me. I will write to you as soon as I get where I am going. So good luck until I hear from you all. Tell all hello.

Lots of Love
Ernest

OCTOBER

October 1942 finds the Second Battle of El Alamein beginning in North Africa. The US defeats the Japanese in the Battle for Henderson Field on Guadalcanal, and the Soviets keep the Germans at bay in Stalingrad.

JUST A FEW LINES

PVT GILBERT FRANKLIN, CO. C 141ST INF REGT, APO36, CAMP EDWARDS, MA
Sunday Night (October 4, 1942)

Dear Ma & Pa,

I got your letter. Well, I am still up here and expect to be here another month and I show do hate it. The reason I haven't written sooner. We had to go on a three-day problem. We went to another island. We had to load on boats early in the morning and land on the island at dawn. The water show was rough and there were a lot of sick men. They got seasick. Well, we got back Saturday Night, and I show was tired. We had to take enough food to last us for three days. I brought most all of it back. I wish you could see it is up up nice. I went for two days without eating anything and I show was sick and week when I got back.

But best of all when I got back, I had a package from Bessie and Fred and was it nice. Cake, candy and good sigratts [cigarettes]. You told me to write to her. I wrote to her two weeks ago, so I guess she must have gotten it by now. She show has been good to me and when you write to her you tell her that I show did like it. I am going write to her tonight. I also here from Jimmie every day and she wants to come to see me again but there is no chance we have to work every day but Sunday and hard to get a pass out the camp.

Well I guess we will be here for another month and it show is cold here, and we only had a blackout to sleep on while we were out, but I didn't sleep any. it was too cold. I don't think we will ever get to go across because they will kill us before then. Ma, I don't write this to worry you because all of us have the same, but I have never made a sick call since I been in the army. You know my back almost kill me at times but there is nothing I can do about it. I never drink anything never have since I been in here. I never go anyplace. I don't have no desire to go. Ma, you said that you wanted a picture of me, well it hard to get anything here. There is no place to have it taken. Ma, it is one thing I would like for you to try and get and that a few candles and send me. We have no way for light at night and you can't get them up here because they sell them as fast as they get them in. Now if it only two or three will help a lot because at night is only time we get to write. I am writing now by one and I think it will be all gone when I get in bed so Love to all.

Gilbert

Written at top: Ma, always write to me at the last address and I will get it and tell all the rest because if I move, they will forward it. That is if you think I have moved.

PVT GILBERT FRANKLIN, CO. C 141ST INF REGT, APO36, CAMP EDWARDS, MA
Monday Night 8 o'clock (October 5, 1942)

Dear Bessie & Fred,

I just got to write you a few lines to thank you for the box you sent me. Bessie, you know I had to go on a three-day problem that was over on another island. We had to get up at about 2 o'clock and walk bout two miles with a full pack and load our boats and it took us six hours to get to the island and we were froze to death. We had got sleep out and didn't have but one blanket, but I didn't sleep because I was too cold. We had to take enough food to last us the three days, and it was so bad I brought most of it back. I went for two days and did eat anything. I wish I could just send you one of these packages of food they give us. One meal is put up in a box. There is on the box supper, dinner and breakfast. It show is put up nice but you can't eat it. For breakfast you get a package of coffee,

3 lumps of sugar, seven hard tachs, that the bread, one little can of meat of some kind, one piece of candy and one stick of chew gum. All the rest is almost alike, but they have a small pack of sigratts (cigarettes).

Bessie I was so tired and hungry when we got back, I was weak but best of all they had mail call and I got the package you send, and did I go for that. I think I eat most all of it at once. You saw my life these can goods I made a fire and warm them and did I eat. Bessie, we have finished all the training we have to up here, but we got word that we will be here for a good while, so we have been fixing our tents up. we don't have any light and any wood or cold to burn. Well Bessie, I show enjoyed the box of things you sent. I show do wish I could come to see all of you. Well Bessie I will have to close because I don't have too mutch light, so I hope to see you soon. Bessie, always write to me at the last address you have, and I will get it no matter where I am.

Yours Truly, Gilbert

Gilbert preparing for training.

Gilbert eating in his tent after the training exercise.

Gilbert in front of his tent on the island at Camp Edwards.

PVT GILBERT FRANKLIN, CO. C 141ST INF REGT, APO36, CAMP EDWARDS, MA
Saturday evening (October 10, 1942)

Dear Bessie & Fred,

    I got your letter and was glad to hear from you and I got the picture and it was good. Bessie you said in one of your letters that you never heard from me while I was in N.C. well, I know for sure that I did write to you and after I got here in Mass. I wrote to you and I wondered why you didn't answer. Bessie, I don't know but I think they are going to put us in camps in Camp Edwards, I show do hope they will it so cold out here.

    Bessie, I show hope Ernest the best of luck and Herman to bet we are all going to have to go across. Our time is short, I think I know when, but I can't say. All I hope is to get a furlough, but they don't say anything about one. I have been in here for five months. Have you heard from Jimmie? I guess it keep her busy writing to me sometimes I get two a day and one every day. I know she gets lonesome and I do too. I heard from home the other day and all was well.

    Bessie, if I could only get some place to have my picture taken, I would send you one, but I am sending you a snapshot. Bessie you asked me for one of my insignia pins. Well, I have only one and I have to have that one. We are supposed to have three, but they don't make them anymore. It takes too mutch metal. so, I am sending you one of my Div. shoulder patches, but if I get any of the pins, I will let you have one. This patch has a T in the center that for 36 the blue in color means Inf. the shape of the patch is an arrow that means Texas as the 36 Div. is a Texas Div.

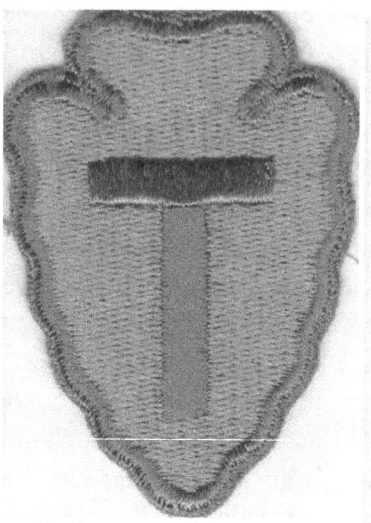

Patch for Texas 36.

PVT GILBERT FRANKLIN, CO. C 141ST INF REGT, APO36, CAMP EDWARDS, MA
Saturday Evening (October 10, 1942)

Dear Ma & Pa,

    Have a little time to write to all of you so I am still in the army. Mom, we are still on the Island and don't know how much longer you will be here, but I hope we can leave from here it's so cold and I'm so sick with a cold I can't hardly hold my hand up. Well, they gave us this Saturday afternoon off the first afternoon we have had off since we've been here. Ma, I got a real nice letter from Bessie and she was telling me about being down there and seeing Herman.
    Well, I think I am the most unlucky person in the world. Herman and Earnest both have been home and I never get any time off. Well, I show will be glad when this war is over, we will never have any piece until it is over. Mom, I have wrote to Herman and Ernest both and I

have never heard a word from either one. Since both have moved, I don't guess they got them.

Ma do you think Ernest has gone over yet? I show hope he hasn't. But all of us have to go and it will be soon, I know we will because we are almost ready. Mom our work isn't so hard now but the way we have to leave we have to be up at 5:30 and it's so cold we are on the edge of the water it is always damp. We are now doing the same thing we did in training. We don't know what going to happen but it got to come up soon. Ma, you said that you wanted a picture of me well I never have time to go anywhere to have one made but I am sending you this snapshot it belonged to Jimmie but will tell her that I sent it to you. That the only one I have made since I've been up here.

Gilbert.

This paper will tell you something about the last problem we had.

The newspaper clipping included was from the Camp Edwards News, dated Wednesday, October 7, 1942. The front-page headline reads, "Lt. Gen. McNair Observes Record War Games Here." The article describes the "games" as a mock amphibious landing. In a predawn raid on the morning of October 2, thousands of troops stormed across Vineyard Sound and "invaded" the historic island of Martha's Vineyard. While the forces landed in three separate areas of the island, paratroopers took the airport at Edgartown. The article describes in more detail the events of the three-day training exercise.

ARTHUR L. JOHNSON

S/SGT H.B. FRANKLIN, 2ND CASUAL CO. C.P.E., STAGING AREA #2, CHARLESTON, SC
(Oct 10, 1942)

Dear Bessie & all,

    Just a few lines to let you know I arrived back here safe and feeling fine. That was some ride I had back home. The train was so crowded and hot. We got back in Reading at 1:45 A.M. We did have a nice time at home and the eats I can't forget them.

    Mama & Papa sure did look well, don't you think? Fred sure did look well and has put on some weight since I last saw him. Well Bessie, since I arrived back here, I have not done anything but sleep and eat. Have you heard from Earnest or Gilbert as yet? I had a letter waiting for me from Gilbert when I got back. But he had the same news. Crying the blues. I think Papa and him write the same kind of letters. Well, Bessie, if you want to you can send me that package. I will accept it with many thanks. The weather sure is warm down here. I put my summer clothes back on and do they feel good. Bessie I was at a soldier trial yesterday and he got 10 years in jail at hard labor with a dishonorable discharge. The crime he committed was going over the hill three times. Very heavy, don't you think? And another boy got 5 years for breaking out of jail. Bessie, when I get to town I will try and send you something from the army. So, I will close for this time. When you find time drop me a line.

Love to All
Your Bro
Herman

P.S. Put this in your scrapbook.

Henry Franklin (Pa), Herman Franklin,
Virginia "Jenny" Franklin (Ma)
in Gretna, VA.

Herman Franklin, wife Cleo, and Micheal
(Mikey) Conlon in Gretna, VA.

Herman Franklin with his sister, Elizabeth Franklin.

PVT ERNEST H. FRANKLIN, 13TH TROOP
CARRIER SQD, A.P.O. 3287 C/O POSTMASTER
SAN FRANCISCO, CA
(October 12, 1942)

Dear Bessie & All,

Well, Bessie, I am now in Calf. I arrived here ok after a long trails man trip. There sure was some pretty on the way up. Well, Bessie, I don't know how long I will be here. You know what I told you in my last letter before I left. Well, I don't think it will be long now, but I am ready. I sure did hate to leave Ohio. I really had a good time while I was there. Bessie, when you get this letter wright straight back if you have time and send it air mail because I would like to hear from you as I might not be here but a short while. Tell me all of the news. Well, Bessie, there is not much that I can say now, so I guess I will close and will write again if I stay here any length of time so the best of luck until I hear from you all. Tell all hello.

Lots of Love
Ernest

My address
Pvt Ernest H. Franklin, 13th Troop Carrier Sqd, A.P.O. 3287 c/o PM San Francisco, California

PVT GILBERT FRANKLIN, CO. C 141ST INF REGT, APO36, CAMP EDWARDS, MA
Tuesday Night (October 13, 1942)

Dear Ma & Pa,

    I wrote you a letter yesterday and last night they told us that we couldn't send any more mail and I had to burn it up. They said that we were leaving, so today at noon they said that it had been postponed for a while. I wrote you a long letter but this one will be short because I am disgusted. I am so worried I don't know what to do. We all thought that we were going to get a furlough, but now we know we won't. I think it a shame we have worked so hard and to think that we won't get a chance to come home. I know we are much as gone now but if you don't hear from me, you will know what has happened, but you still can write to me. Well, Ma, I received the package and show was glad to get it. I am writing by one of the candles now. All the boy show was glad I got them because we can't get them here. I am awful afraid that I won't get the chance to use all of them. The rest of the thing show did come in good but don't send me nothing more because I won't need it. I know when Jimmie hears about this, she will be blue. I was hoping to get a furlough, but I won't now. It show was a sick bunch when we heard what we did. Well Ma, I will thank you again for the package so I will write again soon.

Love Gilbert

This letter was in with others from Jimmie. Based on the contents, it sounds like a second Boston trip. I cannot figure out exactly when that happens, but it sounds like it's right about here.

FROM JIMMIE TO MA
Sunday Night (October 18, 1942?)

Dear Mother & all,

I will try to answer your letter and I know you must think I have been rather slow getting around to it but really my intentions have been very good. I was busy last week getting ready to go see Frankie that I honestly didn't think of anything else. Mother, I surely do wish you could go with me sometime to see Frankie as I know he would love to see you. He really looks wonderful, and we really had a swell time. I met Frankie as I did before in the station. We got a room in the hotel and stayed the night together until nine o'clock on Sunday night. We had such a good time mother, but the time passes so quickly that it almost seems like a dream about us being together.

Saturday we really didn't do much of anything except love each other. Saturday night we went out for a while, then went back to the hotel and talked most all night. I don't think either of us slept more than three hours all night. We had so many things to tell each other, lots. I certainly did enjoy being with Frankie more than anything in all the world. I do love him so much and I miss him so much, and when he left me in the station on Sunday night, I don't think I would have felt any worse if someone had shot me. I cried until time for me to leave, then cried until I finally fell asleep on the train. Mother, I certainly am doing everything on earth that I can to make your son happy cause I do love him so much. He has always been so good to me and mother I still say and will always say that I have the best man on earth. I say my prayers every day and night that we will be back together again soon. When that day comes, I will be the happiest person in all this world.

Mother, I do hope Ernest hasn't gone across yet and I hope and pray that none of them will have to go. I wrote to Herman a long time ago but have never heard from him. I have been intending on writing again but just haven't got around to it as yet. I'm so glad that Herman and Ernest got to come home, even if it was a short visit, I know it helped so much. Sure do wish I could have seen them. How is Mr. Franklin and Elizabeth? Tell them "Hello" for me and to be sure to write to me sometime. I sure wish I could come see you all but don't know just when I can. Tell Elizabeth and Gladys I wish they would come up and see me.

Well, mother take care of yourself and I'm hoping and praying Frankie and I will be together again soon.

Love to you all,
"Jimmie"

PVT ERNEST H. FRANKLIN, 13TH TROOP CARRIER SQD, A.P.O. 3287 C/O PM SAN FRANCISCO, CA
(October 24, 1942)

Dear Bessie,

I received your letter today was pleased indeed to receive it. Well, Bessie, our time is just a matter of days now, before we hit the waves. We thought we would have been gone before now. Our planes are already gone. But we do not know where they are. We are relly taking infantry training now. We go on a hike most every day. We were on a twelve-mile hike Tuesday and you know that walk is pretty tough not being used to it. One boy fell out. But they have got to make it a lot tougher than it is now before they ever see me fall out. If the other can take it, I know I can. We really should be in the pink when this training is over. We have a small pack and are going to be issued rifles. I was on the firing range the other day and out of fifteen shots I made 13 bull's eyes. I hope I can keep that score. And I will bring back a belt full of those little yellow men scalps.

Bessie, I know you were glad to see Herman. I sure wish I could have been there with you all. Maybe it won't be so long before we all can be together again. I got the pictures, and it sure was a good picture of both you and Herman. Bessie, I believe you have put on some weight haven't you. I also got the money, thanks a lot, but Bessie you shouldn't have sent it. I hope someday I can repay you for being so good to me. Bessie, I asked the officer about the other letter you sent me with the money in it. And he said he would see what he could do about it. Although we have but a short while now. But I hope he can locate it. Bessie, it wouldn't be a good idea for you to send be a box because I do not know when or where we will go, and I might not receive it. But I thank you just as much as if you had sent it. Bessie from what you said I guess Gilbert is having it pretty tough. I haven't heard from him for some time. But he didn't know where to write to me.

Bessie, we have some of that field ration issued to us the other time we were supposed to leave. It is made something like a Hershey bar. Bessie you said if I needed anything to let you know. I will Bessie and thanks for the offer but so far, I have made it pretty good altho I haven't saved anything. But Bessie, that is one thing a soldier never think of is saving. I have seen some get paid one day and the next day they are broke, but we all live like brother if one has got money the other one has. Bessie have you heard from Jimmie lately. I haven't heard from her in a long time.

I wrote her the last letter, but she never answered it. I had a letter from home and also one from Gladys this week. They seemed to be getting along ok. Bessie I sure would like to see Micky and C.A. I bet Micky is really a tomcat. Tell them both I said hello. Bessie, I wanted to have a picture made of myself and send one to you all. But ever since I left Miss. I haven't been able to get anywhere in the day to have one made. So if I don't get you one during the battles, maybe I can get you one while I am serving my last six months. By the way Bessie, today is my anniversary six months today was sworn into the army. Well, Bessie, I am not allowed to tell anything about the place I am at so I guess I had better stop. I want to thank you again for the money and picture. Bessie, if you don't hear from me for quite a while you will know the reason why. But I would like to hear from you or after as you can find time to write. So, until I hear from you again, the best of luck to you all. Tell all hello.

Lots of Love
Bro. Ernest

P.S. My address will be the same when I leave.

PVT GILBERT FRANKLIN, CO. C 141ST INF REGT, APO36, CAMP EDWARDS, MA
Saturday Night (October 24, 1942)

Dear Ma & Pa,

I guess I owe you a letter. I owe everyone else. Well, I am still up here on this island and don't know how much longer we will be here. It began to get cold, and I have been sick with a cold and I feel so bad it looks like I can't get better. Ma, I thought I was going to leave and go across and Jimmie come to Boston, Mass to see me last weekend and we show did have a good time. She was so glad to see me, and I know I was. She show has been good to me. I got a letter from her sister today and she said that Jimmie

Mother was in the hospital with some kind of stomach trouble but not serious but don't tell Jimmie. They said that they weren't going to let her know for a while because she had too mutch to worry her. Ma, I am going to get a furlough the first of the month but I don't know whether I will get to go anywhere because my money is short you know, take out that allotment and my insurance I don't have anything left and Jimmie hasn't gotten anything yet. I don't see why I was in hopes that she would get it so I could have some money when I came home, and it takes so much when she comes up to see me.

Ma, I got a letter from Ernest today and he was still in Cal. [California] but expecting to leave anytime. I wrote to him today. I got a nice box of candy from Gladys and it show was good. We almost starve to death here it get to be terrible. Well, I hope it will be a chance to get to come down to see you.

Gilbert

S/SGT H.B. FRANKLIN, 2ND CASUAL CO. C.P.E., STAGING AREA #2, CHARLESTON, SC
(Oct 26, 1942)

Dear Bessie,

I guess you thought I had forgotten you. But I have been transferred to a new company. I like it fine so far. Don't know what my duties, I will have as yet. I received the package all ok and thanks a lot. Will write you a long letter soon.

Herman
Post Hq Command
Med Dept Det
N. Charleston, S.C.

PVT GILBERT FRANKLIN, CO. C 141ST INF REGT, APO36, CAMP EDWARDS, MA
Wednesday Night (October 28, 1942)

Dear Ma & Pa,

    I got a letter from you today and I will try and answer it. Well, we are still on the island, but we got word today that we were moving in barracks in camp Edwards, but my address will be the same. I show will be glad when we move it so cold up here. I was on guard duty yesterday and last night and it rained all night and I got soaken [soaking] wet and I have a cold so bad I can't hardly live. Well, if they don't kill us before we leave, I know I will come back. Ma, you said something about me writing a letter for you to put in the paper well that one I would write would be so hot it would burn the press up. Ma, I am getting a furlough the first of Nov. but it cost so much I don't know whether I will be able to go anywhere. You know I took out insurance and an allotment and they have been taken out every month but one and it only leave me seventeen dollars a month for the rest of the things. I have to have, and you know Jimmie hasn't got a penny yet. I don't see why. You know it would have come in good now that I am getting a furlough. I have never been out of this camp but twice and that was to go see Jimmie. I never have drank anything since I been in the army. Well, I still don't like the army.
    My address will be the same if we move.

Love to all, Gilbert

Equipment ready for inspection.

PVT GILBERT FRANKLIN, CO. C 141ST INF REGT, APO36, CAMP EDWARDS, MA
Friday Night (October 30, 1942)

Dear Ma & Pa,

    I received the letter with the pictures in and the show was good, and did you mean for me to keep all of them. Ma, I thought I would write to you and tell youth I got them. Well, I will for sure leave here Sunday Morning on my Furlough I am going to Washington but from there I don't know what I will do. Time I buy my ticket I haven't had much left you know I don't get much and I think they have done me wrong by not sending what money I have put in. I am going to see why they don't pay it. Ma, don't write to me any more till you hear from me. I only get a week on my Furlough but will try if I can to come to see all of you. Well, we move Monday in Barracks so that will be better.

Love to all, Gilbert

NOVEMBER

In November, the Second Battle of El Alamein ends with Rommel retreating during the night. Soviet forces surround the Germans in Stalingrad, turning the tide. The Naval Battle of Guadalcanal ends with the US suffering heavy losses but keeping control of the sea around the Island. Uncle Ernest arrives in the South Pacific.

> S/SGT H.B. FRANKLIN, 2ND CASUAL CO. C.P.E.,
> STAGING AREA #2, CHARLESTON, SC
> (November 4, 1942)

Dearest Bessie & Fred,

 I guess you thought I forgotten you. But not by a long shot. I have been moved again. Transferred to a new company.
 It is very nice down here. This is a new place just opening up. We are supposed to have 2,000 men when it is completed. And the best of all, I am to be here permanently. Any way this is a permanent party. So, I can relax for a while.
 I am back in the mess hall looking after the food again. It seems that I can't get out of the mess if I want to. Anyway, I can eat.
 Bessie, I received the book, I thought it was very funny and some good jokes. And again, I want to thank you for the package you sent me about a month ago. That cake was wonderful. I had a letter from home to-day and they all three seem to be in the best of health and one from Cleo and she was fine.
 Say are you getting ready for Xmas? I'll bet you are. Now look, I don't want you to get me anything for Xmas. I am telling you in time because you have other places to spend your money.
 I will appreciate a card more than all the trouble you go through buying something.

Well, about the weather down here. It has been like spring. We are still wearing our summer clothes. It is only cold in the evening and mornings. Hope it stays the rest of the year this way.

Has Fred planning ongoing hunting this fall. Wish I was up there to go with him. I will close for this time, write when you can.

love to all

Your bro, Herman.

PS Keep this insignia, don't know if I will need it again.

Herman's Patch.

PVT GILBERT FRANKLIN, CO. C 141ST INF REGT, APO36, CAMP EDWARDS, MA
Tuesday Night (November 10, 1942)

Dear Ma & Pa,

I arrived here in Camp Edwards today 10:30. I left Washington Monday night at eleven o'clock. Well, I show did have a good time Ma. We wrote you a card when we come back and forgot to mail it, but I told Jimmie to write. The company had moved in Camp Edwards and its mutch better than in the tents, but it cold and raining. Well, Ma, I show did have a good time down there and show did hate to leave. I show did hate to leave Jimmie. I know she will miss me because I miss her. I hope to come back sometime soon. Well, I will write more next time.

Gilbert

PVT GILBERT FRANKLIN, CO. C 141ST INF REGT, APO36, CAMP EDWARDS, MA
Friday Night (November 13, 1942)

Dear Bessie & Fred,

I guess I ought to have written to you sooner, but I have been so busy trying to straighten out things. We have moved in barracks, it mutch better but all of us have taken colds since we move its so hot in here and it air condition and you know how that is. I got back on time. I left Washington Monday night at 11 o'clock and got to camp at 10 o'clock Tuesday. I show did have a good time Jimmie hate to see me leave well when I came back, I hope to stay and I hope it won't be long. I haven't heard from home, yet I wrote just as soon as I got here. Well, I will close. Love to all.

Gilbert

S/SGT H.B. FRANKLIN, PORT HDQ COMMAND, MED DET. DPT. N. CHARLESTON, SC
(November 15, 1942)

Dearest Bessie,

Will answer your letter which I received this week and glad indeed to hear from you. This leaves me all ok and hope it finds you all in the best of health.

Today is Sunday, and this has been the most beautiful day you ever seen in a long time. It was like spring. You can still wear your summer clothes down here.

Bessie I'll bet you all had a swell time while Gilbert was at home and I am glad he likes much better than he did before. I know it makes Mama & Papa feel much better.

Bess, you were asking me in one of your letters what A.W.O.L. means. It's Absent Without Official Leave and going over the hill that means desert [desertion] or going away and not coming back to your post. Yes, Bessie I received the other book and thanks a lot.

You ask me if I was wanted back at Fort Jackson. Yes, that was right. But just as soon as they found out I was wanted back there, the Colonel sent me down here and when I first got here, no one wanted me. Now there is a fight between two Company about me each one wants me to work for them. So, you can see how I stand.

Bessie, I wish I could tell you more about this place and only if you could see it. You see this is a Port of Embarkation and you can judge what it looks like.

As news is not so much around here, I will close. Hoping to hear from you soon.

Love to all, Your Bro, Herman.

PVT GILBERT FRANKLIN, CO. C 141ST INF REGT, APO36, CAMP EDWARDS, MA
Sunday Evening (November 22, 1942)

Dear Bessie & Fred,

    I received the package. I was surprised to get it and I show was glad to get it. I also received your letter. I have written to you. I hope you have gotten it by this time. I owe so many letters. I wrote to all of them since I come back. I got a letter from Herman he show is lucky isn't he.

    Well, it looks like we will have to go now. I thought one time that we wouldn't but now I know we will. We are getting ready to leave now. I think it will be between now and the fifteen of next month as far as we can find out all the fellow have to be back off their furlough by the 6th of Dec.

    Bessie, I show did have a good time while I was on my Furlough. I show do wish this war was over so I could come back. It so cold up here we almost freeze, but it's nice and warm inside. They feed much better since we moved. It looks like I can't get enough to eat, I ought to get fat as mutch as I eat. Bessie we are putting on a big display and a parade Monday, Tuesday, Wednesday and I will be in it by some mistake. They picked 36 men from each Co and it so happen that I was one of them. Bessie, we got 300 more trained men for this dive to make it full strength so that a good sign we will be leaving soon.

    Bessie, I guess Ernest has gone over I haven't heard from him. I have written to him twice. Bessie every letter I get from Jimmie she says she is buying something for us to go housekeeping she is sure to do it when I get out. Well, I guess it would be the best and we would be mutch better off. Bessie did Jimmie send you the pictures yet, she sent me the first ones, but I haven't sent them back they were pretty good. Bessie, I have about 8 more letters to write so I will have to close, and I want to thank you again for the package. Bessie, if I leave, I will write you tell Fred hello and also tell the kids I said hello.

Love Gilbert

PVT GILBERT FRANKLIN, CO. C 141ST INF REGT, APO36, CAMP EDWARDS, MA
Wednesday Night (November 25, 1942)

Dear Ma & Pa,

I got your letter. Glad to hear from you. Well, I got a few days to go down to see Jimmie. I only got 4 days to be with her, so her people wanted us to come up to see them, so we decided to go up. We went one day and came back the next. So that way I was on the train most all the time. I spent four nights all together on the train, so you see I didn't get mutch rest. I was down to see Bessie twice. We spent one day with her. I had a very good time. What little time I was there. It was 20 below zero when I got back to camp. I got a letter from Herman and he was home on a furlough. He got 14 days lucky.

Ma, I show would have liked to have come down to see all of you but you know I just didn't have the time and I had promised Jimmie mother I would come to see them and they were so nice to me. Well, I will write you a letter when I get the chance.

Love Gilbert

The following letter is a V-mail. Here, Uncle Ernest tried to fit as much on the paper as possible, so he wrote small and with what looks like a medium nib fountain pen. That made parts of it illegible. I put brackets around parts that I believe are correct. I have put a dash in for each letter I cannot decipher. He finally arrives in the South Pacific. All letters going there are sent to the PostMaster, San Francisco, California.

PVT ERNEST H. FRANKLIN, 13TH TROOP CARRIER SQD, A.P.O. 3287 C/O P.M SAN FRANCISCO, CA
November 27. (somewhere in the South Pacific)

Dear Bessie,

    Where I am, and the set up of the camp I cannot tell, but I am fine and ok. We arrived safely without any [trouble]. it wasn't as ---- leaving ---- on the ships. We only had two meals a day, and salt water to wash in. But since we have landed it is much better we have three meals a day, and plenty of fresh water, there is a [large stream of water close by where we are], and I was in swimming today and it was relly nice Bessie when you wright to me again change my APO number to 502 and I hope to hear from you as often as you can fine time to wright. I will wright as much and on often as I can. Tell Fred, C.A. and Mickey hello and I wish you all the best of health, and a ------ -------, I ------ ----- lot better felt before I left Calf.

Love Ernest

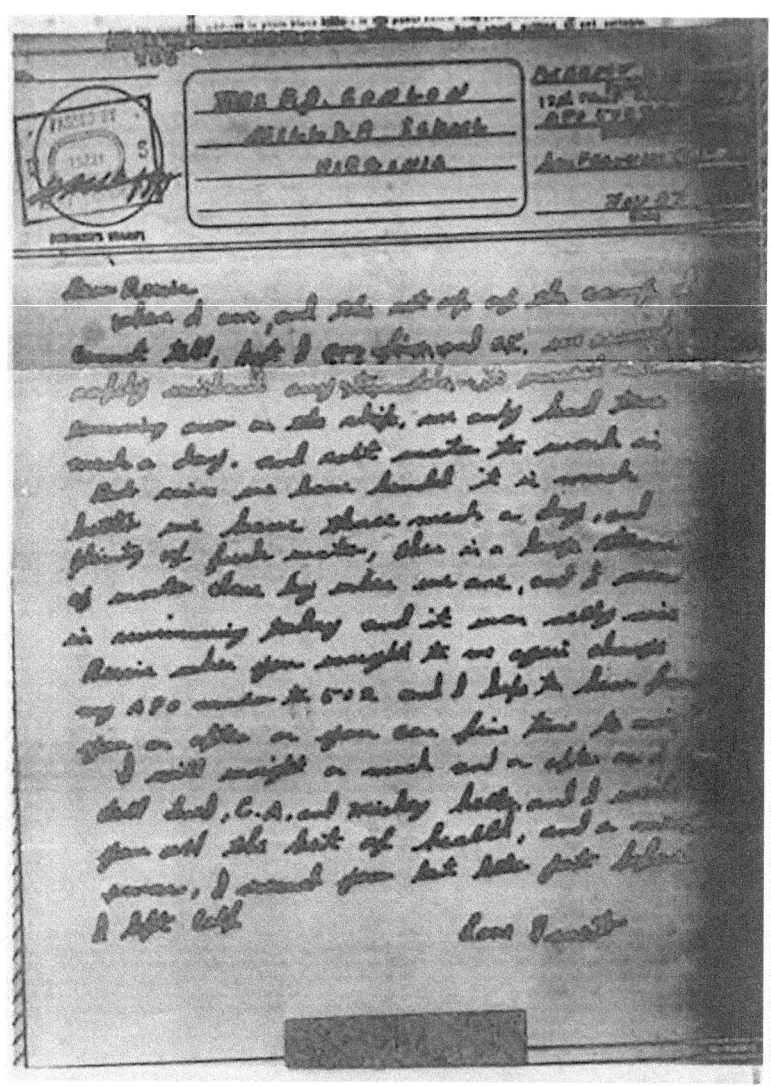

The image of Uncle Ernest's Vmail Letter.

JUST A FEW LINES

PVT GILBERT FRANKLIN, CO. C 141ST INF
REGT, APO36, CAMP EDWARDS, MA
Saturday Night 8:00 (November 28, 2942)

Dear Ma and Pa,

    I will answer your letter I have written to you, I guess you have gotten it by this time. Mom, I show was surprised to hear that Elizabeth had gotten married. Is she going to live with his people? I think it a awful time for anyone to get married, but I did. Mom, it looks like we will have to be leaving here soon I don't know exact when, but it will be after the 15th of next month. Mom, I have been so sick with a cold I nearly cough myself to death I just can't get rid of it. You have to be dead before they will do anything for you. It has been raining for a week up here. We haven't been out for a week until today and it was so cold, we almost froze it was down to 14 this morning. Well, mom, I got a letter from Herman and he is doing good I also got a letter from Gladys and she said that she was well. If you make a fruitcake, will you send me just a little piece. Now I know how hard it is to get things to make them so if you don't make any that will be alright but don't bother sending me anything else I might be here and I might not so if you don't hear from me in a week you will know why. Well I don't feel good, so I am going to bed until I hear from you so long

Gilbert

ARTHUR L. JOHNSON

PVT GILBERT FRANKLIN, CO. C 141ST INF
REGT, APO36, CAMP EDWARDS, MA
Monday Night 8:30 (November 30, 1942)

Dear Bessie & Fred,

I received the papers and your letter with the pictures, and I thought the picture was good and Bessie I show do thank you for the papers. I got them Sunday and read them most the day. Bessie, I had to work all day thanksgiven [Thanksgiving.] I was on KP, that working in the kitchen, but the rest of the Co was off. Bessie I was surprised to hear Elizabeth got married but I think it was an awful time for her to get married don't you and I know from experience although I wouldn't take any two for being married, and I do think I have a good wife don't you from what you know of her? She has been so good to me and I will say you and Fred show have done everything anyone could do and Bessie I don't know why but I can't help from crying when I get a letter from you they are so good.

Bessie, I received three packages from Jimmie today you ought to see a basket of fruit she had sent to me from Woodward & Lothrop it's the prettiest thing you ever seen but the other package I did not open. Bessie there will be no chance for me to send any one anything I only get a little after everything is taken out and we haven't got the allotment yet but gathered still taken my money out. Well, it will be good when we do get it. Bessie we are show to go across soon but as to the date I do not know. But they have stopped the Furlough, and they told us today that today was the last chance to turn anything that that was worn out. We will be here until the fifteen of this month, I am sure. Jimmie knows because she was told.

Bessie, I am sure that Jimmie will send you those pictures because she said that she was having some made for you and Ma. Bessie, I have been almost dead with a cold. We went on a hike this morning five miles and made it in 40 minutes and made it back a little less than that. Boy, I almost gave out, but I made it. Bessie we are having a black out tonight we had to nail blankets over the windows and it so hot in here we can't hardly stand it. It so many men in here it's over 100 men where there ought to be 63. Bessie Now I don't expect anything from any of you because there is nothing, I can have in this army but what you have always give me came in just the right time and was just what I wanted. Well Bessie I will have to go it's time for the lights to go out 10 o'clock. Tell the kids that I show would like to be there Christmas to fix the tree. Tell Fred to take care of that cold. Tell him to get some good licker [liquor] and drink it.

Love Gilbert

DECEMBER

In December 1942, gasoline rationing began at home. Rommel retreats to Tripoli. The first bombings of Naples occur.

> S/SGT H.B. FRANKLIN, PORT HDQ COMMAND, MED DET. DPT. N. CHARLESTON, SC
> (December 1, 1942)

Dear Bessie,

    Here goes again a few lines. I am in the best of health. And hope it find you the same. And the rest of the family.
    Well, about the weather it has been raining here to-day. And a little gloomy. Kinda get a guy down.
    Yes, I guess it seems a little lonesome at home since Elizabeth got married. I began to think she was not the marrying kind. But she fooled the hell out of me.

But things happen so fast now days. Bessie, I did not think she was in love with that Guy. But any way I hope she has a successful marriage and lots of success. How did Mama and Dad take the marriage?

Yes, I received a letter from Gilbert, and he seems to be getting alone fine. And said that he had gained lots of weight.

Bessie thanks a lot for that picture of me. I sent it to Cleo. She puts them all away for me. I received a package from her to-day cigars candy writing paper hankie & sock. Just something to keep up my courage.

I am eating candy now and writing you so it this letter get sticky blame the candy.

Bessie, I am sending you one of my new insignia of my new company. I think it is a little pretty.

Bessie, you can send me another cake if you want to. I don't refuse anything when it comes to eats.

I will close for this time when you find time drop me a few.

> Your Bro.
> Love to all.
> Herman

PVT GILBERT FRANKLIN, CO. C 141ST INF REGT, APO36, CAMP EDWARDS, MA
Wednesday Night (December 2, 1942)

Dear Ma and Pa,

I received your letter and glad to hear from you. Mom, I show have been sick with a cold I thought I couldn't make it this morning. I have the worst cough I believe I ever had. I am going to make a sick call in the morning if I ain't any better. I just can't make it mutch longer. Ma, I got a letter from Herman today and he said that he liked pretty good the new outfit he is in. He said that he had heard from his old company and part of them was in England and part of them was in Egypt.

Well, mom it looks like we will be leaving soon they told us today that if we were absent as much as two days that we would get no less than 20 years in prison. Well, I don't mind going over, but it will be so long before we get back. Well, mom I received three presents from Jimmie you are to see the basket of fruit she sent me it was the prettiest thing you've ever seen. I got a big bar of nuts, a sweater and a pocketbook with some money in it and it also sigrettes.

Mom we got warning today that it was a storm on the way and I think part of it is got here. We didn't go out today it rained all day and tonight you can't get outside for the wind it almost blow you away. It has been raining up here for two weeks. Well mom if I hear from Jimmie this week, I will send you the money to buy the comfort mom I thought of giving $10 for it don't you think you could get a good one for that. Or do you think I could get her something else I want her to tell me what color to get but she doesn't know I am getting her anything. Mom how do you spell Bessie's kids name I just don't know I want to send them a Christmas card.

      Well, I will close so love to both of you,
              Gilbert

PVT GILBERT FRANKLIN, CO. C 141ST INF REGT, APO36, CAMP EDWARDS, MA
Saturday Evening (December 5, 1942)

Dear Ma & Pa,

  I will write you a short letter. I received your letter and the card Gladys sent. I also got a letter from Gladys. Ma, if it all the same to you I will send Gladys the money to get the comfort. Ma, don't you think that nice to give her.

Ma Jimmie got Elizabeth something for Christmas for both of them and I think what she got was nice and for Mike Bessie kid. I think is nice. Now Ma, what Jimmie gets and gives to all of you is from me to because I can't give something too.

Ma, now you and Pa don't worry about Ernest because Jimmie has found out that he is safe where he is, and you will soon hear from him. Now don't worry because I will soon be in his shape. I know we will have go. They are making all our clothes and giving us more shots in the arm. Ma my cold isn't much better, it cold as it can be up here, and I was on guard Friday night and almost froze. Ma now please don't send me much for Christmas because I don't have anywhere to put it just a piece of cake and that all. Now Ma I will send the money to Gladys to get the comfort [comforter]. Well Ma, now don't you and Pa worried because we will all be back soon, I hope. I know how you feel, and I don't think anyone has worried as mutch as I have. Ma, I weigh 133 lbs.

With love, Gilbert

PVT GILBERT FRANKLIN, CO. C 141ST INF REGT, APO36, CAMP EDWARDS, MA
Sunday Evening (December 6, 1942)

Dear Ma,

I wrote to you yesterday, but I received your package and I thought I would let you know I received it. Ma, you don't know how mutch I enjoyed getting it. I open it and I show was glad to get it. I eat last night until I thought I would bust. Well, I don't have mutch news as I just wrote to you. I tried to get a money order to send Gladys but I can't get it until Monday so I guess it will be soon enough. Ma let me know when you here from Ernest and do you still write to him and if you do is it the same address. Ma,

I still have an awful cold I don't think I will ever get rid of it. It no use trying to take anything because we are out in all kinds of weather. Well, I want to thank you again for the package and it was in good shape. Well, I will close so love to all.

Gilbert Franklin

PVT ERNEST H. FRANKLIN, 13TH TROOP CARRIER SQD, A.P.O. 502 C/O P.M SAN FRANCISCO, CA
Dec. 8, 1942

Dear Bessie,

I received your letter which was mailed Nov 16. Was pleased indeed to receive it. This leaves me o.k. hope it finds you all the same. I would have liked very much to have been with you all when Gilbert was there. I am glad he is liking (the army) better. Well, Bessie, it has been raining here for about five days now. Well, I guess Ann and Guy are proud of their new baby. I knew it was to happen, but I didn't think it would be so soon. Do you know if Guy ever got well? Bessie, as I told you before this is not much to write about here. So, I will cut this short. And I hope to hear from you as often as you can find time. Tell all hello and good luck until I hear from you again.

Love Ernest

ARTHUR L. JOHNSON

PVT GILBERT FRANKLIN, CO. C 141ST INF REGT, APO36, CAMP EDWARDS, MA
Wednesday Night Dec. 8, 1942 (actually Dec. 9)

Dear Bessie & Fred,

    I think sometimes I am half crazy, I just can't think whether I wrote to you last night or not. This cold I have has nearly got me. Well, Bessie, I received the package you sent me and I am writing and tell you I received it. I don't have mutch time to write you mutch but will write you more next time. I have written I bet 25 letters since Sunday. Bessie the grown is covered with snow, it has been snowing all day today and we have been out in it and I was wet through when I came in. Bessie so far I have heard that we will be here for about 30 days. Bessie, I show would like to give you and Fred something but I think Jimmie is getting you all something so that will be from me too. She hasn't received anything from the gov. yet. Well, Bessie, I want to thank you again for what you sent me. I haven't open it yet. Tell the kids I said hello and be good and Santa will bring them something.

                                                          Gilbert

PVT GILBERT FRANKLIN, CO. C 141ST INF REGT, APO36, CAMP EDWARDS, MA
Saturday Night Dec. 12, 1942

Dear Bessie & Fred,

    I received your letter, and I received the other package. I show was glad to hear from you. And Bessie those two Christmas cards show was good I had forgotten about the one of Fred and I that show was good wasn't it. Bessie, all of you have been so good to me I just don't know how to thank you. Well, the best news I have heard is that Fred has got him that job and you are going to move back to Arlington. I know Jimmie will be tickled to death. You know I just had to set down and write and tell her. You know there is no one there that she can go to see. The kids I show was surprised to get such pretty cards. Bessie, we went on a night problem [training excercise] last night. We laid out on the grown [ground] most all night. It has been snowing up here all the week but most of it has gone but has been cold today. Well, Bessie, I will stop writing long enough to read this book. They just had mail call and I receive a letter with about fifteen pages.

Well, Bessie, I didn't miss it mutch. It was just 14 pages. Jimmie just said that Kahn's department store and most of all in that block burn up but didn't know the cause. Bessie don't you know Ma & Pa was glad to hear from Ernest I have wrote to him twice but no answer but along as he gets my mail I won't say anything because you don't know how good it is to receive mail and I know how hard it is sometime to answer them. People on the outside will never know what the fellows in here has to go through. Bessie when you do move you let Jimmie know, she will be tickle to death she thinks so mutch of you. Bessie, I have wrote more letters in the past two weeks that anyone I believe. I have gotten so many good things I just had to let them know. Bessie, you know Elizabeth never has written me or Jimmie and told us that she was married so I don't know where to write to her. Tell the kids I show do wish I could be with them Christmas. Bessie last night on that problem I was the Lieutenant's runner, that is take messages for him to different Sergeants so this morning he came to me and told me that he want me to be his runner from now on that I did a swell job. He also said I was the first one to take them right. Well, that made me feel pretty good. Well Bessie tell Fred to take a big drink for me and I hope he does good on his new job. Love to all.

Gilbert Franklin

ARTHUR L. JOHNSON

PVT GILBERT FRANKLIN, CO. C 141ST INF
REGT, APO36, CAMP EDWARDS, MA
Wednesday Night Dec 16, 1942

Dear Ma & Pa,

    I received your letter and the package of candy. I show was glad to get it but Ma, don't send me any more candy now because I have more than I can eat. I think all of them send me candy but I show did think a lot of them. Ma, I sent Gladys a money order for her to get Jimmie's present, but I haven't heard from her, but I guess the mail is so busy is the reason. Well, Jimmie wants to come up to see me over the Christmas weekend, but I don't know whether I will be able to get off. I show would like to see her. Ma, we had a real snowstorm Saturday, and I never seen sutch weather. I went out yesterday at the rifle range and almost froze and we went out today and after we had almost froze to death, they then told us it was too cold so they brought us in. I tell you the truth I don't see how we will stand it up here. We have to go out on a problem tomorrow and stay out all day and the snow is at least 6 in. deep. We will be laying on the ground, that the worse part of it.
    Well, we might as well die over here as to go across and get killed. Ma, I have written to Ernest twice but haven't heard from him yet. But as long as he gets my letters I am satisfied because I know how bad he wants to hear from us. But if you hear from him, you let me know what he has to say. Well Ma, I guess it will be a little blue Christmas without Ernest there. Well we all show would like to be there, but it will be impossible. Well Ma, I will thank you again for the box so I will close. Love to all

                                      Gilbert Franklin

PVT ERNEST H. FRANKLIN, 13TH TROOP
CARRIER SQD, A.P.O. 3287 C/O P.M SAN
FRANCISCO, CA
Dec. 25 (1942)

Dear Bessie,

    I received your letter some time ago was pleased indeed to receive it. Bessie, Elizabeth's marriage was quite a surprise to me, but I hope they can make a go of it. And I wish them all of the happiness in the world. Well, today is Xmas day, but it sure doesn't look like any Xmas I have ever seen before. It is relly hot here now. I guess you all went home for Xmas. If so, I imagine you had a nice time.

    I received a letter from home saying that Dad had gone to work in the plant in Altavista. I am glad he did because that is a lot better place than he was working before and it is not haft as hard work. Bessie, I understand that Gilbert was supposed to leave for overseas duty the 15th, do you know if he went or not? Bessie, we moved about twenty miles from where we were and set up a new camp. There has been quite a lot of work. But it is beginning to look pretty nice now. We have lights now and they really help a lot.

    Bessie our food here is much better than I expected it to be although most of it is canned food. Here lately our worst problem has been bread. But I think in a short order we will have plenty of that. Well, Bessie, there isn't much more to write about so in closing this leaves me ok and hope it finds you all the same. Tell all hello.

                                                  Love
                                           Bro Ernest

CHAPTER 3

1943

JANUARY

Japan continues fighting in western Guadalcanal, but will evacuate by the end of the month. Soviets launch an all-out offensive in Stalingrad. The British capture Tripoli, Libya.

The year opens with Ernest in the South Pacific somewhere—the New Hebrides, we believe—and Gilbert is still in Camp Edwards, waiting to go to Europe.

> PVT GILBERT FRANKLIN, CO. C 141ST INF
> REGT, APO36, CAMP EDWARDS, MA.
> Friday, Noon. Jan. 1, 1943
>
> Dear Bessie,
>
> I received your letter. I think I had written to you but there is so many to write to I just forget.
> I show was sorrow to hear that Uncle Elisha Haden died. Well, I wasn't surprised. Bessie I can feel for you when you went down home because I had a time when

I went down Christmas and I said when I came again I would come to stay. But I show did have a good time.

Well, Bessie, I know Elizabeth was some happy when James didn't have to go to the army. Well, I guess it wasn't mutch drinking since all of us not being there. Well, when I get in at Mrs. Jepson where we live, they had me a quart, so I had plenty to drink and I taken advantage of it you know I have never token anything to drink since I been in the army.

Bessie, you just ought to seen the mess here. Last night they paid me off about ten o'clock and at night I think everyone was drunk and gambling. They had three fights. I never seen sutch a time in my life. They show are paying for it today they got every one on a detail sutch as holling [hauling] ashes & coal and everything dirty and they show are sick. Bessie, Jimmie I think would give that kid of your anything she had told me all the time she was going to get it for him I would give the world to seen him. If you don't move, I think Jimmie will go crazy. Bessie I think I told you that Ernest wrote me. I got one letter from him. I also got a letter from Elizabeth and she said since she got married that no one won't write to her I think she is good home sick well I wrote to her.

Bessie I won't [want] to thank you and Fred for the things you gave me, all my things was nice. Well, how do Fred like his job? I am show glad you are coming back to Arlington. Well, I got a letter from home and all was well. So Bessie I will have to close. I got lots more letters to write. So write when you move. Tell Fred I miss drinking with him this Christmas but hope to be with all of you next year.

Yours Truly
Gilbert Franklin

PVT GILBERT FRANKLIN, CO. C 141ST INF REGT, APO36, CAMP EDWARDS, MA
Sunday Night 7 p.m. (Jan. 10, 1943)

Dear Ma & Pa,

    I received your letter, glad to hear from you. Well, it is awful cold up here but today it warmed up a little. Ma, you asked whether Jimmie ever got the policy from my insurance. Yes she did, she get it the day just before I came back from my furlough and I think you ought to see into Ernest because if you don't have it, it's no good. Just keep writing in no matter what they say, write in and ask whether he taken out any. I also wrote to Jimmie to look up and see if they have any record of it.

    Ma has Bessie moved yet I haven't heard from her in a good bit, but I know she is busy. Ma, do you think that Bessie would let Jimmie stay with her for a while? She just worries me to death to get me to ask Bessie to let her stay with her. Jimmie will pay her good. Ma Jimmie got a raise. She is making good now I show do wish I was out so we could get us some place to stay. She is buying a lot of things for us to have when we go housekeeping if I ever get out. Ma, I don't know how long we will be here, but it looks like it won't be long. I got a letter from Gladys the other day and she said that she was well. Well Ma I guess I had better close I have to write to Bessie.

                                            Love to all Gilbert F

ARTHUR L. JOHNSON

PVT GILBERT FRANKLIN CO. C. 141ST INF.
REGT.APO #36 CAMP EDWARDS MASS.
Sunday Evening (Jan. 17, 1943)

Dear Bessie & Fred,

 I don't know whether I owe you a letter or not, but I will write I have so many to write to and sutch a little time to do it in I just don't know who I owe one. Well Bessie, I received the bag of peanuts and did they come in handy. I have been eating on them ever since I got them the show are good. I didn't know what I was getting. Bessie it hasn't been so cold up here for the last week, but it is raining today, it snowed a little yesterday. We went out every day except Monday. They checked all our clothes and gave us all new, but we haven't got all of them yet. Bessie you ought to see the good clothes they throwed away you know the clothes I wore on my furlough the shirts and pants, well they said to me just take a knife and cut them up and we will give you some new ones you know it a shame. I had a new pair of shoes hadn't been worn but a few times they said you have had them too long to throw them away and get a new pair.
 We are supposed to go oversea pretty soon and one company in the Div. are packed to leave but don't know when they will leave. The Lieutenant called me in the office and asked me whether I was able to go in combat that means go in battle. He had heard that my side had given me trouble. He told me if it gave me trouble to get myself in good shape, we was going over sea. I know we are leaving but where and when I do not know. Jimmie is coming up to see me this weekend if I can get a weekend pass. Bessie, Jimmie told me she had found out where Ernest was and said he was in a safe place but wouldn't tell me where he was, she was afraid to write and tell me because they have been open some of the mail. I haven't heard from him in about two weeks, but I got a package

from Ma and it was a nice cake, peanuts, gum and writing paper.

Bessie, do you think you will get your house back? Bessie Jimmie has worried me to death to ask you if you did move back in your and if you had room would you let her stay with you? Mrs Jepson just treat here anyway. Bessie don't let Jimmie know I said she wanted me to ask you. Now if you haven't the room, just don't say nothing to her. But she will pay you well and help you, she is not lazy. Bessie, I guess I will close. I have been washing today my cloths. Tell the kids I said hello.

Gilbert Frank

How do Fred like his job? Tell him to save me a job. I will be home in 1950. I hope.

PVT ERNEST H. FRANKLIN 13TH TROOP CARRIER SQ. APO 3287 C/O P.M SAN FRANCISCO, CALIFORNIA
Sunday, Jan. 17, 1943

Dear Bessie,

I guess you think I have forgotten you, but it is not that, you know or I told you there is not much to write about, or you know we don't and can't get around here like we did in the states, but I enjoy getting your letter, mail is what we look forward to getting here.

You asked me what kind of mail I get the quickest, well I think air mail reaches me faster than any other mail.

Bessie, I know you are very happy to get to go back to Washington. You had better get another room built to your house by the time this war is over because that is where I think I am going. Bessie you asked me about my voyage on this ship. There is not much I can tell you now, but after it is over, we will get together at a hot dog dinner and I will tell you all about it. Bessie, I don't know why Herman and Gilbert haven't heard from me because I have written them both. I have heard from Gilbert, but never yet have I heard from Herman. Bessie, I had the day off today, so I have been making me some furniture for my tent and cleaning up the area around it. Well, Bessie, I guess Elizabeth and James was very happy since James got a deferment. Bessie if you have a picture of Mickey and C.A. I would thank you a lot of if you would send me one, it has been quite a while since I saw them and I know that they have grown quite a lot Bessie you asked me if there was anything I wanted or needed I would like for you to send me a flash light and a pocket knife, the both I once had, but I lost my flash light and broke my knife, and I cannot get either one here. I hope someday I can repay you all for the favors that I have asked of you.

Bessie, once I get back to the states, I will really know how to appreciate it after being over here. Bessie so far, I have three different kinds of foreign money. Well, Bessie, there is not much more to write about so in closing this leaves me O.K. and I hope the same of you all and until I hear from you good luck. Tell all hello.

Love Ernest

Gilbert makes Private First Class, (PFC).

PFC G FRANKLIN CO. C 141 INF REGT APO #36
CAMP EDWARDS, MA
Saturday Evening, 3 p.m (Jan. 23, 1943)

Dear Ma & Pa,

I received your letter, glad to hear from you. Well, I guess I am as well as I ever will be. I have a falling off so mutch since I have had a cold, I am a little better. It has been awful cold up here. We have about 14 inches of snow and has been so bad we couldn't go out and now it has started to snow again and the way it is coming down I don't know how deep it will be. Well, I have wrote to Ernest twice since I heard from him but I am still going to write to him because if he gets my letter I am satisfied because I know how glad he likes to hear from us.

Ma, where is Warren Franklin? Pa said he was learning to ski and was in a cold climate. Ma, I got a letter from Herman and he didn't have mutch to say. But said he thought he was going to get a Furlough the first of February. Ma, it looks like we will be up here for a while now. We were all ready to leave for oversea, but something happen that we didn't go. Most of everything was loaded and now they are unloading part of it. They are giving some of the fellow's furloughs, but I don't know whether I will even get another. If you see Elizabeth, tell her I will answer her letter as soon as I can. Well Ma I don't have mutch news so I guess I will close. Pa you know I never can think to tell you how glad and I won't to thank you for fixing the little cedar chest. And if I ever get out this army, I will pay you everything I owe you, I have never forgot it and it worries me to think of it because I know you needed it.

Love to all Gilbert

FEBRUARY

The Battle of Stalingrad ends with the surrender of the German Sixth Army. Rommel retreats to Tunisia.

PFC GILBERT FRANKLIN, CO. C 141ST INF REGT, APO36, CAMP EDWARDS, MA
Saturday night, 7 p.m. (Feb. 6, 1943)

Dear Ma & Pa,

    I will answer your letter well I don't feel so good but still going. It has been raining for two days but some warmer we have had a lot of snow about 14 inches but this rain has help to make it go away. Well, I got a letter from Bessie and one from Gladys show was glad to get them. I haven't heard from Ernest in quite a while. Ma, I didn't have Jimmie to come up to see me because I was supposed to get a furlough so I thought it would be best for me to come to see her. I was supposed to get ten days but now they have cut it to four day I get mine the 10th of this month. Ma, I don't see how I can come to see you and Pa, I just don't have the time so here is hope I will get another so I can come to see you. But I will be thinking of you. Ma, it looks like we will be here until the first of April. Ma Jimmie told me that she was trying to find out about Ernest's insurance and she said it was safe so don't bother about it.

    Well, I have a lot more (letters) to write so I will close

Gilbert

PFC GILBERT FRANKLIN, CO. C 141ST INF REGT, APO36, CAMP EDWARDS, MA
Sunday Evening (Feb 7, 1943)

Dear Bessie,

    I received your letter glad to hear from you I knew you were busy why you didn't write.
    Well Bessie, I won't write mutch because I expect to see you next week, I guess. I am supposed to get a six-day

furlough starting Wednesday. Well, I have been awfully sick with a cold but a little better now. The weather is been terrible. We have had about 14 inches of snow but for the last two days it has been raining and most of the snow has left. I heard from Gladys the other day and she was well and said Ma & Pa was just fine. I show would like to see them, but I don't get time to go down this time. I haven't heard from Ernest in a long time, but I still write to him. Well, Bessie, I guess we will be up here for a while at least the first of April. I show wish we could come closer so I could come home over the weekends. Well, Bessie, I guess I will see you soon so I won't write mutch.

Love to all of you
Gilbert F.

PFC GILBERT FRANKLIN, CO. C 141ST INF REGT, APO36, CAMP EDWARDS, MA
Saturday Night (Feb. 20, 1943)

Dear Bessie,

I will drop you and Fred a few lines to let you know I got back. Well, I want to thank you both for the nice time you showed me while I was down, sorry I couldn't have stayed longer. I think about those good ham & eggs we had while I was down there. It was 20 below zero when I got back to camp, and I like to have freeze. Well, Bessie, if you write me just send it the same address but we are moving don't know where we are going. They stopped all the furloughs. It is an emergency move, I think. Well, I will write to you later.

Yours Truly
Gilbert

MARCH

The Battle of the Bismark Sea: the US, and Australia sink eight Japanese troop-transport ships over three days near New Guinea. The Battle of Medenine, Tunisia: Rommel's last battle in Africa forces him to retreat.

PVT ERNEST H. FRANKLIN, 13TH TROOP
CARRIER SQD, A.P.O. 502 C/O P.M SAN
FRANCISCO, CALIFORNIA
March 8, 1943

Dear Bessie,

I hope these few lines find you all O.K. I received your letter. At least I had began to think that I wasn't going to hear from you anymore, but I guess you have been pretty busy moving. I hope you soon get straighten out and settled down again.

Well, Bessie it has been raining here for over a week now, and I mean it is really a mess here now, you haft to take about three steps to count for one it is so muddy and slippery, this is the rainy season of the year here now, and by the time it finishes I guess it will really be a mess here. I received the pictures you sent me and thanks a lot for them.

Bessie I am sorry after you went to the trouble to get the thing, I ask you that they can't be sent overseas. I haven't much time now, but I hope when I write to you the next time, I can send you an approval for them to be sent to me. I had a letter from Herman, and he said he was going home as a leave, Gilbert was also getting a leave. In some of their letter they seem to think they have it tonight, but once they get overseas and go through what we have the last week or so they will soon learn no matter how taught it is it can always be a little worse, after you go throughout the rub for a while you soon get so you don't give a dam, then you are all right.

Bessie will C.A. go to school where you are now or will she wait and start in new this coming year. Well, I guess I will close for this time so in closing this leave me OK and I hope the same of you all, and I hope if you can find time you will wright more after, so good luck until I hear from you.

Love to all.
Ernest

PFC GILBERT FRANKLIN, CO. C 141ST INF REGT, APO36, CAMP EDWARDS, MA
Sunday Night (March 14, 1943)

Dear Bessie

I will write you a few lines. Well, we are still up here but ready to move any time all our things is ready to go but might unpack any time. Well, it snowed most all day yesterday but today it show was pretty. Bessie it looks like we are going this time, but you can never tell. I will be so glad when this war is over, I don't know what to do. We have worked awful hard since I came back. I had to send all my personal things home. Jimmie must stay down there a quite a bit she show do think a lot of you and Fred. Bessie you know when you told Jimmie that Anna May was staying down there for a month Well this is what Jimmie said. Frankie Anna May is staying down here for a month and I wouldn't have told you if Bessie hadn't told me to tell you. Bessie, they have got rid of all the men in this div that 38 or over. Well Bessie, I guess I had better close I have about 3 more letters to write.

Gilbert F

ARTHUR L. JOHNSON

PFC GILBERT FRANKLIN, CO. C 141ST INF REGT, APO36, CAMP EDWARDS, MA
Wednesday Night, 7 p.m. (March 17, 1943)

Dear Ma & Pa,

    I received your letter glad to get it well we are still up here ready to leave any time doing nothing but waiting to leave. We did go on a hike today and when I came in I had four blisters on the bottom of my feet and I can't hardly walk. This is the first time I ever had blisters on the bottom of my feet. Ma, they have taken out all the fellows that was 38 years old or over. I don't know what they are going to do with us but I show do wish they would do something with us so we would know what to do.

    Ma, I haven't heard from Ernest in over two months, but I don't guess he can write mutch. Ma do you ever here from Jimmie her mother wrote me and said she just wouldn't write to her. Well, I guess time she gets in she is tired. Ma, I sorrow you have been sick and hope you get better. Well, it has been raining for two days but been pretty warm. Ma, I think Jimmie stays down at Bessie most of the time. I think she likes down there. Ma, where is Warren Franklin now and is that Mayhew boy still with him? Well Ma I guess I had better close so if my mail stop you will know I have left. So, until I hear from you.

Love Gilbert

PFC GILBERT FRANKLIN, CO. C 141ST INF REGT, APO36, CAMP EDWARDS, MA
(March 21, 1943)

Dear Bessie,

    I received the package, and it was so nice. And the cake is so good I want to thank you for them. Well, I thought I had to work today, but I didn't. And I sleep most of the day. I got a letter from Jimmie today and she had wrote it from down at your house. She must like it down there. Jimmie said she felt at home down there. Well, I guess she gets lonesome. Bessie, I got a package from home and mother had sent me a cake and lots of other things to eat. It looks like when you send me something all of the rest send something at the same time. But I can show get rid of it. I have began to gain some weight again. Bessie I can't write mutch but I will write as often as I can. Tell Fred I wish I could be down there to help him work. Well, I guess I had better close tell the kids I said hello.

Thanks for the package,
Gilbert

PFC GILBERT FRANKLIN, CO. C 141ST INF REGT, APO36, CAMP EDWARDS, MA
Wednesday Night, March 24, 1943

Dear Ma & Pa,

Just a few lines to let you know I received your letter and glad to hear from you. Well, I guess you know I can't write mutch all they want you to say is I am well if you are sick and doing fine. Well, it has been awful cold for the last few days. I had a letter from Ernest yesterday and he was fine said it was awful rainy out there. He said that he had just received a letter from Elizabeth.

Tell Pa I know Jimmie will be awful pleased with the cedar chest. And mother don't send me anything because I don't think I will get it. But the cake was just fine and thanks. Mother, I think Jimmie is a little more satisfied since Bessie have moved back. I think she stays down there most of the time. Well, I wish I could take you up on what you said about coming home and you would feed me on Ham & eggs chicken. Well, someday I hope I can. I guess I had better close.

Love Gilbert.

PORT HDQ COMMAND. MED DEPT DET. C.P.E.
CHARLESTON, SC
March 30, 1943

Dear Bessie,

 I guess you thought I had forgotten you. But never. I lost your address, and I wrote home for it a no [number] of times and I just received it about 2 hours ago.
 So any way I am well and hope you and the rest are well.
 Guess you are glad you have finish moving and settled down to home life again. How does Fred like his job? Good, I know.
 Mother told me that your baby has been sick. Hope he has improved as well by now.
 Bessie, do you get to see Gilbert's wife? If you do give her my regards. I have not heard from him in about a month. Mama thinks that he is on his way across, hope not.
 Believe me, the weather is swell down here, everything is nice and green. But we have had lots of rain. As I am running out of news, I will close for this time.
 Love to all

Your Bro, Herman

APRIL

Germany is forced into the corner of Tunisia. Numerous German troop-transport aircraft are shot down before reaching Tunisia, where they were to pick up the isolated German troops.

PVT ERNEST H. FRANKLIN, 13TH TROOP CARRIER SQD, A.P.O. 502 C/O P.M SAN FRANCISCO, CALIFORNIA
April 10, 1943

Dear Bessie,

I received your letter quite a while ago and was very glad to hear from you. I would have written sooner, but I haven't had much time lately. These few lines leaves me O.K. and I hope it finds you all the same. Well, Bessie, I guess you are just about settled now aren't you, Elizabeth wrote and told me that you thought that Mickey would half to have his tonsils removed. I guess you will dread that won't you. Is C.A. going to school in Arlington now. Bessie, when you see Jimmie tell her I received the present a few days ago that she sent me for Xmas and thanks a lot and I will write her soon. Bessie I am getting the request fixed up for those things and will send it to you in my next letter. Well, Bessie, it is the fall of the year here now, and the night are very cool, but the days are still plenty hot. I guess I will close for this time. So, until I hear from you all good luck. Tell all hello.

Love Ernest

PVT ERNEST H. FRANKLIN, 13TH TROOP CARRIER SQD, A.P.O. 502 C/O P.M SAN FRANCISCO, CALIFORNIA
April 19, 1943

Dear Bessie,

I received your last letter and was very glad to hear from you. I hope these few lines will find you all O.K.

As for myself I am okay. I guess by now you are all settled and straighten out from moving, and I know you are glad because there is sure a lot of work allocated to moving. Well, Bessie, I guess Gilbert is well on his way across the pond by now, as I heard from him some time ago, and he said that they were all packed to leave. I guess he hated to go, but I hope him lots of luck. He can at least come back and say that he is a soldier, the soldiers in the states are referred to as a USO soldier and that is just about right. They don't know what soldiering is until once they get overseas. He doesn't have the best there. You can't mail, you got to keep things moving. Bessie about the question you asked me, I can say yes and no, if you remember what you asked me, oh yes Bessie about my collection I haven't any way of drying them so at the present I haven't any.

Bessie, it seems as if Fred is doing all right for himself. More power to him. Tell him to keep a place reserved, because I might want him for a base in a few years. Bessie about those things you were going to send me, well luck happened to fall my way, and I got them here, but I thank you as much as if you had sent them, and I hope you don't feel bad about it after you had to go to the trouble of getting them for me. Bessie, I understand that Elizabeth has gotten her a job, she used to say that she wanted to go to work, now I wonder how she is liking it. Bessie, what about all of these babies being born? I believe the shortage of rubber is doing more harm than it is good, what about it (ha) (ha)

Yes, Bessie, I remember Wilder and Ray, where are they living at now. Have they gone back to W. VA.? Bessie has any more of Mrs. Allison children gotten married?

Well, Bessie, there isn't much more to wright so until I hear from you good luck tell all hello.

Love Ernest

Having only one side of the conversation, you get an answer but can only surmise the question. "Bessie about the question you asked me, I can say yes and no, if you remember what you asked me." I can only guess Ernest was concerned about the censors, as they could open and read any letter. The USO, United Service Organization, provides entertainment for the members of the armed forces. A USO soldier is not a compliment.

Gilbert is now in the European theater. The 141st Infantry of the 36 division goes to North Africa—Tunisia, to be precise. All letters going to the European theater go to New York.

PFC GILBERT FRANKLIN, CO. C 141ST INF
REGT, APO36, C/O P.M. NEW YORK, NY
April 21, 1943 North Africa

Dear Ma & Pa,

Just a few lines to let you know I am OK. We can't write mutch so I told Jimmie to write and tell you when she heard from me and you write and tell her. Because I won't be able to write to both of you often. We are in North Africa somewhere. The country is wonderful here. Mother, write and tell Ernest & Herman you heard from me. Well, I guess I had better close.

Gilbert

PFC GILBERT FRANKLIN, CO. C 141ST INF
REGT, APO36, C/O P.M. NEW YORK, NY
April 25, 1943 (Easter Sunday)

Dear Ma & Pa,

Today is Easter, but I didn't go to church, I could have but it was raining. I am getting on good, but show am homesick. It a lot of things I would like to say, but I don't know what to. Have you heard from Ernest and how is he getting on. I haven't heard from no one since I left. Well, hope to hear from you.

Love Gilbert

MAY

Remaining German and Italian troops surrender to allies in Tunisia. Americans begin to take back the Aleutian Islands from the Japanese.

The following letter was water damaged, so I could not decipher some parts. I still included it because of a few lines that survived about how rationing was in effect.

S/SGT H.B.FRANKLIN, 2ND CASUAL CO. C.P.E.,
1ST STAGING AREA, CHARLESTON, SC
(May 2, 1943)

Dearest Bessie,

I arrived here last night, <u>Sat</u>. to find my company moved to a new area. You will see by address. Believe me, it did feel funny to go where I was staying and to not find anyone, but I found them. We don't have it as nice as we did, but it will do for a while. We are getting a real hospital and things will [ILLEGIBLE] I have my own mess hall now, that makes it much finer.

I received the package all OK [ILLEGIBLE] I like everything very much. [ILLEGIBLE] you don't have to go to that expense. Because you need everything just now. You sure have been good to me since I have been in service. It made me shed a few tears. I hope to repay everything someday.

I had a very nice trip coming down here, no trouble at all, and I only had one soldier to ride with me about 60 miles. No one on the [ILLEGIBLE] I did not mind. All at [ILLEGIBLE] well. I arrived there at 9.15 [ILLEGIBLE] good time, I think.

I will close for this time. Write soon.

Your Bro, Herman

PFC GILBERT FRANKLIN, CO. C 141ST INF
REGT, APO36, C/O P.M. NEW YORK, NY
May 4, 1943

Dear Bessie,

I guess you thought I wasn't going to write well, it won't be mutch. Well, I received a letter today from Jimmie, the first I have heard since I left and that was mailed April 13th. She said she had been down to see mother I guess she gets awful lonesome I know I do, but this country is beautiful. Do you still hear from Ernest I haven't written to him yet I haven't wrote but a few letters I don't have mutch time and you can't say mutch? You let Jimmie know when you get this letter and tell her I am thinking of her. Tell her to write me V-mail and I can get that mutch quicker They give us some V-mail to write but it's hard to get. I am well but awful homesick to be back. Hope to hear from you.

Love Gilbert

PFC GILBERT FRANKLIN, CO. C 141ST INF
REGT, APO36, C/O P.M. NEW YORK, NY
May 16, 1943

Dear Ma & Pa,

I received two letters from you and about 25 from Jimmie and I show was glad to hear from you. Well, I have very little to say there is nothing mutch I can. I show am glad Jimmie got to come down to see you I show wish I had the chance to come down. I know she had a nice time. Well, I heard from Ernest and he was just fine. I wish I could say that for myself. I am in the hospital but hope to be out soon so don't worry. Mother, I just don't have mutch time to write but will write as often as I can.

Tell all the rest if they don't hear from me that I am still thinking of them. Mother Jimmie and Bessie show did want you to come up to see them, I wish you would.

Love Gilbert

JUNE

The Allies bomb Sicily and the Italian mainland to prepare for invasion. The New Georgia campaign begins in the Pacific. Continued attacks in the Ruhr industrial valley in Germany.

P.F.C. ERNEST FRANKLIN 13TH T. C. S. APO 502
UNIT 1 C/O P.M. SAN FRANCISCO, CALIFORNIA
June 1, 1943

Dear Bessie,

 I think I have written since I last heard from you but probably your mail has been delayed so I will write you again. I hope this finds you all well, as for myself I am O.K. Mama wrote and told me about Mickey and C.A. being sick, I hope they are both well by now. Well, Bessie, it is still plenty warm over here in the daytime, but the nights are really cold. I sleep with about four blankets over me at night and that is none too many.
 Bessie things are much better over here now than what they was when we first got here, we have our own P.X. [Post eXchange] now, and we can get candy, cigarettes and most of the odds and ends that we need now it is really a help, and our food is lots better, we have fresh stuff pretty often now, and I mean that tastes good after eating out of cans for so long
 Well, Bessie, I just finished having all of my teeth fixed last week, I had seven filled in all, and I think I got

a very good job. I think the dentist was just about as easy as any I have ever been too.

Bessie I was in civilization not very long ago. I had two nights and two days there. I was supposed to have been there longer, but things turned up and only got the short while, but I enjoyed every minute I was there, there was plenty of everything there for a soldier and I didn't stand short and the people there was swell.

Bessie have you heard from Gilbert since he landed. I understand that he is in Africa. I guess Jimmie is pretty worried about him, isn't she?

Say Bessie if you don't know where I am you can find out from Elizabeth as she knows, speaking about Elizabeth I guess she and James can settle down now since he didn't haft to go to the army, she tells me that she is working now, but I don't think she likes Arlington so much. Well, Bessie, there isn't much more to wright so until I hear from you the best of luck to you all, tell all hello.

Lots of Love
Ernest

A Post Exchange is a small retail store on the base for the soldiers to purchase items. Originally similar to a small trading post, now they are more like department stores.

S/SGT HERMAN FRANKLIN PORT HDQ
COMMAND MED DET DEPT C.P.E.
CHARLESTON S.C.
(Jun 3, 1943)

Dearest Bessie & Gang,

Just a few lines to let you know I am all OK and hope these few lines will find you all the same. Believe me, the weather is some hot down here just now.

The temperature is about 118 degrees outside and no let up to the weather. But we had a lot of rain last week.

Bessie and about our move, it did not last long. We are back where we started from. And believe me, I don't like it at all. But our hospital is being built and we hope to occupy it on or about Sept 15, then that is where my headache will start.

I had a letter from Mama this week and she said that she has received two letters from Gilbert and that he was well, but he was homesick. I feel sorry for him but that don't help the matter at all.

I hear from Cleo real often, and she is well. As I have some work to do, I will close for this time.

Love to all, Herman

PVT E. H. FRANKLIN 13TH T. C. S. APO
502 UNIT NO 1 C/O PM SAN FRANCISCO,
CALIFORNIA
June 8, 1943

Dear Bessie,

I received your letter a few days ago and was very glad to hear from you. These few lines leave me OK and I hope it finds you all the same. I had just written to you before I received your letter, but I will write you again although there isn't much to write about.

Bessie I am glad to learn that Mickey and CA are both well again, but I guess you will dread having to have their tonsils taken out won't you

Bessie I was very glad to know that Gilbert had landed safely. I have his address, but as yet I haven't written to him, but am going to real soon. I hope he likes it there and I wish him all of the luck in the world.

Bessie, I bet you was surprised to see Herman. I sure would like to see him. I haven't heard from his name in quite some time, he sure gets a lot of time off now doesn't he, do you think he will carry Cleo down there to live with him

Bessie you was telling me about Jimmy Allison getting married, well I think it is just about time, as he was engaged about four or five times before this, and broke them all. Do you know what his brother Charley is doing now? I guess you have heard of the trouble that he was once in so I don't guess they would take him into the service because of it.

Bessie how about Guy and Ann living out on their farm I never would have thought that that would happen. I don't guess they have any more children yet, do they?

Bessie you said that Paul and Helen were expecting a new member. Paul is the one that used to sell those shades, isn't he?

Bessie, I know you will be very proud to get your new heating system installed in your house it will be so much cleaner and just about half as much work keeping your home warm.

Well Bessie, I had today off, so this morning I did my washing I think just about everything I own was dirty. Then after lunch it began to rain, so I went to the hospital to see one of my buddies, so now tonight I am trying to get caught up with my letter writing, so you can see that I haven't had much rest, but I am getting my book work caught up, which I am glad to get the time to do it.

Bessie thanks a lot for the picture. It sure was good. Mickey and C.A. sure have growed haven't they. Mickey sure looks like a tomboy in that uniform. Well Bessie, there isn't much more to write, so until I hear from you again the best of luck tell all hello.

Lots of love to all
Ernest F

JULY

Allies bomb Rome and the U.S. takes Palermo, Sicily, the bombing of German factories continues, and the Battle of Kursk takes place.

Gilbert's company has changed. He is now working with the prisoners of war (P.W.E.). Unless the letter explaining it is lost, he does not tell his parents.

PFC GILBERT FRANKLIN HDQ DETACH A.B.S.
P.W.E. 101 APO 759 C/O PM NEW YORK, NY
July 10, 1943 North Africa

Dear Mother,

    I don't get any mail from you but I will write and let you know I am still over here. Well I am workin every day seven days a week. I get awful homesick and one reason is I don't get any mail. I haven't heard a word since April the first. Mother, you write to Jimmie and tell her to try and find out why I don't get the mail that is sent to me.

    Do you ever hear from Ernest? You write to him and give him my address. Well, I guess I feel about the same. My side gives me a lot of trouble, I guess it will always. Mother, the weather is awful hot in the daytime and cold at night, awful dry and windy. Well, I guess I had better close.

Love Gilbert

PFC GILBERT FRANKLIN 6619TH PW
ADMINISTRATIVE APO 759 C/O PM
NEW YORK, NY
July 21, 1943

Dear Ma & Pa,

    I have been getting some mail from you the last two weeks and I show do hope it continues. Well, I guess I am getting on pretty good I work every day and seven days a week. I am also getting plenty to eat we have a lot of fresh vegetables they grow about the same thing here as they do there only, they have oranges and grapes. Mother I show do wish you could just see how these natives live here, and they are so dirty. I hear from Jimmie real often now, but it was a long time before I heard from anyone. I show am glad you went up to see them. Do Jimmie still worry about me? I show do worry about her, but I hope to come back to see all of you I get awful lonesome. My address is changed again but I am in the same place.

Love Gilbert F.

PFC GILBERT FRANKLIN 6619TH PW ADM. CO PROV. APO. 759. C/O PM NEW YORK, NY
July 23, 1943

Dear Bessie,

I haven't any V-mail to write to you on so I will drop you a few lines. I have begun to get some of my mail, and it makes me feel mutch better. Well, I am working every day I have to work seven days a week. It's awful hot here in the daytime. I guess it awful hot there now. I guess you was glad to see Mother when she came up. And, how was she? Did Jimmie come down any while Mother was there? How is Jimmie doing and do she come down to see you like she used to? I think of her all the time if she thinks of me like I do her. I feel sorrow for her. Well, I know she will see this letter if she knows you get it, so I guess I had better close. Write me all the news.

Love Gilbert
I have a new address but haven't moved.

PFC GILBERT FRANKLIN 6619TH PW ADM. CO
PROV. APO. 759. C/O PM NEW YORK, NY
July 30, 1943

Dear Mother,

    I just received your letter and glad to hear from you well I am getting all my mail now but don't know how long before they stop again. Well, I feel pretty good but working hard I never get a day off. I show will be glad when we all can come home. I just wrote to Ernest I only received one letter from him. And of all things, I got a letter from Herman. Very nice. I get awful homesick to be back but nothing I can do about it. Well, we all will be back some day. Tell all I said hello.

Love Gilbert F.

    Ernest does not mention this in his letter, but he is no longer a Private, but a Private First Class (PFC).

PFC ERNEST H. FRANKLIN. 13TH T. C. S. APO
502 UNIT NO 1 C/O PM SAN FRANCISCO,
CALIFORNIA
July 31, 1943

Dear Bessie,

    I hope these few lines will find you all O.K. as for myself I am, O.K., I guess you will be surprised to hear from me, but I would be more surprised to hear from you, as I think this is my second letter since I last heard from you. I have been waiting for a letter from you so I could answer it, but it has never come, but maybe your people back there are too busy to write, or maybe the mail has been delayed but I am hoping to hear from you in the near future. Well Bessie, Mama wrote and told me that she had been up to visit you, she said that she really enjoyed herself. I am glad that she could get to go, because I know she needed the rest.

Bessie I was in civilization about a month ago on a week's rest leave, and I really had a nice time, it sure was good to live like a human again, when a person stays away from civilization so long he soon gets where he don't give a dam about himself or anyone else

Bessie, do you ever hear from Gilbert now? I haven't heard from him in quite some time.

Bessie I am glad to learn that C.A. and Mickey are well, Mama said that they were just about well when she was there. You have had quite a time with them, haven't you?

Bessie, how is the weather back there, we have had quite a bit of rain here lately, and it has really been cold here at nights. I be dam if I don't nearly freeze some nights, but the days are still plenty hot.

Bessie did Paul H. ever go to the army. I heard that they thought he would haft to go. Bessie does Jimmie visit you as much as she used to. I wrote her a letter not so long ago. Well Bessie, there isn't much to write, so until I hear from you the best of luck to you all.

Love
Bro Ernest H

AUGUST

The US bombs oil refineries in Romania and wins the Battle of Vella Gulf off Kolombangara island in the Solomons. The Battle of Vella Lavella begins. Germany occupies Denmark. Gilbert is now a Corporal. He does not mention it in any letter to his parents or sister. He may have mentioned it to his wife, Jimmie, and she informed the others, but those letters are lost.

ARTHUR L. JOHNSON

CPL GILBERT FRANKLIN 6619 PW ADM. CO
PROV. APO. 759. C/O PM NEW YORK, NY
Aug. 3, 1943

Dear Miss Cynthia Ann,

 I received your letter and thought it was awful sweet. I bet you did have a good time down to Grandmothers. Well, I guess school will soon be starting. Do you like to go to school? I think you wrote a nice letter I guess you will be glad when Mike can go to school, then you will have someone to go with you. Tell him I said hello. Do you see Aunt Jimmie very often? She often speaks about you and Mike. Tell her that you got a letter from me and I was thinking of her and to be sweet. Tell Mother and Dad I will write them a letter.

Love Gilbert

CPL GILBERT FRANKLIN 6619TH PW ADM. CO
PROV. APO. 759. C/O PM NEW YORK, NY
Aug. 3, 1943

Dear Mother,

 I just received your letter today I am like you I haven't gotten any mail from you. Don't worry because you will get it. I write at least two letters a week when I can, but you know we move around so mutch it hard to write all the time. That was a nice letter you wrote I am trying my best to keep in good health. Mother, I got a nice letter from the church back home. Did you attend the service they had in the honor of the boys in service? Mother, Jimmie seem to have had a nice time down there, said she got plenty to eat. Mother, I have never touched a drop of nothing to drink over here I am waiting until I come home then I guess I can't get it HA. Tell Pa to not work too hard because he is getting too old too. Also tell him to save me a big drink when I come, it might be aged by the time I get there. Well, I hope you get this letter lots sooner.

Love Gilbert

CPL GILBERT FRANKLIN 6619TH PW ADM. CO PROV. APO. 759. C/O PM NEW YORK, NY
Aug. 10, 1943

Dear Mother,

    I haven't written to you in a number of days because we have moved. So, my address has changed again. I am getting on pretty good. I have another ratting and like my work fine although we are still workin seven days a week. The weather is awful hot, even the nights are hot, but no rain. It hasn't rained since around April the 5th. Mother, I wish you would send me a few handkerchiefs. I don't have any and can't get any. I think you are allowed to send as mutch as five pounds but just send me a half dozen. Well, do you still hear from Jimmie? I guess my mail will be halt up again. I guess I had better close write often.

Love Gilbert

PFC ERNEST H. FRANKLIN 13TH T. C. S. APO 502 C/O P.M. SAN FRANCISCO, CALIFORNIA
Aug. 22, 1943

Dear Bessie,

    I received your most welcome letter a few days ago and was indeed pleased to hear from you.
    These few lines leaves me OK and I hope it finds you all in the best of health.

Well, I had a letter from home the other day and they said that you and your family was there. I hope you enjoyed yourself while being there, how long did you stay.

Bessie you asked me where I went on my leave. Well, I am not allowed to say. No, I didn't meet anyone there that I knew.

Bessie, I had a letter from Gilbert yesterday he seemed to be getting along OK, he says that he is in a different outfit now.

Bessie that sure was a nice picture you sent me of C.A. and Mickey thanks a lot for it they sure have grown a lot since I last saw them.

Bessie since I have been over here, I have seen quite a bit of this south Pacific and from what I have seen I will take just any old place in the U.S. in preference to any place over here.

Bessie, I don't have any idea when we will get back to the states, but I hope it won't be too long, because these natives are beginning to look white to me already.

Well Bessie, there isn't much more to write about, so I am hoping to hear from you again in the near future and until I do the best of luck to you all

Love
Bro Ernest F

CPL GILBERT FRANKLIN 6619 PW ADM. CO PROV. APO. 759. C/O PM NEW YORK, NY
Aug. 27, 1943

Dear Mother,

I haven't heard from you in a long time. So I am writing to you again. Well it's awful hot here and dry I guess it has been hot there. I got four letters from Jimmie today and she said she had been down to see you. Did she have a nice time? She also said she was going to see her mother. I hope she do because her Dad is so crazy to see her. Do you hear from Ernest and Herman? I never have heard from Ernest. I wrote several letters. Mother, if you will notice my APO no. has changed. I have moved again. Mother, will you get Poppa to put something in my car to keep the moths out? Mother, where is Warren Franklin now? Do you know anyone that [is] over here? If you do give me their address.

Love Gilbert F

PFC ERNEST H. FRANKLIN. 13TH T. C. S. APO 502 C/O PM SAN FRANCISCO, CALIFORNIA
Aug. 28, 1943

Dear Bessie,

I received your letter and was very glad to hear from you. These few lines leaves me OK and I hope it finds you all the same.

Say Bessie you and Mama was kept pretty busy with all of that canning wasn't you?

Bessie you all did have quite reunion didn't you I sure wish Gilbert and myself could have been there with you, but maybe in three or four years if we are lucky, we can be there.

Bessie, you say Herman said that he was anxious to go across. Well, he is just a dam fool to want to go across, and I have told him so, but I don't guess he will be satisfied until he finds out for himself.

Bessie is it very hot there now, it has been rather cool over here for the last few weeks, and it has been raining here for about three days, but it won't be long before it will began to get hot again, and I mean it really gets hot here, the climate is just opposite here from what it is there. When it is winter there, it is supposed to be summer here.

Bessie Russel F. sure was lucky to get such a long leave wasn't he, I bet he was sure glad to get it

Bessie you said in your letter that Mickey was sick, well I hope by the time this letter reaches you that he will be in the best of health, Bessie did C.A. make her grade after moving around so much. I hope she did. I don't guess it will be long before school starts again, will it?

Bessie does Mrs. Allison still live at the same place and if so does she still take in borders. Bessie, do you know if Dug Knisley ever got married? Well Bessie, there isn't much more to write this time so until I hear from you again the best of luck, tell all hello.

Love Ernest F

SEPTEMBER

The Allies sign a secret treaty with Italy. Italy then drops out of the war and clears the way for the Allies' invasion of mainland Italy. As General Eisenhower announces the surrender of Italy, Germany occupies Rome. The Allies take Salermo, Italy, while British troops take Taranto in the heel of the Italian boot. The people of Naples sense the approach of the Allies and revolt against the Germans.

CPL GILBERT FRANKLIN 6619 PW ADM. CO PROV. APO. 759. C/O PM NEW YORK, NY
Sept. 1, 1943

Dear Bessie,

I received your letter today and you don't know how glad I was to get it. You know it has been a good while since I heard from any of you. I don't see why Mother haven't been getting my mail because I write at least two letters to them a week. I guess you are having a quite a time down home. I got a letter from Jimmie saying she had been down there but she didn't say she went with you, but I haven't gotten all my mail. I also got a letter from Jimmie and she was up to see her mother and dad. She said her father was in bad shape I don't think he will live long. Bessie it is a little cooler here now I am getting on OK. Will be glad when I can come home. I show would like to see your kids tell them I said hello Bessie you take care of Jimmie for me see that she don't get sick. Tell her I am thinking of her and to be good till I come home. Tell Fred I hope to warm by the heating plant this winter.

Love to all
Gilbert

PFC ERNEST H. FRANKLIN. 13TH T. C. S. APO 502 C/O PM SAN FRANCISCO, CALIFORNIA
Sept. 5, 1943

Dear Bessie,

I received your letter and was very glad to hear from you, and that you had a nice trip back home. I hope these few lines find you all OK as for myself, I am OK.

Say Bessie you and Mama did quite a bit of canning while you was down there didn't you.

Bessie that was a pretty good joke you all pulled on the Scruggs wasn't it. I guess that will teach them a lesson.

Bessie, we used to have mice running all over the tent at night, and eating everything we put down, but a few days ago we got busy and killed six of them in the tent. I found a nest in my cloths and they had ate holes in a pair of pants and shirt and made a nest and it had one baby one in it. We have killed two more since we killed the six, now we hardly ever see any of them. I think we have killed most of them now. I hope so anyway.

Well Bessie, I guess it is beginning to get cool back there now isn't it? We have had quite a lot of rain here for the last few weeks, in fact it is raining tonight. Bessie I am not doing so bad now. I am getting flying pay now, which makes my pay ninety-six dollars a month. I don't know how long this will last, but I hope it continues.

Bessie, I guess Mama and Dad are getting along OK aren't they, I haven't had a letter from them in quite a while, the last letter I think was written around August 10, but I guess the mail isn't coming through so good

Bessie, when you write to me again you can leave off that unit number. It doesn't haft to be on my address anymore. Bessie, I don't think it will be long before I will be having a new address but when I do, I will let you know. Bessie I am sending you a little snapshot, it is not very good, but I hope to send you a better one soon. Well Bessie, I guess I had better close for this time, so until I hear from you again the best of luck. Tell all hello.

Love Ernest F

CPL GILBERT FRANKLIN 6619 PW ADM. CO PROV. APO. 759. C/O PM NEW YORK, NY
Sept 6, 1943

Dear Mother,

I got two letters from you today and one of them was written in June, so you see I don't always get you mail. So, don't worry because you will get the mail sometime. And I have written to Ernest two or three times he will get them soon. Mother, I think I wrote and told you we was getting plenty to eat. They grow the same things over here as we do back there. They have lots of grapes, figs and oranges. It hasn't rain in five months awful dry the weather is fine now cool at night. I will try and send you a card if I get a chance to get any. Mother, I have written to Elizabeth once or twice, I never hear from her. But if

I don't hear from them, I write just the same so tell all them I still think of them. I was at church Sunday I go as often as I can.

Love Gilbert

S/SGT. H. B. FRANKLIN. PORT HDQ
COMMAND. MED DET DEPT C.P.E.
CHARLESTON, SC
(Sept. 10, 1943)

Dearest Bessie & Family,

    Just a few lines to let you know I have not forgotten you all It seems like I can't get around to write to anyone. I have been putting off writing to you until I am ashamed of myself. But any way Bess. I think of you often. And wish I was up there with you.
    Well, the weather has turned a little cooler down here. And I am glad of it.
    About two weeks ago I sprain my ankle and it is still swollen up and I am still limping on it. Believe me, it has been some sore.
    Bessie, I have not forgotten about the cap I promised you I have just keep putting it off mailing it. You don't care what color braid it have on it do you.
    Have you heard from Gilbert or Earnest lately If so, write me the news? I have not heard from them in months.
    Bess I am sending you some negatives. We took in Va. I had forgotten about them. After you are finished with them, send them back to me as I want to have Gladys a set made.
    How is Frank doing now fine, I hope?
    So, when you find time, write.

Love to all,
Herman

CPL GILBERT FRANKLIN 6619 PW ADM. CO
PROV. APO. 759. C/O PM NEW YORK, NY
Sept 11, 1943

Dear Mother,

    I know I have written to you more times than you but long as you hear from me I know all of you are ok. I just got a long letter from Jimmie and one from Gladys Mother you know the letter you wrote and sent Gordon Martin address well if I had got it in time I could have seen him he was here in sight of us but they had moved when I got the letter. The letter was almost two months old. I haven't seen any one since I been over here. I have my name most everywhere in the Red Cross I often try to find someone I know but haven't yet. Mother, don't send me anything for Christmas. It takes so long to get it. I would like to have some cigarettes. Well, we are having some pleasant weather. Tell all I said hello.

Love Gilbert

CPL GILBERT FRANKLIN 6619 PW ADM. CO
PROV. APO. 759. C/O PM NEW YORK, NY
Sept 17, 1943

Dear Bessie,

    I haven't got a letter from you in a good while so I thought I would write to you. Well, I just received two letters from Ernest, and they were four months old, but I was glad to hear from him. I also got a letter from Mother that old. Well, how is the kids and Fred and yourself? I show would like to see the kids. Bessie, why did Jimmie move? She never did tell me, and do you know the place? You know I think all of them forgot my birthday. I don't get the mail from Jimmie like I use to. Write me a long letter. You write sutch good letters and tell me a lot of news.

Gilbert

PFC ERNEST H FRANKLIN. 13TH T. C. S. APO 502 C/O PM SAN FRANCISCO CALIFORNIA
Wednesday, 43 (Sept 29, 1943)

Dear Bessie,

I received your letter yesterday and was very glad to hear from you. Well Bessie, it is beginning to get pretty dam hot over here again, but I guess it is getting pretty cool there now isn't it.

Bessie has C.A. started to school yet, and when will she go this year.

You said that Paul H was leaving for the army, did he sign up for the air corps, if he is drafted how does he know that he will be in the air corps.

Bessie what is Gilbert in now. I never hear from him, and I have heard that he has been transferred.

Bessie I received the package today and thanks a lot for it, as for you sending me something for Xmas thanks a lot for the offer but there isn't anything that I really need.

Bessie you said that Jimmie had moved. Did she move down with the two girlds that she used to live with, or is she living with this man and his wife that she used to live? And Bessie, is her sister's husband Paul still living in the big house on Downing street? Bessie does the buses still run their regular schedules into D.C. with all the gas rotations.

Bessie you said that you hoped that I didn't worry too much about Elaine S. getting married, well that is my least worries. I don't have much time to think of stuff like that now. Bessie, do you remember Mr. Star that boarded at Mrs. Elisann? If so do you know if he ever had to go to the army? Well Bessie, there isn't much more to write this time so in closing this leaves me OK and I hope it finds you all the same, and until I hear from you again the best of luck, tell all hello.

Love
Ernest

OCTOBER

The Neapolitans complete their uprising and free Naples from German occupation and the Free French liberate Corsica. Allies cross Italy's Voltorno line. Naval battle of Vella Lavella.

> CPL GILBERT FRANKLIN 6619 PW ADM. CO PROV. APO. 464. C/O PM NEW YORK, NY
> Oct 11, 1943

Dear Mother,

    I just received a letter from you today, glad to hear from you. Well Mother, I am getting on. I didn't write to you for a week because I was too busy. I got a letter from Ernest and he was fine. I also got a letter from Gladys and Elizabeth and I will answer them real soon. Mother, I don't expect anything for Christmas. It takes so long to get things from there. Mother, I have a new APO #464. So, you let the rest of them know when you write to them. You tell James and Elizabeth I show do thank them for what they did to my car and you also.

Love Gilbert

JUST A FEW LINES

A newspaper cutout was among the letters.
Uncle Ernest is second from left.

This is the first letter from Gilbert, where he states that he is in Italy. The 141st landed south of Naples in Salerno, Italy. Although Gilbert is not in the 141st, his unit follows where they go.

CPL GILBERT FRANKLIN 6619 PW ADM. CO
PROV. APO. 464. C/O PM NEW YORK, NY
Oct 22, 1943 Italy

Dear Mother,

I just received your letter today was glad to hear from you. Well, I show do have a bad cold and look like I just can't get rid of it. I just had a letter from Bessie and one from Jimmie. Mother, what Shelton boy that poppa wrote me and say he was missing. He said he was in Washington. Well, I am some place in Italy. I guess it is getting cool there now. It very good weather here, cool at night and warm in the daytime. I don't have mutch news so I will close.

Love Gilbert

CPL GILBERT FRANKLIN 6619 PW ADM. CO
PROV. APO. 464. C/O PM NEW YORK, NY
Oct 25, 1943

Dear Bessie,

I received your letter today, and show was glad to hear from you. How do Paul like the army? He show was lucky to get where he is. Well, it will either make you or kill you. I had two long letters from Jimmie today also. They are all awful late. She said in one of them that she had been sick with a cold and had hurt her foot. You write me and let me know how she is. Well Bessie, I am in Italy somewhere Herman ought to be here. I don't see any difference in the people than in Africa just as dirty. Bessie I am working every day seven days a week the weather is nice here it gets cold at night but warm in the daytime. Tell the kids I said hello and I hope to see them soon.

Well, write me a long letter and tell me the news. Tell Fred to save me a job.

                          Love Gilbert

PFC ERNEST H FRANKLIN 13TH T C S APO 502
C/O PM SAN FRANCISCO, CALIFORNIA
Oct 26, 1943

Dear Bessie,

    I received your letter today and was very glad to hear from you, and to know that you all was OK, as for my-self I am OK.
    Well Bessie, it is really getting hot here now. It is as hot here now as it is back there in July, and summer has just started. You should see my suntan. I go without a shirt most of the time, and I am just about as brown as a negro man.
    Bessie you said that Gilbert didn't seem very pleased with Jimmie moving. I think I understand the reasons, but you know how funny Gilbert always was. I don't think he has anything to worry about.
    Say Bessie, Paul sure was lucky to get station at Bolling Field wasn't he. I bet he sure was glad to get station there. I don't guess his child has been born yet has it, is he going to try for O.C.S. after his basic training.
    Bessie, I wanted to try for a pilot before I came across, but my eyes were twenty-thirty, and I couldn't make it, but now the requirement has been lowered to twenty-thirty and I might try again. I don't know for sure yet, since flying quite a bit I think I would like the excitement being behind the stick.
    Well Bessie, I think I have been to civilization again since I last wrote to you. I was there for only two days and nights and I think I lived two months in that short time. I really had a nice time. Bessie you asked me if I was near

any tavern, well we are about thirty miles from any tavern. I guess we are just about as far back in the sticks as we can get, when we first got here we had to cut down trees in order to get our tents up, yes Bessie we can get bananas but to send them back there would be impossible. Bessie there isn't much to hunt for here but deer and wild hogs, of course there is a plenty of seafood here. You asked me if I would like to move to a new location, yes indeed if it was a better place than what this is, but I am afraid that you will be getting a new address from me in the near future, and it is by far a worser place than where I am now. Bessie where I am now the jungles are very dense, but I have seen plenty of them. I guess you know what troop carrier means, so you can judge from that whether I have been in any enemy territory or not. Yes Bessie, the gift you sent me has already came in handy and thanks a lot for it. Bessie, you shouldn't have sent me anything for Xmas, but since you have, I thanks you a million, and I hope that I can return your kindness someday.

Well Bessie, I guess I had better stop for this time so tell all hello and the best of luck until I hear from you again.

Love
Ernest F.

CPL GILBERT FRANKLIN 6619 PW ADM. CO PROV. APO. 464. C/O PM NEW YORK, NY
Oct 30, 1943

Dear Mother,

I have gotten so many letters in the last two days I don't think I will ever get caught up. I have been so busy I just haven't had time to write. Well, I am ok working every day. I think I have heard from everyone except Ernest. I show do like to get a lot of mail. Mother, you said in one of your letters that you had me a quilt for my birthday did you send it to Jimmie. Well, I don't know what would be any better than that and I want to thank you. Mother, I got a new letter from Elizabeth and I will answer it when I get the chance. I think Ernest is getting on fine I show would like to see him, but I guess I better close.

Love Gilbert

CPL GILBERT FRANKLIN 6619 PW ADM. CO PROV. APO. 464. C/O PM NEW YORK, NY
Oct 31, 1943

Dear Bessie,

I just received your letter yesterday, and show was glad to hear from you. I don't get mutch time to write. I have been working pretty hard. I don't never know when Sunday comes. Bessie I just got the letter that Jimmie wrote telling me why she had moved. But after all, I still don't like it. But if she is satisfied it tickles me to death. I got the cigarette lighter she sent me about five months ago. It show was a nice one. Bessie, I got about 40 letters in two days I don't think I will ever get caught up with my writing. I show would like to see that boy of yours. I bet I could have some fun with him. Do Cynthia Ann like to go to school? And do she go alone? Bessie I would like for you to get Jimmie something for Christmas. You get what you think she want and I will send you some money when I get paid. Get her something nice. I have the money and I will send it, payday.

Love Gilbert

NOVEMBER

Marines land in Bougainville, Solomon Islands. Battle of Empress Augusta Bay of Bougainville Island. The Red Army Liberates Kiev. British troops, in Italy, reach the Garigliano River. Allies take Castiglione, Italy. RAF bombs Berlin.

CPL GILBERT FRANKLIN 6619 PW ADM. CO
PROV. APO. 464. C/O PM NEW YORK, NY
Nov 1, 1943

Dear Bessie,

I answered your letter, but I had something else to tell you I am sorrow I wrote and told Jimmie what I did, but if you was in my place, you would too. She thinks the world of you and Fred and the kids. Bessie I would like to send some money to you to put away for me and I don't want anyone to know it but you and Fred. I don't care what you do put it in the bank in your name. You get Jimmie something nice for Christmas because I have enough money to pay for it. Now when I send the money, I will also write a letter telling you. Now I don't know when I will send it, but I hope this week.

Love Gilbert

We either have a missing letter, or the details were in the one from Bessie that I do not have. Not having the whole story leaves us to only speculate at what he wrote and told Jimmie. Did Bessie find out from Jimmie and mention it in the letter to Gilbert?

JUST A FEW LINES

CPL GILBERT FRANKLIN 6619 PW ADM. CO
PROV. APO. 464. C/O PM NEW YORK, NY
Nov 5, 1943

Dear Mother,

    I have begun to get your mail now I hope you are getting mine. I just got two letters from Jimmie and she said that Herman had call Bessie to see if they had got any mail from me. Mother, don't you worry if you don't get my mail because I will write as often as I can. You know I move so often is the reason. Well, I am ok and working every day seven days a week. I got a letter from Cleo and I will answer it soon. Mother, I never did receive any of the package you sent me, but I know I will sometime. I didn't get to see Gordon Martin. He is in Sicily. I got a letter from him and he was fine. I like here better than Africa. Write me a long letter. The V Mail is too short

Love Gilbert

Gilbert is now a Sergeant, but he does not mention it as when he made Corporal.

SGT GILBERT FRANKLIN 6619 PW ADM. CO
PROV. APO. 464. C/O PM NEW YORK, NY
Nov 6, 1943

Dear Bessie,

    I guess you will be surprised to get so many letters from me. Well, yesterday I wrote and told you I was going to send you some money to put away for me? Well, I got two money orders, one hundred each $100. I am sending one today and I will send the other tomorrow. I made them in your name. Now you put it away and don't let anyone know I have it. But take out enough to buy Jimmie a nice present I don't care what it cost.

Love Gilbert

SGT GILBERT FRANKLIN 6619 PW ADM. CO PROV. APO. 464. C/O PM NEW YORK, NY
Nov 13, 1943

Dear Bessie,

    I just received the V-mail today so after all I think we get everything that is sent to us. I want to thank you for them. But now we are getting plenty. Bessie, you let me know when you receive the two money orders. Don't let Jimmie know I sent it to you because I won't [want] to buy her something when I come back. I got a letter from Herman today and he must have a home in the army. He was telling me about going fishing and hunting. Well, just wait until I get back. Bessie this is a pretty country, but you ought to see how the people live. I thought the people in Africa was dirty, but they are clean to the people here.
    Write me a long letter.

Love Gilbert

SGT GILBERT FRANKLIN 6619 PW ADM. CO PROV. APO. 464. C/O PM NEW YORK, NY
Nov 15, 1943

Dear Mother,

    I just received a letter from you today and I was going to answer it and they brought me a package you had sent me. It was the handkerchiefs. I was glad to get them. Mother, I think I will get to see Gordon Martin tomorrow. He is going to meet me at the camp. Did you say Warren Franklin's son over here?, You send me his address. I might get the chance to see him. Well, it is getting cold here. It has been snowing in the upper part of the country. I was in hopes we wouldn't have to be over here this winter, but it looks like it now. I got a long letter from Ernest and one from Herman they both was well. I got a snapshot from Ernest he looks well. Mother, I don't see why you don't get my mail. You know I moved and they for one reason.

Love Gilbert

SGT GILBERT FRANKLIN 6619 PW ADM. CO PROV. APO. 464. C/O PM NEW YORK, NY
Nov 23, 1943

Dear Mother,

I haven't heard from you in two weeks. I don't know what the trouble I only received one letter from Jimmie. I received the package with the cigarettes, and I want to thank you for them. Now I know I will get the mail you are sending sometimes, don't let that worry you. Mother, I went on a pass today and I had a wonderful time sightseeing. Well, we will have turkey for thanksgiving, but I had rather do without turkey to be home. Mother, I am ok working every day and I show will be glad when this war is over. Do you ever hear from Jimmie her mother is there with her?

Love Franklin

FROM MARY ELIZABETH SIMMONS, AKA, JIMMIE
Thanksgiving night 9:30 p.m. (Nov 25, 1943, based on calendar)

Dearest mother and Dad,

    I guess you thought I was never going to write to you, but I guess Bessie told you my Mother was here. She left Tuesday night and gee! I did hate for her to leave. She was so much company for me and we did quite a bit of sightseeing even though it was awfully cold.

    Mother, I don't know if you have heard from Frankie lately or not. I had two letters from him Tuesday and he is a Sergeant now. Gee! Mother, I am so proud of him I don't know what to do. I just finished writing a big long letter to him and telling him all the things I have to be thankful for today. Even if we can't be together, I am thankful that he is mine, and that he is well. Oh! Mother, I will be so glad when Frankie comes home, I don't know what to do. It has been over nine months now since I saw him, and it honestly seems like nine years. I do hope it wouldn't be long until he can come home.

    Have you heard from Ernest lately? He is in New Hebrides, an island near the Fiji Islands. Frankie writes real often but once in a while the mail gets slowed up a little and then I don't hear from him for a while then I really get worried, but he is very good to write. Here a few weeks ago he got 35 letters in one day and a cablegram I sent him. He also got the cigarette lighter I sent him way back in June. He was so tickled over it.

    I was up to Bessie's last night. They are all fine and getting ready for Xmas. I have just about all my Xmas shopping done. I think about five or six more gifts, then I will be through. I will be glad when I do get through as it is so hard to shop here the stores are so crowded you just have to push your way through. I think my mother liked it up here and said she was coming back next spring if she possibly could at all. My Daddy is quite a bit better and has been walking around a little in his room. I certainly do wish he could be better and get out of there.

Mother, how have you all been? Have Gladys and Bay been home lately? I sure do wish I could come down and spend Xmas with you but as civilians won't be allowed to travel, I guess I will just stay here. Mother wanted me to come home so bad, but I just don't see how I can. I sure would give anything in this world if Frankie could be home for Xmas. That would be the best Xmas present I could ever have. Gee! Mother, I miss him so much I don't know what to do.

Mother, I do hope you aren't mad at me for not answering your letter sooner, but I'm sure you understand. I worked every day and the nights pass so quickly while mother was here that it seemed like they just flew by. I hope you will forgive me and please don't wait as long to write as I did.

I hope you have all had a nice Thanksgiving and I'm sure that we all have a lot to be thankful for.

Answer soon and all my love to all of you –

Jimmie

PFC ERNEST H FRANKLIN 13TH T.C.S., 403 JC G. APO 708 C/O PM, SAN FRANCISCO, CALIFORNIA
(Nov 25, 1943)

Dear Bessie,

I hope there few lines finds you all O.K. as for myself I am O.K. Well Bessie I have moved to a new location and it is really one hot place, here sweat is dropping off of me now, while writing this letter, but we have a little better set up here than we did at the other place. Well

Bessie, today is Thanksgiving, but it sure didn't seem like it. I had to work today as usual, but we really had a good dinner, we had turkey and all that goes with it. Bessie, I received the package that you sent, and it was really nice, everything that you sent me was useful and I sure do thank you for it.

Bessie, I had a letter from Gilbert the other day and he is in Italy now said that he was getting along OK. Bessie, I started this letter about two days ago, but I had to stop so I will try and finish it now

Bessie you have never seen it rain as much anywhere at it does here we stay west most all of the time

Bessie, I want to write C.A. a few lines so I will cut this short.

Dear C.A.,

Gee but I was surprised to receive your letter but was very pleased to receive it. Say C.A. you must be quite a smart girld to write such a nice letter, and you are in the second grade at school that is just fine. If I don't hurry and get back, I won't know you when I get back. CA you should be over here to get some coconuts, I am living in a grove of them, and you should see these little black boys and girlds over here.

C.A., I bet old Sani Clause will really be good to you this year since you haven't gotten any whippings in school. I hope your cold is well and you are back in school when you receive this letter. I hope to see you and Mickey soon, so keep smart until I see you.

Love Ernest

SGT GILBERT FRANKLIN 6619 PW ADM. CO
PROV. APO. 464. C/O PM NEW YORK, NY
Nov 28, 1943 Italy

Dear Mother,

    I haven't heard from you in sometime. But I know I will soon. Well, this leaves me ok. I just received a Christmas package from Gladys, and you tell her it was just what I wanted. I also got a long letter from Elizabeth. I like to hear from her. She writes a long letter and a lot of news. I don't see why all of you don't get my mail. I write to one of you every night. Sometimes I write as many as five letters in one night. I got a letter from Ernest and he was fine. Mother, I haven't seen Gordon Martin yet, but he is here clost [close] to me, but I hope to see him before we move again.

Love Gilbert

SGT GILBERT FRANKLIN 6619 PW ADM. CO
PROV. APO. 464. C/O PM NEW YORK, NY
Nov 29, 1943

Dear Bessie,

    I will answer your letter I received the other day. I know this is about five letters I have written to you. I guess you haven't gotten them. You must have a lot of company now if Jimmie stays down there too mutch you let me know and I will write and tell her to not go so often. What did she think of Cleo? And how long did Cleo stay with you? Bessie look like I just can't get any mail from Mother, I did get a package from her and one from Gladys. I think all the Christmas package are going to get here before Christmas. We are getting them every day. Bessie the picture you sent was good I have wrote to

Jimmie to send me one of her but I never received any. I got a long letter from Elizabeth and I show do like to hear from her. I haven't heard from Ernest in a long while. Bessie you ask Paul whether he knows his general orders. I bet he is some guard. Tell him I will trade places.

Love Gilbert

SGT GILBERT FRANKLIN 6619 PW ADM. CO PROV. APO. 464. C/O PM NEW YORK, NY
Nov 30, 1943

Bessie,

I received the birthday card and the dollar you sent me. When did you send me the card? It was dated Oct 6. I just want to know. I show do won't to thank you. It look like our mail is hard to get to us. I haven't heard from anyone in over a week except today I got a letter from Jimmie. Has Jimmie's mother been down to see you yet? How do she like there? Is Paul station clost to home and how do he like the army. Tell him I wish he was with us. Well Bessie, it is began to get cold here I show do hope I can come home soon. You write me a long letter now I think you owe me three or four letters.

Love Gilbert

DECEMBER

American Marines land on Cape Gloucester, New Britain. The US sends troops to Europe to prepare for Operation Overlord—the invasion of Normandy—under the lead of General Eisenhower.

SGT GILBERT FRANKLIN 6619 PW ADM. CO
PROV. APO. 464. C/O PM NEW YORK, NY
Dec 3, 1943

Dear Mother,

 I just received a letter today, the first I have had from you in three weeks. I show was glad to hear from you. Well, my cold is better I am working every day. The weather is cold and rainy, it looks like winter now. Mother, you sent Lyne Payne address to me I might get the chance to see him. I never did see Gordon Martin, but he is real clost to me. I got a nice letter from Gladys today. I just wrote to her and Elizabeth. Mother Jimmie wrote and told me she and Bessie were awful busy Christmas shopping. Well, I don't worry any now. Mother, I show do get tide [tired] and want to come back. Well, I hope to be there next Christmas. I got a Christmas card from Ernest it was nice. Write me a long letter.

Love Gilbert

SGT GILBERT FRANKLIN 6619 PW ADM. CO
PROV. APO. 464. C/O PM NEW YORK, NY
Dec 4, 1943

Dear Bessie,   ITALY

 I don't know how many letters you owe me. I guess the reason I say this is because I just don't get yours. Well, I am writing this one to thank you for the Christmas package. I received it today, and it was so nice. I got the one Elizabeth sent yesterday. All of it comes in good and I won't to thank you. Bessie is it a chance that you can send me some more films I know they are hard to get. I never did get my Kodak [camera] but I have a friend's. Bessie, did you ever get the money order I sent you? I sent two, but in separate letters. Well, I hope all of you a happy Christmas and hope to see you next Christmas.

Love Gilbert

SGT GILBERT FRANKLIN 6619 PW ADM. CO
PROV. APO. 464. C/O PM NEW YORK, NY
Dec 5, 1943

Dear Mother,

    I just received the letter with the picture of Ernest. It was good. He show do look like his self. I don't see why you don't get my mail I just can't get any mail from you I get Jimmie mail. I just got the Christmas package Elizabeth sent me and it show was nice you tell her I received it and I am going to write to her tonight also. I am in Italy somewhere so you was wrong. Mother, I bet that kid of Bessie is nice. I show would like to see him. Well, I am ok working every day.

Love Gilbert

SGT GILBERT FRANKLIN 6619 PW ADM. CO
PROV. APO. 464. C/O PM NEW YORK, NY
Dec 10, 1943

Dear Mother,

    I received five letters today, but I didn't get any from you. I got one from Cleo, one from Gladys and three from Jimmie. Well, I feel good working every but have a bad cold. Gladys sent me the letter he [Ernest] wrote and had put in the paper it was good. I also received the picture. I show would like to see him. Mother, I met a fellow from home today I knew. His name is Eugene Hedrick, he lives between Chatham and Gretna. Tell father if he see any of his people

I seen him. I got a letter from Gordon Martin and he is here clost to me but I just can't find him. Well Mother, I hope all of you a happy Christmas and hope to be with you next Christmas. Write me a long letter and tell me the news.

Love Gilbert

SGT GILBERT FRANKLIN 6619 PW ADM. CO PROV. APO. 464. C/O PM NEW YORK, NY
Dec 15, 1943

Dear Mother Italy,

I just received your letter and show am glad to hear from you. I don't see why you don't get my mail. I write at least twice a week. I just got a letter from Herman I think he has had it nice. Mother, the weather is good here, but it has been raining a lot. It awful pretty here and they raise most everything we do there, lots of nuts, oranges and lemons. Tell dad to save the whiskey because I haven't had a drink since I been over here. But I will make up for it when I get back. I will show you how to down on that new floor you have. I am sure Gladys will like her new job. Well Mother, don't worry when you don't get mail from me because I will be here.

Love Gilbert

PFC ERNEST H FRANKLIN 13TH T.C.S., 403 JC G. APO 708 C/O PM, SAN FRANCISCO, CALIFORNIA
Dec 16, 1943

Dear Bessie,

I received your letter yesterday and was indeed pleased to hear from you. I enjoy very much getting a nice long letter like that. Well Bessie, these few lines leaves me OK, and I hope by the time that you receive this letter that it will find you all O.K.

Say Bessie, it seems as if you have been having a little company lately. Where does Jimmie's mother live now since her husband is in the hospital?

By the way Bessie, Jimmie is really going in for the best now, isn't she? I hope that she doesn't disappoint Gilbert by spending the money that he sends home. I don't know what kind of place he is in, but if it is at a place like I am, he deserves every cent that he makes and then some. Well Bessie, Gilbert is doing all right for himself now isn't he, as he is a sergeant. I am glad to see somebody get ahead.

Bessie, you asked me have I liked my new place. Well, we have a little better set up here, but I had rather be at the other place. Bessie is Pete Conlon in the navy, there sure is a lot of navy where I am now.

Bessie, how is Paul H taking the army, does he like it? I bet it will be hell on him when he has to leave Gravelly Point.

Bessie, Mickey must really be militantly minded I sure would like to see him in his uniform. I bet he is really a tom cat.

Well Bessie, I had a letter from Herman the other day, the first time that I had heard from him in about three months. He seemed to like his new place just fine. I am like Gilbert, he (Herman) really has it soft in the army. I am catching hell now, but whenever I get out of this army, I am going to raise some hell.

Bessie you said that you had received a letter in regard to the money that you sent me that I never received well while I was at Calif I received a form and had to sign it, saying that I had never received the money, it has really been a search for it haven't it, maybe you will soon get it. Well Bessie, there isn't much more to write this time, so until I hear from you again, the best of luck to you all.

Love
Ernest F

SGT GILBERT FRANKLIN 6619 PW ADM. CO
PROV. APO. 464. C/O PM NEW YORK, NY
Dec 17, 1943

Dear Bessie,

    I received a package from you today and I want to thank you for it. I received three. You know it has been a long time since I got a letter from you. Did you get the two letters I sent you? Bessie, I guess you have all your Christmas shopping done now. I know you will time you get this letter. Well, we are having some good weather here now. I have an awful cold look like I just can't get rid of it. How do Paul like the army now is he still doing good? I got a letter from Herman he has moved in his new place. I think he likes where he is. Well, Bessie, write when you can.

Love Gilbert

SGT GILBERT FRANKLIN 6619 PW ADM. CO
PROV. APO. 464. C/O PM NEW YORK, NY
Dec 23, 1943

Dear Mother,

    I don't have mutch to write. I haven't heard from any of you in a long time. I received a package from Gladys and one from you and it show was nice. I don't know how to thank you for it. Mother, I get a letter from Gordon Martin most every week, but we haven't seen each other yet. It has been awful rainy here but not too cold. I guess it is cold there. Well Mother, I hope all of you a Merry Christmas and hope to be with you next Christmas.

Love Gilbert

SGT GILBERT FRANKLIN 6619 PW ADM. CO
PROV. APO. 464. C/O PM NEW YORK, NY
Dec 26,1943

Dear Mother,

    I haven't heard a word from any of you in three weeks. So, I don't have mutch to say. I was awful blue Christmas. I didn't work, I just stayed around the camp. We had an awful nice dinner turkey with dressing pie and cake candy nuts and a package of cigretts. Well, I am working every day, but I have an awful cold. I have found out where Gorton Martin is, so I am going over to see him when I get a chance, he is clost by. Write and tell me what kind of Christmas you had.

Love Gilbert

SGT GILBERT FRANKLIN 6619 PW ADM. CO
PROV. APO. 464. C/O PM NEW YORK, NY
Dec 28, 1943 Italy

Dear Poppa,

    I have been trying to write you a long letter, but I just don't do it. You know I have a lot of the V-mail forms so it so mutch easy to write them. Well, I haven't heard from any of you in about three weeks until today I got two letters, from you and one from Elizabeth. You don't know how glad I was to get them. I haven't heard from Ernest in a long time. I write to him real often. You know I got all of my Christmas package before Christmas and they was all nice. We had an awful nice dinner Christmas turkey and everything to go with it. I didn't work that day, but it didn't look like any Christmas. Pa, I get awful homesick, but I know there is Nothing I can do about it. I show will be glad when we can come back. The country here is awful pretty, and the weather is began to get cool. You asked me about the water it is good here but in Africa it was awful. They raise most everything here as they do back home. Poppa I would like to send you some pictures, but they won't allow us to. You wait till this war is over and then I will get you all the pictures you want. Pa I wrote Swannie Shelton a letter did he ever get it. Well, I show do hope I will be back home next year. I like my work and work every day it not too hard. Well, Poppa, I guess I had better close. I am sending you two five cents pieces of money we used in Africa.

Gilbert

CHAPTER 4

1944

JANUARY

The First Battle of Monte Cassino. Allies land troops in Anzio, Italy. In the Pacific, the US Army shells and bombs in the Marshall Islands to prepare for a full-scale invasion.

The year opens with Ernest in the South Pacific. Gilbert is still in Italy.

SGT GILBERT FRANKLIN 6619 PW ADM. CO
PROV. APO. 464. C/O PM NEW YORK, NY
Jan. 1, 1944

Dear Bessie,

I received a V-mail letter from you today written Dec 8, the first I have heard from you in months. I show was glad to hear from you. I also got the Christmas card it was good. Did you ever get the train going for Christmas? I will never forget the time I had with that train. Where did you get that V-mail did you make it? Well, tell Paul and Helen I said hello. Bessie, I think that was good what you did with the money. Do you think that what I should have done? I have some more I would like to send. Bessie do Jimmie need any money and is she saving any now if she don't need any I will send it to you. Because I don't know what will happen when I come back. Well, I hope to hear from you.

Love Gilbert

SGT GILBERT FRANKLIN 6619 PW ADM. CO. APO. 782. C/O PM NEW YORK, NY
Jan. 7, 1944 ITALY

Dear Mother and Dad,

    I don't have mutch to write about. I am getting on ok. I have been in the hospital for about two weeks, leaving tomorrow in fine shape. I had a cyst taken off my lower lip. Now don't worry about it because I am in fine shape. How is the weather there now? It has been cold here for the last few weeks. Have you heard from Ernest I haven't heard from him in a long time? I don't get any mail at all. Mother that Price boy is closE to me but we don't have time to go anywhere. We have to work seven days a week.

Love Gilbert

SGT GILBERT FRANKLIN 6619 PW ADM. CO. APO. 782. C/O PM NEW YORK, NY
Jan. 11, 1944

Dear Bessie,

    I received your letter telling me you received the money. Now I wasn't worried about you not getting it and I know you will take care of everything. Well, I bet Paul is a proud fellow I show would like to have seen him shoveling coal. Jimmie didn't want mutch for Christmas. You know I wish she wouldn't get the ring because that what I wanted to get her when I come back. Well, I guess she thinks I won't even get back. Bessie, I think she ought to be pleased with what you gave her. Bessie, I have been in the hospital for two weeks but now I am out. I had a cyst on my lip. Everything is ok now. I never did tell Jimmie, but I will write to her and tell her. Bessie, we don't get mutch mail now, but it will soon be coming.

Love Gilbert

SGT GILBERT FRANKLIN 6619 PW ADM. CO. APO. 782. C/O PM NEW YORK, NY
Jan. 21, 1943 (actually 1944)

Dear Mother,

I just received four letters from you today I knew I would get them sometime. I am always glad to hear from home. I also got a letter from Gladys. You know I haven't seen Gordon Martin yet, but I am hoping to see him. You ask me whether I ever have any time off. I haven't had any time off since I been here. You know the picture well it could have been because that the places, I received a letter from Ernest but he seem to not like where he is. Well it real cold here but nothing like there we [ILLEGIBLE] most every day and it snow up on the mountains. Well I guess I had better close hope to be back sometime soon.

Love Gilbert

PFC ERNEST H. FRANKLIN 13TH TCS, 403RD TCG. APO 708 C/O PM SAN FRANCISCO, CALIFORNIA
Jan. 25, 1944

Dear Bessie,

I received your letter today and was indeed glad to hear from you. You said that you all had a very nice Xmas. Well I had a very quiet one, I was off that day so I went swimming that afternoon, and to a show that night, and that about ended my Xmas, but we did have a very nice dinner that day.

Say Bessie, that sure was a nice picture that you sent me. Thanks a lot. C.A. and Mickey sure have grown a lot since I last saw them. From what you say, I bet Mickey is really a cat, but I sure would like to see them both. Can Mickey talk any yet? Yes Bessie, I received both of the packages that you sent me, and thanks a lot for them, the film that you sent me was the right size.

Bessie it sure seems as if it is hard for Guy to get settled don't it, he always was as nervous as could be.

Bessie speaking of Jimmie I sure am sorry that she is acting like she is, because I think I know her and Gilbert better than anyone else. Because I lived with them and ran around them before they got married, there was something that happened that I don't think anyone knows but me and them two, and there wasn't anything that Gilbert wouldn't do for her, and I know hell will really be raised if he comes back and don't find things like he think they should be. I wrote her a number of letters but she never answers them. No Bessie I will never say anything to Gilbert about what you have written me.

Bessie, I received the Xmas card that you sent me with the picture on it, it sure was nice, and I thank you a lot for it. Tell Fred that I said I thought that he made a very nice-looking soldier, and that beer put the finishing touch to it all. Bessie the other day I was as hungry as could be and I was thinking about the week-in [weekend] that we came up to your house at Miller School and I was eating all of those hot dogs, and I came near getting home sick. I don't like to write my troubles to anyone, but sometimes it really looks dark for us over here. I try to keep my mind bright, but I be dam if it don't get low sometimes, no place to go, the same old two and three all of the time.

I guess it adds up to staying away from civilization so long. Well Bessie I don't guess there is much more to write this time so until I hear from you again the best of luck, tell all hello.

Love
Bro Ernest

SGT GILBERT FRANKLIN 6619 PW ADM. CO. APO. 782. C/O PM NEW YORK, NY
Jan. 26, 1944

Dear Bessie,

I haven't heard from you in a good while so I thought I would write you a few lines. Well I am working every day. It has been cold here but I don't think it will stay cold very long. I get a letter from Ernest the other day and he was just fine. Bessie how is Jimmie and is she doing good. I get awful worried about her I don't hear from any of you mutch. You write me a long letter and tell me all the news. Do Jimmie ever come down to see you. She told me that she was going home for Christmas but I heard that she didn't. How is the kids tell them I hope to see them soon. I would give the world to be back there. I get so homesick I don't know what to do.

Love Gilbert

FEBRUARY

The Second Battle of Monte Cassino in Italy. In the Pacific, the US Navy bombs a major Japanese naval base in Truk Lagoon, the Japanese equivalent of Pearl Harbor. The Allies attack Leipzig, Germany for two straight nights. US Navy planes attack Saipan, Guam, and Tinian in the Mariana Islands.

SGT GILBERT FRANKLIN 6619 PW ADM. CO.
APO. 782. C/O PM NEW YORK, NY
Feb. 6 1944 Italy

Dear Bessie,

I received your letter and was glad to hear from you. The picture show was good. I received eight letters, but all was from you, Gladys, Elizabeth, and Mother. I don't never hear from Jimmie. I guess she has all she can do to play basketball and bowling. Well I worry a lot, but I guess it don't do any good. Bessie, I took out a bond one a month. I am going to send you some more money sometime this week. I am sending you the card back. Bessie I never did get the Kodak but if you send me the film, I can use them because a fellow here will loan his Kodak to me any time. Bessie, I don't see why I put the wrong address on the letter I sent you. Bessie I will send Jimmie some money and the rest to you. But after this I won't have mutch to send because I am buying a war bond which cost $18 a month and that don't leave me mutch. Bessie, I show do wish Helen dream was true, but I don't have a mustache. But if that would do any good I will. Bessie, I got two letters from Ernest and he was just fine. Bessie you must not get all my letters because I wrote and told you that I had been in the hospital, but I am all OK now. Bessie I would give the world to be back home I get so homesick I don't know what to do Bessie I will send the money to you sometime this week I will write you also. Well I hope to see all of you soon. Tell all I said hello tell Helen and Paul I hope to see them soon.

Love Gilbert

SGT GILBERT FRANKLIN 6619 PW ADM. CO. APO. 782. C/O PM NEW YORK, NY
Feb. 9 1944 Italy

Dear Bessie,

I just received your letter with the second card for me to sign. Now I just sent the first one yesterday, but it might be wrong, so I am sending you the other one. I just got one of the letters yesterday and the other today. I just received a letter from Herman the first in over four months. He also sent me a picture of him and some of the rabbits he had caught. Bessie, I know you must have fixed the Christmas package up nice. But Jimmie must not have liked it, she never did write and tell me about it. Bessie, I wish you would go to her and see if she is mad, I never do hear from her. I have only received two letters from her in two months. Bessie, I am sending you $150 to put with the rest of the money. I am also sending Jimmie $50. Bessie, I am sure you will take care of everything and any way you do is the right thing for me. Bessie, that picture you was asking about well that is right. Bessie, I bet that kid of yours is some boy. I show would like to see him. Well Bessie I just wrote to you yesterday, so I don't have mutch news so until next time.

Love Gilbert

SGT GILBERT FRANKLIN 6619 PW ADM. CO. APO. 782. C/O PM NEW YORK, NY
Feb. 14, 1944 Somewhere in Sunny Italy

Dear Mother & Dad,

I received two letters from you and show was glad to hear from you look like you are the only one I get any letters from. Well I have been working awful hard for the last few weeks. And I have an awful bad cold now but hope to get rid of it soon. It has been awful cold here the last few weeks. I guess it is cold there now. Mother you asked whether we get plenty to eat. Yes, we do all we want but nothing like it's cooked back home Mother I write two or three letters to Gladys before I even heard from her. I try to write to all of them as often as I can. But when I don't get any mail, I don't have mutch to write.

Love Gilbert F

SGT ERNEST H. FRANKLIN 13TH TCS, 403RD TCG. APO 708 C/O PM SAN FRANCISCO, CALIFORNIA
Feb. 15, 1944

Dear Bessie,

I received your letter and also the valentine today and was very glad to hear from you. Bessie in my last letter to you I didn't mean to sound so down in the dumps, but you know you just haft to get it off of your chest sometimes. Bessie that sure was a good picture you sent me of Mickey, and I sure thank you a lot for it. I got quite a few good compamments [compliments] on it, he sure has grown since I last saw him.

Say Bessie, Gilbert sure has a hard time with his health don't he, but I am glad to learn that he is OK now.

I haven't been hearing from him much lately. I just had a letter from home today and they said that Herman was there, he is some lucky to get so many leaves isn't he.

Bessie I am sure sorry that Jimmie is acting like she is, as she thought so much of Gilbert, no Bessie I wouldn't right and tell Gilbert how she is acting, because I have seen too much of that happen to the boys over here and it really gets them down, I can see where you stand, either way you it might cause hard feeling to one or the other of them. Bessie I believe if I were you I would try and have a talk with her, and tell her if she didn't lay the facts down, that you was going to wright and tell Gilbert just how she was acting, as he is always writing and asking about her, and you are tired of lying to him, maybe this will set her wise and she will come to her senses.

Bessie, she might be trying to use you for a news spreader to cause them to break up, so if I was you, I would try and stand off as long as I could in letting Gilbert know about it. Bessie I am in not much of a position to give any one advice, but I hope that I have given you a little helpful advice and whatever the outcome is I hope it is in your favor.

Bessie you said that you had just had a birthday. I wish there was something that I could send you, but as there isn't, I hope that you had a very nice one, and I wish you many more to come.

Bessie I thank you more than I can say, for wanting to send me something, but really Bessie it is just taking a chance on your part because a lot of this stuff we never get, and I can get most of what I need here you just keep writing to me and I will appreciate that more than anything you could send me, well Bessie there isn't much more to wright this time so until I hear from you again the best of luck. Tell all hello.

Love Ernest

ARTHUR L. JOHNSON

SGT GILBERT FRANKLIN 6619 PW ADM. CO.
APO. 782. C/O PM NEW YORK, NY
Feb. 20, 1944

Dear Cynthia Ann & Mickey,

I received your Valentine and it show was nice. The two pictures show do look like both of you. I guess you got the one I sent to you. If you didn't you will. Well how is everything. Cynthia are you going to school every day, and do you like? What do Mickey do while you are at school? I bet he finds enough to do. I guess he will be a big boy by the time I get back. Do you ever see Jimmie? Tell her I show do miss her letters. And her too. You both take good care of my Jimmie because I will soon be back. Well I hope to see all of you soon.

Love Uncle Gilbert

DRAFT OF TELEGRAM SENT FROM BESSIE
TO GILBERT.
(Based on letters, I'm assuming it was sent
Feb. 24, 1944)

No news of you for some time. Are you all right worried about you. Please write or telegraph.

Letter on way from Jimmie asking Divorce. My opinion she thinks you do wrong thing she get her freedom and your insurance. Await my letters.

You are more than ever in my thoughts at this time. Are you all right worried about you? No news of you for some time.

DRAFT OF LETTER/TELEGRAM SENT FROM BESSIE TO CHAPLAIN FRAY.
(I believe this was also sent on February 24.)

Dear Chaplain Fay:

I am writing to you on behalf of my brother, Sergeant Gilbert Franklin,
(insert address)
Gilbert had written me for information as to the reason he had not been hearing from his wife. I visited her and learned she feels their marriage was a mistake and that she is writing him to request a divorce. Her letter is going to be a great shock to him as he has had no inkling of this other than a decrease in the number of letters he has been receiving from her.
Gilbert is of a somewhat melancholy disposition, and I rather fear his immediate reaction to the news when he receives it. He is not religiously inclined, and for that reason may not seek you out, which is why I am placing the matter before you so that you can take the initiative with him if you feel it proper to do so. Please be assured that we - his parents, sisters, and brothers - will deeply appreciate your efforts in attempting to help Gilbert; it is difficult for us to be of much real help to him at this distance, and we feel that he is in need of friendly and sympathetic counsel at this time.

Sincerely yours,
Bessie Conlon

LETTER FROM BESSIE TO GILBERT.
February 24, 1944

Dearest Gilbert:

    I am sorry to have to write you this when you are where you cannot talk the matter over with your family, but I think your recent letters have shown you felt that something had changed Jimmy a good deal, and it hurts me terribly to have to tell you that you are right.
    I have been trying to get in touch with Jimmy but have been unable to do so since she has been out when I called and failed to return my telephone calls. I am still trying to see her and will write you more fully when I do. I want you to know this so that you will fully realize the information I have did not come from Jimmy direct but from other sources.
    I should like to break this to you gently, Gilbert, but I don't know any other way to let you know that I understand Jimmy has written you a letter saying that she would like to get a divorce. I understand the letter has already been mailed, which is why I am writing you in such haste and hope that this may reach you before you get her letter.
    I want very much to say something to comfort you, but I know what a dreadful shock this is going to be to you and that there are no words which will ease the burden that has been placed upon you. I just want to bring this thought to your mind - that you are in no way responsible for what has happened - your conscience is clear, and you have nothing with which to reproach yourself. Be sure we all feel very deeply for you, Gilbert, and I will write you again as soon as I have further word.

                                          Your sister, Bessie

While the following letter was written and sent before Bessie's above, I hope Bessie's wish was granted and that Gilbert received hers first, before Jimmie's.

LETTER FROM JIMMIE TO GILBERT.
Feb. 23, 1944

Dear Frankie,

No doubt you have been wondering why you haven't heard from me so I will try to explain just why. You know Frankie. I do hope you will understand this letter. If you remember quite some time ago, we made the agreement that if one of us changed our mine bout the other one we would tell each other so here goes. You see I have stayed in so long and I am so tired of staying in that I don't know what to do. I have done a lot of thinking before writing this letter but Frankie I just don't love you anymore and I feel that our marriage was all a mistake. I know this I is probably all a surprise to you, but I wanted to let you know first that from now on I'm going out and have a good time as everyone else doing. You know Frankie I have never felt the same towards you since last February when you were last home. Just about every letter I have written you since then has be very difficult to write and I feel there is no use trying to go on. I hope you will understand and appreciate my telling you first and let me know how you feel about a divorce. I would also like for you to let me know what personal belongings you want me to give to Bessie to keep for you. I do want to be as fair with you as I possibly can, so please let me know what to do. Frankie, I do hope you will understand, and I wish you all the luck in the world. Please let me hear from you as to what I should do with your things and –

Lots of Luck
Jimmie

ARTHUR L. JOHNSON

DRAFT OF TELEGRAM SENT FROM BESSIE TO GILBERT. Approx. FEB 24
SGT. GILBERT FRANKLIN NO A.P.O. 782

Keep letter from Jimmie. For advice see either Legal Assistance Officer, Staff Judge Advocate, or your stations or nearby post adjutant before answering Jimmies letter. Be brave, you are lucky, Details on way.

SGT GILBERT FRANKLIN 6619 PW ADM. CO. APO. 782. C/O PM NEW YORK, NY
Feb. 25, 1944

Dear Bessie,

I received the cable graph the next day after you sent it I got it at noon. That's fast going I wish I could go back that fast. Well I show was glad to get it because I don't get any mail. You know I haven't heard from Jimmie but once in two months I don't see why. Is she mad or what the trouble? Now if she doesn't won't [want] to write she can say so. I get letters once in a while from Mother and Elizabeth. She must be spending her time with the 4F.*
I sent you the money and the cards you wanted to sign about the same time, were they right?

*A 4F is a reject from the draft.

SGT GILBERT FRANKLIN 6619 PW ADM. CO. APO. 782. C/O PM NEW YORK, NY
Feb. 25, 1944

Dear Mother,

I will answer your letter I just received I got a letter from you and Elizabeth once in a while. I never do hear from Jimmie. I got one letter in two months from her.

Well this month has been the coldest since I been here. I will be glad when it gets warm. Yes, I think I have been in the hospital my part. They was good to me and there are all nurses from back there. Miss Boss, you know her, was to be in Danville. She is clost to where I am, but she isn't in the same hospital. Mother I am allowed to wear three stars in my ribbon. Ernest said he had two. Well I don't have mutch news so I will close.

Love Gilbert

SGT GILBERT FRANKLIN 6619 PW ADM. CO.
APO. 782. C/O PM NEW YORK, NY
Feb. 27, 1944

Dear Bessie,

I received the second Radiogram they show are fast. I get them the next day after you send them. I got both of the Valentine you sent with the pictures in. They show are good. Paul look like a rookie with that haircut and those long draws on. I don't never wear mine how do he like the army by this time. That was a good picture of Jimmie I show do wish I could see her. It show do worry me because she don't write I don't know what the trouble I know I never did say anything to make her mad. You tell her to please write or send me a Radiogram. Did she get the money I sent her?

Love Gilbert

ARTHUR L. JOHNSON

SGT GILBERT FRANKLIN 6619 PW ADM. CO.
APO. 782. C/O PM NEW YORK, NY
Feb. 29, 1944. Italy

Dear Mother & Dad,

I just received your letter today I show was glad to hear from you. I got your letter in eight day that awful good. Mother I have been working every day not so hard but long hours. You know it worries me because I can't hear from Jimmie, I haven't heard from her in over a month. I don't see why I can't hear from her if I could only get a letter once in a while it would help. I thought that was Herman Moon. I will write to him and let you know. I haven't heard from Ernest in a long time. You know it take a long time to get a letter from him. I write to him often as I can I show would like to see him. Mother we are getting plenty to eat over here. Now we get fresh meat every day. It looks like the spring is coming it was awful pretty today we have had a lot of rain. You said Ernest was where they trade things for wines well, he would be as well off with one from there as he would with one back there. From what we hear from them. Mother you said Earl Scruggs was to go in the Army well now that all of us had to go at the same time I don't care who they take now. Mother you can but I will come to see you and papa first and I will go see Elizabeth because what she has done for you and poppa is worth as mutch as I have done and I think that a lot. It look like I have throwed two years of my life away. You told me in one of your letters that you had the house finished. I guess I won't know the place. It won't take me long.

Love Gilbert

I believe "where they trade things for wines" is referring to Ernest being near a local trading post for the island.

MARCH

In the Third Battle of Monte Cassino, the small town of Cassino was destroyed in the bombing. The eruption of Mt. Vesuvius—March 17 to 23—disrupts army activities in the area and damages a plane station at Pompeii Airfield near Terzigno, Italy. Fighting continues on the Island of Bougainville in the Pacific. The Red Army continues to advance in Ukraine.

SGT GILBERT FRANKLIN 6619 PW ADM. CO.
APO. 782. C/O PM NEW YORK, NY
March 1, 1944

Dear Bessie,

I received your letter you wrote Feb 10. You know it almost made me sick when I read it. I don't know what the trouble I don't never hear from her at all. The last letter I hear from her was the one she wrote while she was in New York just a few lines. That the only letter I have gotten since Christmas. I know I haven't said anything to make her mad. I sent her $50 I never did hear she whether she got it or not. Bessie will you go to her and find out what the trouble and let me know. I never did think she would ever do that way. You know I never did want her to move when she did. Someday I will tell you. Bessie that package I sent her cost me $75 and she never did tell me whether she got it. You know it bad enough to be over here than for her to do that way. Bessie now will to you tell her to write me a letter and tell me what the trouble. The picture of the kid show is good. I wish I could see him. I never hear from Ernest. I get a letter once in a while from Mother and Elizabeth. Bessie I am at the same place it was just my APO no. change. I never see any one from my old company, but they are close to me. Well Bessie I will write to you again I am so upset I don't have mutch to say.

Love Gilbert

SGT GILBERT FRANKLIN 6619 PW ADM. CO.
APO. 782. C/O PM NEW YORK, NY
March 4, 1944

Dear Bessie,

I don't hardly know how to write this letter it's the worst thing I ever did. Not knowing anything. I received your Radiogram and your letter too. I also received two from her. You know I just don't know what to think of sutch a thing. I will keep the letters for a while then I will send them to you. Now you get everything that belong to me. My diamond ring, watch. Radio. And the title to my car. I want everything I sent from Africa. And also, the things I sent from Italy. Bessie you tell me what to do but I will not give her a divorce, but I want everything that belongs to me but get them first before I write to her, I have worried to death and she has ruin my life. Bessie, I don't know mutch more to say so I will write to you tomorrow.

Love Franks

SGT GILBERT FRANKLIN 6619 PW ADM. CO.
APO. 782. C/O PM NEW YORK, NY
March 5, 1944

Dear Bessie,

I just received the V-mail letter you wrote 22 Feb. I show was glad to hear from you. I never hear from anyone but you Mother and Elizabeth. I did get a letter from

Gladys. I guess she is awful busy. I know you will take care of the money I sent you. I have never heard whether Jimmie got the money I sent to her. You know she hasn't been writing me so mutch since I came to Italy the letters, she wrote wasn't mutch. It worries me so I don't know what to do. I have been the truest person on earth I never go anywhere. Never drink a drop. If I just knew what the trouble it might help. Write soon.

Love Gilbert

SGT GILBERT FRANKLIN 6619 PW ADM. CO. APO. 782. C/O PM NEW YORK, NY
March 9, 1944

Dear Mother & Dad,

I received your letter and Elizabeth both. Well I am getting on ok I have been awful homesick, but I guess I will soon get over it. I heard from Gladys and Bessie both Mother I wrote to Herman Moon but never hear from him. And that Hedrict boy is here clost to me I seen him this other day but didn't get to talk to him so if you see his people tell them he is ok. Mother if Bessie write you anything which I hope she does don't say anything. I will tell you later or you write and ask her.

Love Gilbert

SGT GILBERT FRANKLIN 6619 PW ADM. CO. APO. 782. C/O PM NEW YORK, NY
March 13, 1944

Dear Bessie,

I received your long letter today I have been waiting for it. You know that almost kill me, little did I even think of anything. I have never said anything out the way. I always told her if she needs anything to go to you and I know she could get it. I began to worry after Christmas because I didn't get the mail mutch then when I did get a letter it wasn't mutch. I never hear from her mother or sister either. Bessie, I gave her everything I ever made. I never was away from here since I met her. I just can't hardly believe it that has ruin my life to just think at the people back there and how we use to go around and everyone thought so mutch of us. Well I haven't eat or sleep any since I got the news

Bessie you know I have been the best thing I can to her. That's what hurts me. All her letters were good that I get. She use to always say in her letters that she hasn't never done anything that she didn't want me to but then after Christmas she stopped that. I began to think when I got the letter from her when she went to New York something was wrong. She said she thought that I would be the first one to take her there. But she was on strictly business. She told about going to some big drives and she would write and tell me the good times. I didn't think so mutch of that, but still I was worried. I wish I had saved that letter, but I didn't you know it hard to save anything here. Bessie, I haven't written anything to her. I was waiting for your letter. I don't know what to write. It came to me sutch a shock Bessie it so mutch I could write but you know how it is. What should I do I want her to suffer for this?

I will be willing to give her the allotment. But I won't give her a divorce. Should I?

Bessie, I had just sent her a bunch of flowers for Easter you know we had to put it in time to get them. My bank is in mine and her name. I will have my insurance change. Now the things I would like to have all of them. All the things I sent her while I was over here, I show did want Mother to have the camera I sent. Bessie you let all of them know but tell them to not write to me about it. I only read her letter once I Just can't stand to read it. I just can't believe it. Do you think her mother knows how she is doing? At first, I thought she must have done it. Well Bessie I have all of you to think of and will all the time but now I don't care how long I stay over here. I feel like now that I can do something for all of you. Write me as often as you can. Write me your advice.

Love Gilbert

An allotment is a part of the soldier's paycheck set aside and paid to the spouse. The only way to stop it is to divorce, but the Army will reduce Gilbert's wages.

SGT GILBERT FRANKLIN 6619 PW ADM. CO.
APO. 782. C/O PM NEW YORK, NY
March 13, 1944

Dear Mother & Dad,

Just a few lines to let you know I am well. I will write you a long letter this week. Well I have been worried because I didn't get any mail but now I have been getting it. I guess you have heard what Bessie had to say. What do you think of it? Was it a shock to me? Well I took it.

Love Franklin

SGT GILBERT FRANKLIN 6619 PW ADM. CO.
APO. 782. C/O PM NEW YORK, NY
March 15, 1944

Dear Bessie,

I guess you have gotten my letter by this time. I don't know whether I wrote you enough. Well don't worry about me because it don't do you any good. You know

I never did ever think of sutch a thing and I can't hardly believe it now. What could have caused her to do sutch a thing it never was a word ever said in any way. Well I have had everything changed in mother name, except the allotment and I can't do that. Bessie you get everything that belong to me if you have to go to the law. Bessie, I want the tie pin you give me and I have a wooden picture I sent I want to get everything, clothe and all. Write me after.

Love Gilbert

SGT GILBERT FRANKLIN 6619 PW ADM. CO. APO. 782. C/O PM NEW YORK, NY
March 20, 1944

Dear Mother and Dad,

I will drop you a few lines I just got a letter from all of you and was glad to hear from all. Mother it looks like I made a mistake and will never know why. It show was a quick notice. I never did even think of sutch a thing. Well don't you worry just for me. I know I will come back and I want to see all of you. I have made my Insurance and bonds over to you. That all I could. All hurt me is the thing be said that she said about me and you know that isn't so. Well it show did hurt me but I guess I will get over it. You write me a long letter telling me you will forget all about the thing.

Love Gilbert

Mother I got an answer from Herman Moon and he OK

SGT GILBERT FRANKLIN 6619 PW ADM. CO.
APO. 782. C/O PM NEW YORK, NY
March 21, 1944

Dear Bessie,

I don't know whether I owe you a letter or not, but I will write to you. I just got a letter you typed but it was late getting here. Well Bessie how is everything now. And have you gathered my things yet. I only wrote one letter to her and told her to give everything to you and that all I said. If you get them, you can have the spread [bed spread/comforter] that spread cost me $95 and if you get the cameo give Mother the big one. I got that one for her. Did she even say whether she got the money I sent? Well, all my insurance and bank is in mother name. You write me and tell me what to do. Now you just forget everything because I know how everything is. Bessie do you need the letter I got I just haven't sent it so if you do let me know.

Love Gilbert

Bessie, tell Paul & Hellen I got their letter and I will answer it.

SGT GILBERT FRANKLIN 6619 PW ADM. CO.
APO. 782. C/O PM NEW YORK, NY
March 25, 1944

Dear Bessie,

I received your letter and Fred's both now I will write to you first so tell Fred to not feel hurt. Because I will answer his too. I also got two letters from Mother. Bessie, I have began to get over all of it now but it still worries me. Now I want you to try and get everything I have there. All the thing I sent from over here. The title to my car. My Little teddy bear diamond ring, watch, the tie pin you gave me, and the one Herman gave me, my Radio, the little cedar chest. I would like to have the picture I had taken while I was in the army. Bessie now I wrote and told her to give you everything. I only wrote a few words and I have never wrote any more. I said when she gave the thing to you, I would write again. Bessie if you can't get my thing you find out how you can and let me know. I don't want you to worry over anything because you know I show didn't do anything I just hope to come back. everything has been changed except the allotment and that can't be changed. I wish I could.

When you get this letter, you let Mother know how I feel. Of all the chances I took I took the wrong one. Well I am more satisfied over here than I ever was. Bessie I would like to send you those letters, but you know how it is but if you need them I will. It nothing mutch in them just like you said. All I want is my thing and I won't be satisfied until you get them. Bessie do you know whether my Kodak was sent to me I never did get it. The picture of the kids show was good that boy will be a man before I get back. I will write to the kids when I get a chance. Well I have to answer mother's letter so you write to me nice often because I will be looking for you to.

Love Gilbert

SGT GILBERT FRANKLIN 6619 PW ADM. CO. APO. 782. C/O PM NEW YORK, NY
March 25, 1944

Dear Mother,

I just got two letters from you March 2 and the 9. Well I show am glad to hear from you. Mother I think it is the right thing for you to tell me what you think, and I will always believe you. I would never get mad with any of you what you said. That show was a shock to me and it's bad enough to be over here. I can't say so mutch and can't do anything. Don't worry I won't drink anything. All hurt me is thing was said about me and you know it wasn't so. I haven't written to her but once, and just a few words telling to give me the things of mine. Mother I show am glad you got the cameo. It took me a long time to get a good one so if you can have a pin made for it. You know you can't get them in a setting over here they don't have the material. I will pay for it if you have it fixed. If I get the chance to get Bessie one I will. I told her if she could get the spread I sent, she could have it. The things cost so mutch. The spread I sent to Jimmie cost $50. Mother Now just forget everything because I am through and I am waiting till Bessie get my thing, before I write again. Now I won't loose any more sleep over it.

Love Gilbert

PFC ERNEST H. FRANKLIN 13TH T.C.S., 403 JC G. APO 708 C/O PM SAN FRANCISCO, CALIFORNIA
March 26, 1944

Dear Bessie,

I received your letter a few days ago and was indeed pleased to hear from you. Well Bessie, these few lines leaves me O.K. and I hope that it finds you all the same. Well Bessie, I was over in Auckland N.Z. a few days ago and I had a very nice time. I have also been to Sydney Australia and I like Australia a much better than I do N.Z. but both places are very nice, and I would like very much to be station at either place. It sure is hard to come back to these Island after being over there for a few days, but at any rate it is good to see civilization again. Bessie it seems as if we guys will haft to stay over here about two years before coming back, if so, I only have seven more months in a way that seems a long time, but it will pass pretty fast.

Well Bessie I sure was sorry to learn about Jimmie, that really bums me up, from what you say she must be nothing but a two-bit whore. I think I would be tempted to kill that bitch if I could see her, and I am going to make it my business to look her up whenever I get back there. You said that she was trying to hold her honor. Well I guess about the only kind of honor she has left is the honor of satisfying the most men, but some day she is going to see where what she is doing will never pay. I know it is going to be hard on Gilbert, because he really trusted and believed in her.

Bessie, I received the birthday cable gram that you sent me, it was sure nice of you and thank a lot. Tell C.A and Mickey, I received the valentine they sent me, it sure was cute, and thanks a lot, tell them I said to be smart and when I get home I will come up to see them and we will go out and have a good time. Well Bessie I guess I had better stop for this time so until I hear from you again the best of luck.

Love Ernest F

SGT GILBERT FRANKLIN 6619 PW ADM. CO.
APO. 782. C/O PM NEW YORK, NY
March 27, 1944

Dear Fred,

I will answer your letter. Yes, I was surprise to hear from you. Well I wouldn't write either if I had someone to do so. Fred I just got a letter from Bessie and I don't see why she hasn't gotten my letters I know I have written at least five telling her what to do. I have been waiting for a answer. I told her to get everything I have and keep it for me or send it home. That all that bothers me is what thing I have, be show and get the title to my car. I have had everything changed in mother name except the allotment and I can't do that. So don't worry about me. Just wait till I come back.

Gilbert

SGT GILBERT FRANKLIN 6619 PW ADM. CO. APO. 782. C/O PM NEW YORK, NY
March 29, 1944

Dear Bessie,

I just got your letter telling me you haven't received mine. Well I don't see why because I have written you a lot. Now don't worry because I can have everything, I want done right here. I don't have to see anyone. I had everything changed the day I got the letter. Except the allotment and there is nothing I can do about that unless she is Free. But I want everything I have before I do. And I want you to try and get them. I only wrote one letter to her and told her to give you everything of mine. I have already forgotten about the whole thing except what she said about me.

Love Gilbert

APRIL

Allies bomb Budapest, Hungary and Bucharest, Romania ahead of the advancing Red Army. Air raids continue in the Caroline Islands, including Truk Lagoon.

ARTHUR L. JOHNSON

SGT GILBERT FRANKLIN 6619 PW ADM. CO.
APO. 782. C/O PM NEW YORK, NY
April 2, 1944

Dear Bessie,

I just received two letters from you one March 6th and 20. I don't see why you don't get my mail I have written two or three every week and have been waiting for the answer I wrote you. I just can't write you what I want to so you will have to just do what you think is the best. I haven't never heard from J- and none of them. I will never know what was the trouble. I think it all came from Becky. Bessie, I have had the Bonds and Insurance change. And when I get a chance, I will go see about the other you know over here you don't have the chance to do like back there. All you can do for me I will show be glad. Now don't you worry about the thing because I have made up my mine and you know me well enough when that is made it goes. And that mean I am through. I show would like to get everything before I do anything. You ask Fred about the title to my car and what can be done about that. I wouldn't believe anything Mrs Mo- said. Bessie, I wrote to Paul and Helen. I just got a package from Gladys and it was put up so nice and all the things were nice. Bessie, I wish you would send me those films, I would like to have as many as you can get that all. I would like you to send me. Did Fred get the letter I sent him. Bessie it show is pretty weather here now and I hope it will stay that way. Well you write me as often as you can so don't worry thing will be ok.

Love Gilbert

We believe Becky is a friend of Jimmie's. It looks like Gilbert thinks she is the cause of all the trouble. Not having any other letters, we can only surmise what happened and why he believes it.

SGT GILBERT FRANKLIN 6619 PW ADM. CO.
APO. 782. C/O PM NEW YORK, NY
April 10, 1944

Dear Bessie,

    I received the Radiogram Easter morning thanks. Well I haven't heard from you in a good while. I have been waiting to hear whether you got my things. I never did write to her but once and I never did get any answer. Did she get the flowers I had sent to her? Well it has me in sutch a place I don't know what to do. You write and tell me what the best thing to do I just in a place I just can't find out anything. Hope to hear from you soon.

Love Gilbert

SGT GILBERT FRANKLIN 6619 PW ADM. CO.
APO. 782. C/O PM NEW YORK, NY
April 11, 1944

Dear Bessie,

    I received your letter today was glad to get it. I have been looking for it a long time but when you don't get mine, I know why I did get an answer. Bessie I just wrote to you last night, so I don't have mutch to say. You have been so good to me I just don't know how to thank you. And I am so far away I can't do mutch. But what you do I know is right I am also sending you a letter to give to Jimmie. Bessie, I hate to send those letters but if you want them I will, but she said to tell her what thing to give to you and I did she didn't want anything of mine.

Love Gilbert Franklin

Bessie I just don't know what I do have there.

In the same envelope, a letter to Jimmie.

April 11, 1944

Dear Jimmie

I am sending this letter to Bessie to give to you. I didn't know where you were now. And I thought maybe it wouldn't get to you. You said in your letter to tell you what thing to give Bessie. The title to my car my diamond ring, watch, radio, my tie pin, the little cedar chest, the little teddy bear, the picture on the board I sent from Africa, the bed spread and little box and things I sent from Italy. Give her all my army cloths and civilian clothes, what pictures I had taken while I was in the army. Now I know you don't want them. I would like to have everything belong to me.

Gilbert Franklin

PFC ERNEST H. FRANKLIN 13TH T.C.S., 403 JC G. APO 708 C/O PM SAN FRANCISCO, CALIFORNIA
April 13, 1944

Dear Bessie,

I think I have had two letters from you since I have written but I haven't had much time in the last week for writing. I hope these few lines will find you all in the best of health, as for myself I am OK, well Bessie it has been raining here again today, we have had rain most every day for the last few weeks, we stay wet most of the time, rain doesn't mean anything when there is work to be done.

Bessie you asked me what I thought a woman needed with a diaphragm for birth control, well the only thing I can figure is that she wants to make some dirty money, do you think I am right?

I had better never get my hands on that bitch after those statements she made, and if she is around there when I get back, I think I will get to see her. Bessie, I think Gilbert is doing the right thing by not giving her a divorce now don't you, let her go through some of the hell that he has gone through.

Bessie, I received the Easter card and also the Radio gram they were really nice and thanks a lot. I also received C.A. letter, tell her I will answer it in a few days, it was sure sweet of her to write to me.

Bessie a bunch of us boys went to a Frenchman home last night and had supper. He served wine, and a five course dinner. We really had a nice time and I enjoyed it very much.

Bessie you can take it from me this Mrs. M. is not what she is cut out to be, she has had quite a bit of family trouble herself, there is a lot that I could tell you, if I could see you. I never said anything before because it was none of my business, but now it doesn't matter, and when I see you I can inlite [enlighten] you a quite a bit that you never knew.

Well Bessie I have just had a letter from home, and they all seemed to be getting along O.K.

Bessie, I have been to quite a lot of these advance bases lately, and from the look of thing I will get to see quite a few more before I get back. I wish I could tell you about them in my letter, but as I am not allowed to I will haft to wait until I get back and see you, as I am out of news I guess I had better bring this to a close, so the best of luck to you all until I hear from you again

Love Bro Ernest F

"Bessie a bunch of us boys went to a Frenchman home last night and had supper." The same Frenchman the one in the book *Tales of the South Pacific*?

SGT GILBERT FRANKLIN 6619 PW ADM. CO.
APO. 782. C/O PM NEW YORK, NY
April 19, 1944

Dear Cy Ann,

I just received your letter today I was glad to get it. You show can write good. Do you like to go to school? I bet you have a good time. You said that Mickey broke Mothers flowerpot I wonder whether that the one I dropped one time. I bet he got a spanking. Tell him to be a good boy till I come back and I will teach him some tricks. Tell Mother I will write her a long letter tomorrow. And you be a good girl and I will bring you something when I come back.

Love Gilbert

SGT GILBERT FRANKLIN 6619 PW ADM. CO.
APO. 782. C/O PM NEW YORK, NY
April 19, 1944

Dear Mother,

I just received two letters from you. Well I am ok working every day. I show do hope you feel better now since you have had your teeth taken out. Mother I haven't heard from Bessie but once since I wrote to you and she didn't have mutch to say. Well you want to know how I feel. Well I just hope I get the chance to come back. I might be sorrow. But I think I could settle it in a few minutes. I feel just like you do about the whole thing and I know how you feel. So just forget about the whole thing but I will write you about the same thing after tomorrow.

Love Gilbert

CHAP. (LT. COL.) PATRICK B. FAY BASE
CHAPLAIN P. B. S. BASE HQTRS. P. B. S.
APO. 782 NYC.
24 April 1944

Dear Mrs. Conlon:

    Met your brother and talked over the situation with him. Sent him to the Judge Advocate for further advice. Seems to take a very common sense attitude in the whole matter.

Patrick B. Fay
Lt. Col. Chap

After the letter of April 19 to his mother, I get the feeling that Uncle Gill was not honest with the chaplain.

SGT GILBERT FRANKLIN 6619 PW ADM. CO.
APO. 782. C/O PM NEW YORK, NY
April 25, 1944

Dear Bessie,

    I received the letter you sent me, but I just haven't had enough time to get all together what I want to. So, you just wait, and everything will be ok. I know you have been to a lot of trouble. And Magdalene I don't know how to thank her and some of these days I hope to be back there I will show you how mutch I appreciate what you and her have done for me. Now you will hear from me soon. Don't worry over nothing because everything will be ok.

Love Gilbert

Magdalene is Bessie's sister-in-law, Fred Conlon's sister. She earned her law degree and passed both the Virginia and District of Columbia Bar exams in 1933. She could not start practicing law until 1943, when the war caused a shortage of male lawyers.

SGT GILBERT FRANKLIN 6619 PW ADM. CO.
APO. 782. C/O PM NEW YORK, NY
April 25, 1944

Dear Mother,

I guess you think I am not going to write. Well I have been awful busy. I am ok and working every day. We are having some pretty weather here all the time in bloom. It makes me home sick. I just got a letter from Gladys and she said everyone was well and said you was feeling good. I show am glad you feel better I want you to be good and well when I come back because I am coming there to stay and I mean to stay. How happy when that day comes

Love Gilbert

SGT GILBERT FRANKLIN 6619 PW ADM. CO.
APO. 782. C/O PM NEW YORK, NY
April 28, 1944

Dear Bessie,

I won't write mutch to let you know I got your letter. You asked me whether I got your Easter telegram, yes, I did. I thought I wrote and told you. Bessie, I guess you think you will never get the letters you are expecting well it took me a long time to find out what I wanted so you will soon get it. Now you do what you think is the best. I have the money in the bank, and you use it and if you need any more let me know. I would like to get all of this cleared up before I even come back. Bessie now you have a list of the things I want.

Gilbert F

Bessie, what is mother's middle name?

MAY

D-Day plans and preparations are ongoing. The Fourth Battle of Monte Cassino ends in victory for the Allies. There is an increase in bombing targets in France to prepare for D-Day. The Allies take the airfield in Burma. The Allies break out of Anzio and link up with troops from the south to force the Germans back.

SGT GILBERT FRANKLIN 6619 PW ADM. CO.
APO. 782. C/O PM NEW YORK, NY
May 3, 1944

Dear Bessie,

    I will write you a few lines I hope you have received the letter I sent you. I know you have been waiting for it. But it takes time to get everything together. I hope you will have all the information you want. You know I got a letter from Elizabeth in five days. I just received a letter from Ike Mayhew he was fine but didn't like so mutch. Bessie don't you think I did the best thing after I had studied over the whole thing, I thought that was the best. Because I was so far away, and the easiest way is the best. You know I heard from the Insurance Co. and the change I made had been approved. So now I think I will have a second beneficiary after what you said I will make it in your name. I never did hear from the bonds. Bessie do you know whether Jimmie got the flowers I sent her Easter. You know I sent them about two months before

Easter. I got a letter from Marguerite last week and it was a nice letter. She didn't know anything and said she knew J. was writing and said her mother told her that she wrote every night. Now I don't know what to think. Well I know what I am going to do. Bessie, I know you and Mag. will do all you can. Tell Mag. how mutch I thank her. How is the kids wish I could see them? I hope to soon.

Love Gilbert

SGT GILBERT FRANKLIN 6619 PW ADM. CO. APO. 782. C/O PM NEW YORK, NY
May 3, 1944

Dear Mother,

    I will answer your letter I got a few days ago. I wrote to poppa the day I got your letter so I thought I would wait a few days to write to you. Well I am well working every day. The weather here is wonderful, everything is green and pretty. I just got three letters from Elizabeth one of them came in five day that quick service. She said that she had miss one with getting my letter. Well you know what I have had to go through with that the reason for it. Well I hope all of it will soon be straighten out. I guess Bessie will write you about it. I haven't heard from Ernest in a long time only what you write me. Mother my insurance I had changed over to you has been approved but now I want to have Bessie the second beneficiary. Don't you think that ok? Mother I got a letter from Ike Mayhew I show was glad to hear from him. I think he is a little homesick. He said he was fine. I also got a V-mail letter from Herman awful short he was home on a furlough. He don't know how luck he is. Well Mother I don't have mutch news so I guess I will have to close I am sending you a list of the fellows in my Co that got the good conduct medal.

Love Gilbert.

There were four pages of typed names, but the only one that matters is listed here:

```
    HEADQUARTERS PRISONER OF WAR ENCLOSURE NUMBER 326
      6619TH PRISONER OF WAR ADMINISTRATIVE COMPANY
                          APO 782
                       26 April 1944

SPECIAL ORDERS )
                :
NUMBER     53)

     PAC AR 600-68 the following named Enlisted Men of this
     Organization are awarded the Good Conduct Medal.


     NAME                    RANK        ASN


     FRANKLIN, GILBERT C.    Sgt
```

SGT GILBERT FRANKLIN 6619 PW ADM. CO.
APO. 782. C/O PM NEW YORK, NY
May 6, 1944

Dear Mother,

I just received your letter was glad to hear from you. Well I am getting a lot of mail now. I just heard from Ernest and it has been a long time since I heard from him. He wrote me a long letter he was fine. I think the boys over there get a lot more time off than we do over here. Well I like to see anyone get some time off I think it helps a lot. Mother I guess Bessie will write and tell you what I had decided to do. And I think it is the best I got a letter from Herman. I have a lot of writing to do I will write you a long letter when I get a chance.

Love Gilbert

SGT GILBERT FRANKLIN 6619 PW ADM. CO. APO. 782. C/O PM NEW YORK, NY
May 8, 1944

Dear Bessie,

I received your letter and the V-mail both. I don't see why you don't get my mail I write to you two or three times a week. That the reason why I don't know what to write. I hope you have received the letter I sent you. And when I do, I don't know what to write. I hope you have received the letter I sent you. Bessie, I don't know how I had my bank made out, but I think I have from 18.75 paid up. I heard from the insurance, but I haven't heard from the bank. I think the last thing is to stop the bank. It is so many things to do and I don't know the time. I show will be glad when everything is settled. I got a long letter from Ernest and he was fine. Bessie if you can send me the films. I have taken some pictures, but haven't had these develop.

Love Gilbert

SGT GILBERT FRANKLIN 6619 PW ADM. CO. APO. 782. C/O PM NEW YORK, NY
May 11, 1944

Dear Bessie,

I just received your letter telling me that you had gotten most of my things. Well I show am glad! I wished you could have gotten all of them. Well I hope to get them someday Bessie. Now that I have written you the letter tell you what I thought was best and also writing how I don't know what to do I will wait till I hear from you. If you think it is best to not sign the papers if she sends them, you wire me. But I won't until I hear from you. Bessie, I have stopped all my bonds now. Bessie if you think it is best to make her sweat it out, I won't sign anything I will just write and tell her I had decided I didn't want to.

Love Gilbert

SGT GILBERT FRANKLIN 6619 PW ADM. CO. APO. 782. C/O PM NEW YORK, NY
May 14, 1944

Dear Mother,

Today is Mother day and I am thinking of you wish I was there with you. Well I am in hope I will be there next year. It a wonderful day here. Mother I just received poppa's letter yesterday with the stamp. I also just got Elizabeth letter with Gordon Martin address. It has been coming a long time. I also got a nice letter from Bessie letting me [know] she had gotten part of my thing. She show has been nice about trying to help me. I think it worries her more than it does me. Well Mother I am sending you a poppy in this letter also a picture.

Love

P.S. Mother I just got a letter from you today that you wrote to Ernest. So I guess he will get the one you sent me. I won't send it to him. I will write and tell him.

Love Gilbert

SGT GILBERT FRANKLIN 6619 PW ADM. CO. APO. 782. C/O PM NEW YORK, NY
May 21, 1944

Dear Bessie,

I haven't written to you so often because I don't know what to write I don't get your letter so good and I like to wait till I get them to find out what to write. Now I got one of the V-mail letters you sent me the second page. I thought I might get it today but didn't. Bessie you know what I wrote you to do if J. didn't, well don't do anything yet just wait until I hear from her and if she send me the paper to sign I will write her that she will have to give you the rest of the things don't you think that the best. You send me Mother's middle name. I haven't had the will made yet.

Love Gilbert

SGT GILBERT FRANKLIN 6619 PW ADM. CO. APO. 782. C/O PM NEW YORK, NY
May 21, 1944

Dear Pop,

I received your letter and Mothers I show was glad to get them. I get a letter from one of you every day and it show do helps a lot. Well I am well, but we are working pretty hard right now. Thing look good over here now. Poppa the little dog I had well she had three little puppies and they show are pretty. I sent you a picture I hope you get it. I just got a letter from Ernest and he was just fine. You can bet we will have a good time when I come back. I am going to stay there with you and Mother the rest of my times. I think I only made one great mistake but I will never do it again. Tell Mother I will write her next. I have to write to Elizabeth.

Gilbert. F

SGT GILBERT FRANKLIN 6619 PW ADM. CO.
APO. 782. C/O PM NEW YORK, NY
May 23, 1944

Dear Bessie,

I never did get the first part of your last letter. I guess I will soon. Bessie I never did hear from J. and I don't care if I don't. I wrote and told you to just forget about the letter I sent you. I have decided to not sign anything until I get the rest of my things. Don't you think that the thing to do? Well Bessie it has been awful pretty weather here. Ernest says it awful hot where he is. Well I guess I had better close. Bessie, I sent you a V-mail letter with an air mail stamps let me know whether you get them sooner.

Love Gilbert

SGT GILBERT FRANKLIN 6619 PW ADM. CO.
APO. 782. C/O PM NEW YORK, NY
May 25, 1994

Dear Bessie,

I just received the first part of your letter today. You know it is hard for me to write and tell you what to do because it takes the mail so long. But I wrote to you in one of my letters tell you to hold off everything until I heard from J. I haven't heard a word yet. I think the best thing is to not sign anything until she gives you the rest of my thing. What do you think? And in the same time I think things will change in the meantime. I think it will be a time soon that I won't have to pay the allotment. So, in that way I would like for her to suffer also. When I get a chance, I will send you some more money but don't let anyone know I have it. If you find out any good news let me know You try to find out if I can stop my allotment.

Love Gilbert

SGT GILBERT FRANKLIN 6619 PW ADM. CO.
APO. 782. C/O PM NEW YORK, NY
May 29, 1944

Dear Bessie,

I haven't heard from you since I got the first part of your V-mail letter. So I thought I would write you a few lines Well I am well working pretty hard now. I like to keep busy I just hope it stays this way. Bessie, I have the ring you asked me about but just don't say anything. I never did hear a word from J-. I have decided to not sign anything until I get the rest of my things. Bessie, I wish you would write to Mrs. Charles T Miller she will tell you about her Son. But don't tell her about J-. Their address is (Charles T Miller, S- 6th St, Bangor Pa) Write when you can

Love Gilbert

SGT GILBERT FRANKLIN 6619 PW ADM. CO.
APO. 782. C/O PM NEW YORK, NY
May 31, 1944

Dear Bessie,

I haven't heard from you in a good while. But I got the package you sent me, and it was in good shape. I show was glad to get it. I want to thank you for it and when I take some pictures, I will send you some. I just received a package from Gladys today. She sent me some Peanuts and they was nice. Bessie if you do get any more films you send them to me that the only thing I want. Now you have some money of mine and you use it. I don't care if you use all of it. I will send you some more soon.

Love Gilbert

Bessie you send me Mothers full name I forgotten it.

JUNE

Operation Overlord (AKA D-Day) starts with the daily bombing of Cherbourg and Normandy, France. The Allies enter Rome one day after Germany declared it an open city (a city without defenses, free for peaceful occupation). On June 6, U.S. and Allies invade Normandy, France. In the Pacific, US marines land in Saipan. Free French liberate Elba. Allies capture Assisi, Italy. The US Fifth Fleet wins a decisive battle over the Japanese in the Battle of the Philippine Sea. The month ends with American troops liberating Cherbourg.

There are no letters between May 31 and June 11. While Gilbert typically wrote about twice a week, with D-Day occurring early in the month, it can be assumed that, if there were any letters, they were lost.

SGT GILBERT FRANKLIN 6619 PW ADM. CO.
APO. 782. C/O PM NEW YORK, NY
Jun 11, 1944

Dear Mother,

I haven't heard from you in over two weeks, but I know I will soon. Well I am ok working every day. I just got a letter from Gordon Martin and he was fine. I show would like to see him. I almost forgot to tell you I got a letter from Herman well I think that the second I have heard from him in six months. He was telling me what a nice time he had on his furlough. Things are going good over here now we have to work pretty hard but if it will help to get this war over, I am willing. Mother I am sending you a picture of Herman Moon and myself. You show it to Pete. It was taken when he came down to see me. I haven't heard from him since he came down.

Love Gilbert

SGT GILBERT FRANKLIN 6619 PW ADM. CO. APO. 782. C/O PM NEW YORK, NY
June 12, 1944

Dear Bessie,

I haven't been writing so mutch for the last few weeks. I have been so busy. You know I haven't heard from you in about three weeks. But I know I will hear from [you] soon. All the mail has slowed up. I did get a letter from Herman and one from Elizabeth. Well things over here looks good for us now we are working hard now. Bessie, I think I wrote and told you to send me Mothers middle name if you haven't, send it to me. I have forgotten it. I don't have mutch to say I haven't never heard from J-. yet. It's not worrying me though. Bessie if you do get any more films send them to me. I wrote and told you I received the package you sent me thanks a lot. I will try and send the money sometime soon. Tell Fred and the kids I said hello.

Love Gilbert

SGT GILBERT FRANKLIN 6619 PW ADM. CO. APO. 782. C/O PM NEW YORK, NY
June 16, 1944

Dear Bessie,

I received your letter today the first I have heard from you in three weeks. I thought it must have been something wrong. I haven't heard from Mother either. You know I got a letter from Elizabeth and she said in the letter that you had to do all your work and Cynthia Ann was mutch better. But she didn't tell me that she had been sick or nothing. I had began to get worried. I haven't been getting mutch mail from anyone. I did get two letters from Herman. I was surprised. Bessie I never did hear from J, so I have decided to let everything be until I get the rest of my things. So if she writes me I will tell her she will have to give the rest of my things before I sign anything. The reason is because it a lot of time and so mutch writing. Now if you think any better way let me know. Bessie if you have my watch there keep it running as mutch as you can. Now if the rest of my things in your way you can send them home. But if they aren't I had rather you would keep them. I show am sorrow the kid has been sick. Glad she wasn't any worse than she was. Elizabeth has a time trying to get her a place I hope she can get her a good place. She is so good to mother and dad. How long did Poppa stay up there with you. Bessie, we have awful busy the last month and thing look good for me now I have an awful cold and it so hard to get rid of it. Bessie you write me all the news. Tell the kids I said I hope to see them Christmas.

Love Gilbert.

PFC ERNEST H. FRANKLIN 13TH T.C.S., 403 JC G. APO 708 C/O PM SAN FRANCISCO, CALIFORNIA
Jun 20, 1944

Dear Bessie,

I received your letter today and was indeed pleased to hear from you, and to learn that C.A. was out again. Bessie you have sure had a lot to worry you lately, and I sure hope that things will soon be straighten out for you.

Bessie I can understand why you haven't written sooner, and I should have written, to you before now, but if I can receive a letter, I have a little to write, answer the question in it otherwise there just isn't anything to write about here.

Bessie Dad sure seemed to have enjoyed his stay while at your house I think he want to go back up when he can.

Bessie what grade is CA in now, and how is she doing in school? I would sure like to see her, and Mickey. I bet they have sure grown since I last seen them. I understand that you have had C.A. hair cut short, how does she look with short hair.

Say Bessie, Elizabeth has been moving around quite a bit lately hasn't she. I just had a letter from her, and she has just moved again, she said that they had tried to find them a place to buy, but as yet haven't been able to do so.

Bessie I finally got the picture I had made and sent them to Mama, and she is going to send you one. I hope that you like it, but don't be disappointed because you remember this old mug of mine, you can't except but so much

Well Bessie things are looking pretty good over here now, but as for me coming home any time soon, I would be afraid to say when, and don't be surprised if you get a new address from me in the near future. Bessie you said that it was rather cool back there now, well we have been having some pretty nice weather here lately it is supposed to be the beginning of winter here now, but about the only difference you can tell is that it is cooler at night.

Say Bessie when you were talking about Dad and Fred drinking that beer I had to stop and have one, as we get about twelve bottles a week here, but it is always hot I wouldn't harley know what a cold beer would be like, so Bessie when I get home I am planning on coming up to your place, and if you have anything in your ice box you had better watch it, because I think I am going to be awful thirsty.

Bessie, I had three letters from Gilbert last week and he seemed to be getting along OK. I think he is taking it about Jimmie pretty good.

Bessie, for the last few days I have really been home sick I don't know why. I guess one just have days like that. I have been over here nearly two years now, but sometimes it seems like ten. Well Bessie there isn't much more to write this time, so I hope to hear from you again in the near future, so until I do, the best of luck and tell all hello.

Love Bro Ernest F

SGT GILBERT FRANKLIN 6619 PW ADM. CO. APO. 782. C/O PM NEW YORK, NY
June 21, 1944

Dear Bessie,

 I just received the letter you wrote the 25 of May. It looks like it takes a long time for us to get answers. Bessie, I know you have done a lot for me, but I think I might as well have everything as it is because I just don't have the time to do the thing that is right. After all I haven't heard from her. Now I think she is waiting for to do something. I show would like to settle everything before I come back but I never will sign any papers until I get the rest of my thing. And I know when I do come back, I will get them or I will know why. Bessie your write and thank for the letter [?was?] wrote for me. Little did I ever know it would be so mutch trouble. I will write you a long letter.

Gilbert Franklin

SGT GILBERT FRANKLIN 6619 PW ADM. CO. APO. 782. C/O PM NEW YORK, NY
June 28, 1944

Dear Mother,

 I think I owe you two letters so I will try and answer one of them. I am well and working every day. We have a lot of work to do now but I don't mind it. Mother I went up to see if I could find the Hedrick boy, but he is not with the same outfit he was with. He has been sent to the ninth replacement depot. He left last week but one of the fellows said they saw him today and he was fine and I told them to tell him to write to his people. I just got a letter from Ernest and I show was glad to get it he was fine. He said he just got two letters from me the first in two months I know I write real often to him. I also got a letter from Gordon Martin. I found his old address and I write to him and he has answered it he is ok and doing good Mother you said that you got one of the bonds well I guess Jimmie got the other I think I had five but she can't get the money for them. I stopped all of them. And the Insurance has been changed because I got a letter from them telling me it had been changed. Did you ever get the picture of Herman Moon and myself? I also sent Gladys and Elizabeth one. Mother you aught to see my flower garden I have I am going to take a picture of it and send it to you. I will send you some seeds. The wether here is wonderful warm in the day and cool at night. We are getting plenty to eat Fresh vegetable all all kinds of fruit. I got the package Gladys sent me and it was nice. Well it getting late so I better close.

Love Gilbert

Tell Papa I will write him a letter tomorrow

Gilberts Flower Garden.

SGT GILBERT FRANKLIN 6619 PW ADM. CO.
APO. 782. C/O PM NEW YORK, NY
June 30, 1944

Dear C. ANN,

I just got your letter and it show was nice. I was sorrow to hear that you had been sick but I guess you are well now. Did you make your grade I hope you did? Well it won't be long before Mickie will be going to school with you. Are you going down to grandmother to stay a while? I hope to see you before the summer is over. Tell your mother I will write to her the first of the week. Now be a good girl and write to me again.

Love Gilbert

JULY

The Allies' advances continue in Italy, France, the Eastern front, and in the Pacific.

PFC ERNEST H. FRANKLIN 13TH T.C.S., 403
JC G. APO 708 C/O PM SAN FRANCISCO,
CALIFORNIA
July 7, 1944

Dear Bessie,

I received yours and C.A. letter a few days ago and was indeed pleased to hear from you.
Well these few lines leave me O.K. and I hope that it finds you all OK.
Bessie, I guess you all are having some red-hot weather back there now aren't you, the weather over here isn't too bad now at night it is rather cool.

Bessie was there a big fourth up there this year. I guess there was quite a bit of excitement when they announced the [ILLEGIBLE] wasn't it.

Bessie do you think you will get down to see Mama & Dad this summer.

I have had a letter from most all of them but Gilbert this week and they all seemed to be getting along OK.

Bessie, do you ever see Jimmie now, and do you think Gilbert will give her a divorce? He harley ever says anything about her in his letters to me.

Bessie you said that you had you a garden, where is it in your back lot. I had a letter from mama, and she said that she was getting all kinds of vegetable now.

Well Bessie it was a long wait, but I finally made another step and I hope the next one won't be a long coming, as this and was.

Well Bessie I will stop now as I want to wright C.A a few lines so I hope to hear from you again in the near future, and until I do the best of luck.

Love Ernest F

July 7, 1944

Dear Cynthia Ann,

I received your letter and sure was pleased to hear from you. C.A., you must be quite a large girld now, as you are writing letters. I sure would like to see you and Mickey.

Your mother wrote and told me about you finishing your grade. I sure am proud of you and when I get back, I am going to buy you a nice present.

C.A., when I get back, I have a lot of stories to tell you about the little black boys and girlds I have seen over here.

C.A., I sure sorry to learn that you had been sick but am very happy to know that you are well again.

Well C.A., I guess I had better close for this time. So, stay sweet an smart and you and I will have a swell time when I get back.

Lots Love, Ernest F

Gilbert gets another stripe, he is now a Staff Sergeant.

S/SGT GILBERT FRANKLIN 6619 PW ADM. CO. APO. 782. C/O PM NEW YORK, NY
July 7, 1944

Dear Bessie,

I was going to write to you the first of the week, but I just put it off. Well I haven't heard from you in a time. I know you have been awful busy. Did Cynthia Ann get the letter I sent to her and how is she? Bessie, I have some pictures I am going to send you soon. I had a nice time, yesterday I had an all-day pass and I went sightseeing. I took some pictures. Now I need some more films so when you get a chance to get any you do so. Now Bessie I have been aiming to send some money for you to put in the bank so one day this week I will send it. Now anytime you need any of it you use it. Well Bessie I have another stripe, I got it the first of the month now I am as same as Herman. I show am proud of it.

Love Gilbert

JUST A FEW LINES

S/SGT GILBERT FRANKLIN 6619 PW ADM. CO.
APO. 782. C/O PM NEW YORK, NY
July 11, 1944

Dear Bessie,

    I know I haven't been writing to you like I ought to but I have been awful busy. Well I am fine and working every day. I have had an awful cold but better now. I show am glad your kids are ok now. You know I thought something had happen when it was so long before I heard from you. Well I guess Paul think he is a soldier now and I know how he feels to get his rating? You tell him I also got another one and I felt like celebrate but I didn't. You said that Dug Knisley was in the navy, did she say how he liked. Rita Conen isn't losing any time. Well I hope he has better luck than I did which I know he will. Bessie you said you had two rolls of films well I show do hope you send them to me. I am going to send you a picture just as soon as I can. I sent Mother, Gladys and Elizabeth all one, but I haven't forgotten you. I have been trying to send you some money to put in the bank for me, but I just haven't gotten to it. It a few things yet I have to do I haven't did. Mother wrote and told me she got one of my bonds, so I guess J- got the next so I had them stopped. I have never heard from her and I never did write any more. I guess I will let everything be as it is. I only hope it won't be long before I can come back. Bessie don't you think I will worry about what money I have in the bank because I know you have it safe because what you have done for me I know you did the right thing. You at any time you need any of it you use it. Yes I did get mother name I was glad to get it now I can finish my business. Well if you hear any good news let me know. I show did think a lot of C.A letter did she get the answer. I am going to send her something when I get a chance.

                                                          Love Gilbert

ARTHUR L. JOHNSON

S/SGT GILBERT FRANKLIN 6619 PW ADM. CO.
APO. 782. C/O PM NEW YORK, NY
July 11, 1944

Dear Mother,

 I will try and write you a few lines I know I haven't been writing as often. Well I haven't been getting so mutch mail from any of you. I just got a letter from Gladys Bessie and Myrtle [?Haden?] and you tell her I will answer it soon. Mother I received the box of nuts yesterday and they show was good. I think we will get our beer this week and I will have nuts and beer. They give us one bottle a week and it show do go good. Well my cold is mutch better you know how hard it is to get rid of a cold in the summertime. Mother the flower seeds you asked me to send you well I can't send them they won't allow you to. I show do have a pretty flower garden Mother we are getting all kinds of fresh Vegetables and fruit. We just got some peaches today but they isn't so good we have plenty to eat and nice weather.
 Well how is Johnnie making out with the mess he is in. He must be sorrow as he can be. Do they hear from Warren F.? I guess he will see plenty. You know I heard from Gordon Martin before I got his address, so I have written to him again. I just got a letter from Herman Moon and he was fine. Mother look like you still have as mutch company as you use to. How about Charlie Jackerson I got one letter from him, but I didn't answer it, all he talked about was how his boys keep from going in the Army. Well Mother I don't have mutch new so I want to thank you for the package. How is Elizabeth getting on I haven't heard from her in a good while? Did you get the picture I sent you? Write me a long letter and tell pa I will write to him tomorrow

            Love Gilbert F

In the letter dated June 20, 1944, Ernest states he gets 12 bottles of beer a week. Here, Gilbert gets only one bottle a week. I guess even in the winter; the South Pacific is hotter than an Italian summer?

S/SGT GILBERT FRANKLIN 6619 PW ADM. CO.
APO. 782. C/O PM NEW YORK, NY
July 20 1944

Dear Bessie,

    I guess you are like me you don't have mutch time to write. I just received the small package with the card in it. Well I am ok working every day. I just got a picture from home one of Ernest and it show is good. I don't get so many letters from Mother, but I guess she is awful busy I get a letter from Elizabeth most every week. She show do help mother a lot. I got a letter and three pictures from Herman and he looks well. Bessie by all means I am going to send some money for you to put in the bank for me. I have been trying all this month, but I just don't get to it.

    Bessie you don't think you will get to go down to Mothers this summer I know she would love to have you. They wrote and told me that Cleo was down there, and Herman was out to see them. Well how is Paul since he made corporal? I guess he full his self. Tell him he ought to be over here there are plenty wine and lots of pretty women. You can't talk mutch to them you have to show them. HA. Bessie I am sending you a small package it's not mutch, but I want you to have it for what you did for me. It's a cameo and a broach and I also sent Cynthia Ann a Rosary. I hope you like it. Bessie, I think I have everything finish up. I am sending mother a will and you one of the carbon copy to filed. I will write you both.

Love Gilbert

S/SGT GILBERT FRANKLIN 6619 PW ADM. CO.
APO. 782. C/O PM NEW YORK, NY
July 25, 1944 Italy

Dear Mother,

Just a few lines to let you know I am fine and working every day. I just received three letters today, one from Cleo and one from Elizabeth and Poppa. Mother I sent you a small package and in it is something for Elizabeth and Gladys I hope they like it. Mother you wrote and said that you had received one bond. Well I don't think you will get any more because I had them stopped. I guess J-- got the others that the reason why I had them stopped. Now in this letter I have my will so you have it put in a safe place. Now I am sending Bessie a file copy so she can keep it so if anything should happen to this one.

Love Gilbert Franklin

S/SGT GILBERT FRANKLIN 6619 PW ADM. CO.
APO. 782. C/O PM NEW YORK, NY
July 26, 1944. Italy

Dear Bessie,

I just received your letter was glad to hear from you. I knew something was the trouble because I didn't hear from you. But I got a letter from home and they told me that your kids had been sick again. I hope they are better now I show would like to see them. I bet that Mickey is some boy he will be a man before I get back. Bessie, I don't see how mother stomach it with so mutch company and they wrote and said Charlie Jackson was coming I would guess only thing if they could get water in the house. I could fix it up when I come back if they would just get it in. I just got a letter from Gladys and she said she was going up to see you I hear from her after. You ought to let Mickey go down to mother this Summer it will do him good and I know mother would be tickled to death to have him.

You know I haven't heard from Ernest in a long time, but it takes so long to get his mail. Bessie, I show am glad you are taken care of my things. I hope it won't be long before I can use them, things look good for us over here. Bessie I am like you sometimes I began to think of the same thing, and I don't know what to do with myself. I don't know what I will do when I get back it's going to be hard to keep me straight. Bessie, I think it would be best to get the letter and you keep it. I just sent you a letter I hope you get it. I also sent one to mother. Bessie, I do have a flower garden and they show are pretty I wish I could send you some of the seeds, but I am not allowed to send them. I hope you get the package I sent you and like it. And the films you just send me what you have that will be ok. Tell Fred and the kids I hope to see them soon.

Love Gilbert

AUGUST

With Florence liberated, the Allies begin landings in Southern France. Romania breaks with the Axis and surrenders to the Soviets. The Allies liberate Paris.

S/SGT GILBERT FRANKLIN 6619 PW ADM. CO.
APO. 782. C/O PM NEW YORK, NY
August 6, 1944

Dear Bessie,

I will answer your letter I show was glad to hear from you. Well I guess Gladys had a nice time. I heard from her and she said she did. Bessie I can't change my allotment, it's just like Paul said. I found out so I will have to let it be. I know you have done a lot for me in that way so just forget it. I show am glad Ernest got another stripe I know how he feels I haven't heard from him in a good while. I got the picture Mother sent me of him it show was good. I wrote him to send me one but I haven't heard from him. I sent you a snapshot I hope you have gotten it its not so good but the best I can send you now. The fellow with me is in the co we were both awful tide [tired] when it was taken. Bessie, I show do hope you and Fred go down to Mother. And I also hope Fred get the water in it will be so mutch help for them.

I just wrote to Poppa to not work so hard he don't have to do it. I bet Cynthia Ann was disappointed because she couldn't go back with Gladys. Well tell her when I come back, I will take her and Mickey with me. You said Cynthia Ann letters isn't worth three cents well they are worth a million over here and I am glad to get them any time. I bet that Mickey is some boy. I wish I was there I bet I could teach him something don't you? Bessie I have seen a lot of thing here it is some wonderful thing to see here. Bessie the only film I can use is 120 so if you have any just send them don't waste any time trying to get any. Bessie, we have plenty to eat here but I could go for one of them grilled sandwich any time. Bessie, I hope you will like the camera I sent you. I sent the other one too. Bessie I am sending you $150.00 to put in the bank. Well I guess I better close.

Love Gilbert

Ernest is now a Corporal. He referred to his promotion as "another step" in his letter of July 7, 1944.

CPL ERNEST H. FRANKLIN 13TH T.C.S., 403
JC G. APO 708 C/O PM SAN FRANCISCO,
CALIFORNIA
August 8, 1944

Dear Bessie,

I received your letter a few days ago and was indeed pleased to hear from you. I hadn't had any mail for about three weeks until I received yours and two other our mail had been held up somewhere.

Well these few lines leaves me ok, and I hope that it finds you all in the best of health.

Bessie, I was sorry to learn that you had to have CA tonsils removed but maybe now she will be in better health I sure hope so, you have had quite a time with your children in the last year or so haven't you.

Bessie I sure thank you for the picture you sent me of C.A. & Mickey, it sure was good. You sure have two cute kids. I would give anything to see them. Bessie what have you had done to C.A. hair it sure looked good in that picture

Bessie I am glad that you got the picture that I sent you, and that you liked it.

Bessie you asked me if Gilbert could stop his allotment now that he had made staff. I can't tell you for sure just how it works now, but this is how I think it works, he can stop his allotment through the [?gan.?] but since he hasn't got a divorce I think he is allowed about thirty eight dollars extra for quarter, and if J. should request to help I think he would haft to sent it to her, but he would still draw his full amount as staff, you see if he should get a divorce he wouldn't get that extra money for quarter. I sure hope he can soon get things straighten out with her.

Bessie I sure hope that you can keep Dad in the notation of putting water in the house because I know it will be a lot of help to them.

Well Bessie I had a letter from Herman today the first time I had heard from him in a long time he seemed to be getting along OK, only he was working pretty hard, he seemed to have had enough of army life now, you know how he used to say, that he liked it, well he doesn't like that anymore.

Well Bessie there isn't much more to wright this time so tell all hello, and until I hear from you again the best of luck

Bro Ernest F

S/SGT GILBERT FRANKLIN 6619 PW ADM. CO. APO. 782. C/O PM NEW YORK, NY
August 15, 1944

Dear Bessie,

Just a few lines to let you know I received the films and your letter I want to thank you for them. Well I am awful busy and haven't had the chance to write you a long letter I just received Cynthia Ann letter and it was nice I will answer it soon you tell her I got it. Bessie, I got a real nice letter from Mary. Jimmie Sister. She want me to send her your address I haven't answered it yet. She don't seem to know mutch and real mad about everything. Bessie did you get the package I sent you. Bessie I just ran into a fellow back home Marian Lewis, the brother to the girl Ernest was to go with. Well I will write more next time.

Love Gilbert

S/SGT GILBERT FRANKLIN 6619 PW ADM. CO.
APO. 782. C/O PM NEW YORK, NY
August 20, 1944

Dear Bessie,

    I received two letters from you, but I will answer the V-mail letter first. Bessie I don't think the two middle name make any difference. So, don't send it back to me now. It took six months to get that mutch done. But you can find out if it makes any difference. You know I would have to change mother's too, but I am sure it ok. You don't know how mutch trouble that has been to me. Bessie you will notice I have a new APO no [number]. Did you get to go down to see mother? And how is the kids. Tell Cynthia Ann I will answer her letter real soon. Bessie, I got a real nice letter from Mary, Jimmie sister I wish you could read it. She wants your address, but I haven't sent it yet.

Love Gilbert

CPL ERNEST H. FRANKLIN 13TH TCS, 403RD
TCG. APO 708 C/O PM SAN FRANCISCO,
CALIFORNIA
August 23, 1944

Dear Bessie,

    I received your letter a few days ago and was very glad to hear from you and to know that you all were getting along ok, as for myself I am ok.
    Bessie I had a letter from Mama and she said that you didn't think you would get to come down for your vacation, but I sure hope that you can and know it would be a relief for you, since you have had so much sickness and worked so hard.

Say Bessie speaking of those peaches, if they are what I think they are [peaches in brandy], you had better save some of them until I get back, because I think I am going to need all of that kind of stuff I can get, to forget some of this mess over here.

Bessie right at the present, I am not working so hard, but I guess it will start up again soon, there isn't much to do over here when you have time off, or there isn't any tavern to go to, and everything in GI, and you know you would like to get away from that when you have time off. But we do have some real good shows over here. I go three or four time a week, I think a lot of picture are shows over here before they are back there.

Bessie speaking of Gilbert I haven't heard from him in a long time now but its like you said it takes our letter a long time to reach each other.

Bessie, I think that was pretty dam low down in Jimmie telling Mr. Kinsley what she did don't you, I think she is going to be in for a letdown when Gilbert gets back, because I understand he is going to see her once more.

Say Bessie that was quite a picture on the letter you sent me. I thought it was real cute, that's really something to howl at. You should see us boys over here howl!! but only at the moon.

Bessie if later on you shouldn't hear from me for quite a while, I guess you will know what the reason is. Well Bessie there isn't much more to wright this time so until I hear from you again the best of luck. Tell all I said hello.

Love
Bro Ernest F

Gilbert is now in France. This letter is the first where he mentions it.

JUST A FEW LINES

S/SGT GILBERT FRANKLIN 6619 PW ADM. CO.
APO. 667. C/O PM NEW YORK, NY
August 29, 1944

Dear Bessie,

    Now I have a chance to write you a few lines. Well I am some place in France and like [it] fine. I think I wrote and told you I received the film and I show was glad I got them before I left. Did you get a chance to go down to Mother? Bessie, things show do look good over here now I hope it won't be long before we all will be back. You said Mrs Knisley was going to get married well I would have thought she would have been before now. I remember very mutch what Mr. Knisley said, and I often think of it. Well I just hope I will get back there safe I think I can find out a lot. And it will be just to bed. Bessie, this is awful pretty over here and the weather is fine. Tell C.A. I will write to her soon.

Love Gilbert

    The following pictures seem to be on the move from where they were in Italy to southern France. They are in no particular order.

On the back of this one it says "Lt. Col Buckley 1944"

SEPTEMBER

The Allies liberate Brussels and Luxembourg. The Americans reach the Sigfried line, the west wall of the German defense. In the Pacific, the US takes Ulithi Atoll in the Caroline Islands.

> S/SGT GILBERT FRANKLIN 6619 PW ADM. CO.
> APO. 667. C/O PM NEW YORK, NY
> Sept. 1, 1944. Southern France

Dear Bessie,

I received your letter Aug 15 the first I have heard from you. Now I think our mail will be better. I also received a letter from Elizabeth. Look like you have a time trying to get down to Mother the summer will be over before you get there. Bessie, I forgot to keep the receipts of the money order, but I knew it would get there. Well when I do come back, I will have a little after all I have lost other ways. I never did find out about the bonds. I had only the one mother got. Bessie, I didn't won't [want] to put you to any trouble getting these letters I don't think they will be any good to me when I get back. I think I can settle everything awful quick. Tell C.A. I will try and answer her letter tomorrow. Well I will have to close.

Love Gilbert

> S/SGT GILBERT FRANKLIN 6619 PW ADM. CO.
> APO. 667. C/O PM NEW YORK, NY
> Sept. 6, 1944 Southern France

Dear Bessie,

I received your letter and the birthday card yesterday. Well this is my third birthday in the army, and I show do hope the next one is home. I want to thank you for the present you gave me. I know I can use it when I get back. Well at last you got down home I show am glad you did get to go because Mother show did want you to come. I bet Mickey had a time while he was down there. It show is nice that Fred got what he did done I don't guess he got mutch rest while he was down there. Well I hope I can pay him back some way. All of them have been good to Mother and Dad since we all have been away

Bessie there is nothing that shock me anymore. I wouldn't be surprise of anything happen back there. I hear of sutch thing every day we get the low down from back there. Bessie, I wrote to papa and told him to stop work but it don't do any good, he don't have to do it. I think I am going to stay with them when I come back and he won't have to work then I will make him stop. Bessie you asked about Christmas presents well there is nothing that I can think of now but don't send any candy, gum or anything like that we get all we want. Bessie, I like here so mutch better than Italy. Things look almost like back home and the people are so clean and the weather is nice and warm. Plenty grapes and wine. I hope you got the package I sent you and you will like it.

Love Gilbert

S/SGT GILBERT FRANKLIN 6619 PW ADM. CO. APO. 667. C/O PM NEW YORK, NY
Sept. 28, 1944

Dear Bessie,

I haven't forgotten you. I haven't written to any one I have been busy and been moving a lot. I haven't heard from you in over three weeks and when you don't get any mail, I don't know what to write. I am well and working every day. It has begun to get cold here I show do hate to have to be over here this winter. But I like here better than

Italy, its awful pretty country, plenty of grapes and wine and a lot of beer. And the girls are pretty. Bessie, I don't have mutch to say so I will have to stop.

Love Gilbert

S/SGT GILBERT FRANKLIN 6619 PW ADM. CO.
APO. 667. C/O PM NEW YORK, NY
Sept. 28, 1944

Dear Mother,

I guess you thought I had forgotten you well I haven't. I have been awful busy and moving a lot. Well I am well working every day. I haven't heard from any one of you in over three weeks and I show do miss my mail. You know when I don't get any mail, I just don't know what to write. Well it has began to get cold here, but I like mutch better than I did in Italy. I hope we will be home before the real cold weather gets here. Have you heard from Ernest he owes me a letter I haven't heard from him in a long time? Do you know whether Gordon Martin is over here I can't hear from him?

Love Gilbert

OCTOBER

Allies bomb Aachen, Germany, and the Americans capture it. It is the first battle on German soil, and the first German city to be captured by the Allies. In the Pacific, Australia and the United States' Third and Fifth Fleets celebrate a major victory in the Battle of Leyte Gulf, the largest naval battle in the war.

S/SGT GILBERT FRANKLIN 6619 PW ADM. CO.
APO. 667. C/O PM NEW YORK, NY
Oct. 2, 1944

Dear Mother,

    I guess you thought I have forgotten all of you. Well I haven't written to any of you I have been so busy. And today is the first I have heard from any of you in over a month. I got the birthday card and your letter and thanks for the money, but I will have to wait until I come back to spend it because it isn't any good over here. Did Herman Moon tell you about the place I was? Well it is mutch better over here but it so cold here. I am still doing the same kind of work and plenty of it now. I haven't seen anyone I know here yet. I haven't had a chance to find out who is here. Well I will write a long letter next time.

Love Gilbert

S/SGT GILBERT FRANKLIN 6619 PW ADM. CO.
APO. 667. C/O PM NEW YORK, NY
Oct. 4, 1944 France

Dear Bessie,

    I have began to get settled down again. So now I will try and answer some of the letters I have gotten. Well I am working every day and feel fine. I like here mutch better than I did in Italy, but it is awful cold here and windy. Bessie you said you like the thing I sent you I am glad you do. I wish I could have sent you a lot more, but things are so high. That cameo I sent you is the best you can buy. You know Gladys sent me a package with some films in but I have never received them yet. Herman also sent me a package, but I haven't gotten his yet. Bessie you know the over sea cap I have then the winter one I wish you would try and get me one like it 6 5/8 and send it to me. But if you can't send me the one there now don't send anything to me for Christmas because it takes so long to get here, and I have plenty of everything but films—HA!

Bessie, I guess you was surprise when Margo & Paul come up to see you. Well I know they would if they could find you. I know they didn't have anything to do with it. I think the world of Margo I never did write to them, but I will, but I will not say anything about what happen. I don't care what you write because there is nothing, they say that worries me because all J. has said is not true. Bessie did you get the post card I sent you when I get a chance, I will send you some more. Tell Fred there are plenty of beer and pretty women and I mean pretty. Tell Paul H. this is the place he ought to be

Love Gilbert

S/SGT GILBERT FRANKLIN 6619 PW ADM. CO. APO. 667. C/O PM NEW YORK, NY
Oct. 7, 1944 Southern France

Dear Mother,

Just a few lines to let you know I am well and working. You know I haven't been writing like I aught to but we are awful busy. I hope we will get settled down. Well it has been awful cold and rainy here for the last week. It look like the winter is here I guess it has begun to get cold there now. I just had a letter from Bessie and Gladys but it looks like I just can't hear from Ernest. I wrote to Warran F. but haven't heard from him. I am a long way from him. I don't guess I will get to see him. And Red Debo is where Warren is. Mother you tell that Heduct boy, that the Mess sergeant that use to with the M.P. Co he was in is with us now. He show was lucky to get back so quick. Well it looks like I will be here until it is all over with and when that is, I don't know. Mother did you ever the other package I sent you there wasn't mutch in it but just a few things. I have a few more things I want to send when I get a chance. I think I wrote and told you I received the picture of you and Dad. You show do look well and haven't you gained a lot of weight. I think Poppa is a little thin you tell him he better quit working so hard because I want him in good shape when we come back. Well there is nothing I need we are getting plenty to eat and everything we need now. So tell all of them I will write to them

Love Gilbert

Red Debo would be a family friend and is in the same place as Warren Franklin, a cousin. The Heduct boy should be a family friend and was where Gilbert was at some point. From the letter, we can only deduce that he is now at home for some reason.

S/SGT GILBERT FRANKLIN 6619 PW ADM. CO.
APO. 667. C/O PM NEW YORK, NY
Oct. 13, 1944 France

Dear Bessie,

I just received your letter written Sept 19. It looks like I can't get any mail. I never did receive any of the package Gladys and Herman sent me. Well I am working every day we have plenty of work now. We have a very good place but not like back in Italy. And the weather here is cold and rainy I don't know what it will be like when winter comes. I often heard that France was a pretty country and I can say it is for what I have seen. And the people are nice. And plenty beer wine and pretty women. You asked me how I like the women over here well so far fine I can't talk mutch France, but I can use my hands and make signs. I like here fine I have seen plenty but there is a lot back there that I haven't seen, and I am ready to come back there any time. Bessie the statue I sent you was given to me by a British solider and the cup was the first thing I got when I landed in Italy. I will tell you about it when I come back. Bessie, I haven't gotten the chance to write to Marg, J's sister, but I will. I still think a lot of her and Paul. I know they would come to see you because they wrote me a letter and said they was going to find you. Bessie I will write mother a letter but I think my happy days are over. Well I think Gladys got a good break don't you and I think she will make good. You tell C.A. I owe her a letter but I will write to her soon. And Magdalene I will write to her. Bessie you send the films to me just like you did the other ones. And I have some money I want to send you to put in the bank

Love Gilbert

S/SGT GILBERT FRANKLIN 6619 PW ADM. CO. APO. 667. C/O PM NEW YORK, NY
Oct. 15, 1944 France

Dear Bessie,

Just a few lines I think I answered your letter, but I lost it and it had Mag [Magdalene] address in it and I want to write to her so will you send it to me again. Well I don't get mutch mail and haven't never got the package Gladys and Herman sent me. I hope I will get them because they both had films in them. Bessie there are the prettiest women here I ever seen but I show don't like the weather here it is cold and rainy. Bessie, we show do get plenty to eat over here we have fresh meat every day. Well Bessie I started this letter yesterday so now I will try and finish it. I just got a letter from Mother and she said that Uncle Jimmie died. Well I guess it will be a lot more before I come home. Bessie, I seen Ray Prier yesterday he is here clost by, but I think they will move soon. Why haven't Mother heard from Ernest. I just can't get any mail from him. Bessie you send me my cap if you can't get one. How is Paul doing and is he still at the same place he ought to be over here plenty of beer and all the women he want—HA! Bessie I will send you some money to put in the bank this week. I am sending you a picture of some friend and I drinking beer.

Love Gilbert

S/SGT GILBERT FRANKLIN 6619 PW ADM. CO. APO. 667. C/O PM NEW YORK, NY
Oct. 17, 1944 France

Dear Poppa,

Just a few lines to let you know I am thinking of you and Mother. Well I am ok working every day It has been a little warmer this week but a lot of rain You tell Mother I just got her letter and will write soon. Pa there was a fellow come up to me today and said how are you Gilbert and I didn't know him at first and it was Ray Price he is here clost to me. His outfit just came in but they won't be here long. I didn't have long to talk to him I might get to see him again tomorrow. Well it looks like this war will never end I get awful homesick at times. We are getting plenty to eat and good too. You know I haven't heard from Ernest in a long time. Mother said in her letter that Uncle Jimmie Franklin died what was his trouble. Do you work long hours like you use to? I don't see why you and Mother don't quit that hard work. I am sending you a couple picture. The other fellow are in the co we are drinking beer they have plenty of beer here but not so good.

Gilbert

S/SGT GILBERT FRANKLIN 6619 PW ADM. CO. APO. 667. C/O PM NEW YORK, NY
Oct. 23, 1944

Dear C. Ann,

I just received your letter today and I show was glad to hear from you. Well I guess you are going back to school by this time. How is Mickey I guess he is a big boy now. The drawin you sent me show is good do you do mutch drawing in school. How do you like Paul and Helen little girl. Well how is your mother and dad. Tell mother I haven't heard from her in a long time. I did receive the (Washington evening star) she sent me. Tell her I said thanks.

Love Gilbert Franklin

CPL ERNEST H. FRANKLIN 13TH TCS, 403RD TCG. APO 920 C/O PM SAN FRANCISCO, CALIFORNIA
Oct. 28, 1944

Dear Bessie,

I guess you think you are not going to hear from me anymore, but I have been moving around so much lately that I haven't written anybody much. I was in Australia for about six weeks, and I really had a nice time down there, it was six of us and T.D. down there and we had a little apartment it was almost like be a civilization again, but now I am back in the Islands. I am in the Netherlands East Indeas [Indies] and it is really hot here, but we have a very nice camp and very good food, which makes a great help.

Well Bessie it will soon be two years that I have been over here, and it doesn't look much like I will be home any time soon either, it sure seems like a long time.

Bessie I just had a letter from home, and they told me that Uncle Jimmie F. had died, they didn't give me any details do you know what his trouble was.

Bessie what did you think of Lillian F. having a baby. I thought that was the worst thing I had ever heard of. I can't see what is the matter with people back there, you know she has ruined her life for good and not only hers but her peoples. Well Bessie there isn't much to wright this time but will try and do better the next time so until I hear from you again the best of luck to you all.

Love
Bro Ernest F
My APO is 920

We can only guess that Lillian Franklin was not married.

NOVEMBER

In France, General Patton takes Metz and French troops free Strasbourg. The US bombs Singapore. There is an effective stalemate in Italy because of weather and heavy rains.

The following letter was damaged, possibly by water; this is the best we could decipher.

>S/SGT GILBERT FRANKLIN 6619 PW ADM. CO.
>APO. 772. C/O PM NEW YORK, NY
>I am in the same outfit but our no has been
>change to (6832)
>Nov. 6, 1944

Dear Bessie,

I owe you two letters and I don't have mutch time to write so I will write you a few lines. I don't hear [?from any?] of you very often. I want to [ILLEGIBLE] you that

I got one of your package the one that had the things Mrs Handbeck sent. They were all nice and I thank you. I wish you would send me her address I have forgotten it. Bessie did you get the money order I sent you I forgot to write and tell you I was sending it. And about the cap I had to laugh when I read the letter when you was trying to find just what I wanted. Now it doesn't make any difference what color the braid is on it because I can change it. Now don't you go to any more trouble to get one. I know you like to do anything for us, but I don't have to have it. Now I want to thank you for the trouble you have done for me. Bessie [ILLEGIBLE] sent you a box with a little [ILLEGIBLE] in it. I hope you will like it when you get it, be careful in open it. I also sent Gladys and Elizabeth one. I would like to send you some post card, but they have stop us from sending them. Did you get the one I sent? Bessie, I wrote to Marg, Jimmie's sister but I haven't heard from her. Well I have so many letters to write I guess I had better stop. You tell Paul I asked how does it feel to be a Sgt. I show am glad he made it. Tell Helen I said hello.

Love Gilbert

S/SGT GILBERT FRANKLIN 6619 PW ADM. CO. APO. 772. C/O PM NEW YORK, NY
Nov. 10, 1944

Dear Bessie,

I just received the two rolls of films and a letter from you. It must took you a week to write this letter. Now I am not saying it is too long because that's the kind I like. Bessie I will try and send you some more money because I think I will need it when I do get back. Now if you need any of it just spend it. The pictures I sent you was taken here in France. You know I would send more but

I try to send all of you some. And in that way, it takes a lot of them. Bessie the picture you sent me of Poppa and mother it was good, but I think Poppa has began to look old I think he is working too hard I have written to him several times and told him to quit working so hard. Bessie you can bet I am not spending any of my money on these women over here. I have been fooled once. Well the difference in the weather here and Italy is France is cold as H-- What time it isn't raining the wind is blowing. Bessie, Ray Price didn't come to see me, I just happen to run into him one day. I was glad to see him. I didn't even know him he spoke to me twice before I knew him. He has moved a good ways from me now. Lena never hears from Johnnie well you can't hardly blame him I feel sorrow for her but I still think I had the worst deal. You know when I read what you wrote I was so mad I don't know what to do. I feel sorrow for myself because when I do come back I don't know what I will do. Bessie I am sorry you went to a lot of trouble trying to get me the cap. I should have explained it to you. I guess I have cost you a lot, but I will pay you back when I come back. Paul ought to be over here he could get plenty to drink it cost plenty too. Well I guess I had better close I want to thank you for the films. I think I wrote and told you that I got one of your package. Tell Mrs Handback I will send her a letter thanking her for the thing she sent me.

Love Gilbert

PS Bessie I forgot to tell you we had ham this week and it was good. And we have chicken for tomorrow.

S/SGT GILBERT FRANKLIN 6619 PW ADM. CO.
APO. 772. C/O PM NEW YORK, NY
Nov. 16 1944 France

Dear Poppa,

    I will try and answer your letter. I haven't been writing so mutch. I have been busy, but I always have time to write if I would. Well I have a bad cold and feel bad. But I have been taken some medicine and I think it has help me some. We have had some good weather the last week, but it has been awful cold here. It's a lot difference in the weather here than in Italy. Well Poppa I got a letter from Elizabeth and she said she had moved again well I hope she will buy this time. She said that you had bought your Christmas licker [liquor] I wish I was there to help you drink it. We can get plenty to drink over here most anything. You know I don't care for any of it. But I don't know how I will be when I get back. I hope I never drink any more. Poppa did you ever get the water cut in? I don't see why they wait so long. Well when I get back, I will fix it up like it aught to be. You tell Mother I received the package she sent me, and I show was glad to get it. Tell her I will write to her tomorrow. I got a letter from Gladys and she had gotten back from Richmond she said that she liked fine. Well Poppa I show do wish I could be back there with you. Bessie sent me a picture of you and Mother, and it was good but what was the green on your face Bessie told me and I don't blame you I guess I had better close.

Love Gilbert

JUST A FEW LINES

S/SGT GILBERT FRANKLIN 6619 PW ADM. CO.
APO. 772. C/O PM NEW YORK, NY
Nov. 20, 1944. France

Dear Mother,

 I haven't heard from you in a good while. I hope everything is good. I am well all ~~is~~ except I have a cold. Mother I received the package you sent me, and it was nice and all the thing was good you must know I had a cold who address the package for you. Because my name was spelt wrong. Well it won't be long before Christmas. I guess you are ready. I wish I was there with all of you. I hope to be there Next Christmas.

Love Gilbert

S/SGT GILBERT FRANKLIN 6619 PW ADM. CO.
APO. 772. C/O PM NEW YORK, NY
Nov. 25, 1944

Dear Bessie,

 I think I owe you a letter although I haven't heard from you in a good while. Well I have a bad cold and I just can't get rid of it. I got a letter from home and mother had been sick with a cold. How is the weather there it has been nice here for the last week not so mutch rain? Bessie I received the package with the Kodak in you know I had began to think that's what you was sending me. It was nice for you to send it to me but I am afraid I will lose it but I will try my best to keep it. Is it hard to get films for it? Bessie did you get the picture I sent you. I will try to send you more when I can. How is Fred getting on with his work? I guess he has plenty to do. I wish I could be there to help him. Well when I get back, I don't know what I will do. I think I will go stay with

Mother. How is Paul doing and is he station at the same place. I guess he is getting tide of the army now. How was Thanksgiving back there you ought to see the dinner we had. Turkey and everything to go with it. Our food over here is wonderful. I couldn't ask for nothing more. Well I guess I had better close. Tell the kids I said hello.

Love Gilbert.

DECEMBER

The Battle of the Bulge in the Ardennes Region begins and will continue into January. The Soviets begin the siege of Budapest. The battle for the Philippines continues.

Ernest is now a Sergeant but he does not tell anyone yet other than in his return address.

> SGT ERNEST H. FRANKLIN 13TH TCS, 403RD TCG. APO 920 C/O PM SAN FRANCISCO, CALIFORNIA
> Dec. 5, 1944

Dear Bessie,

I will take time out to write you another letter. I have written you two since I last heard from you. I don't know if you received them or not.

Well I hope this finds you all in the best of health. I guess you are beginning to have some pretty cold weather up there now ain't you, has it snowed any there yet.

Well Bessie I am now in the Netherland Dutch Indea now, and it is really a hot place here. I think it must be the next thing to hell, and the most of the time it is dry and dusty.

Bessie are you expecting to have a big Xmas this year? You know this will be my third one overseas, how many more I will spend over here I don't know, but I sure hope this will be the last one.

Did you have a very nice Thanksgiving it was just another day here, but we did have a very nice dinner turkey and all that goes with it.

Bessie is Paul H. still in the states or did he go overseas. I hear that they are sending quite a few of the old men overseas now.

Well I just had a letter from home and one from Elizabeth and they all seemed to be ok.

Bessie how are your children getting along fine I hope, tell them all I said hello, so until I hear from you the best of luck

Love
Ernest F

SGT ERNEST H. FRANKLIN 13TH TCS, 403RD TCG. APO 920 C/O PM SAN FRANCISCO, CALIFORNIA
Dec. 12, 1944

Dear Bessie,

I received your letter today and you don't know how pleased I was to hear from you as it had been over two months since I last received a letter from you.

I was glad to learn that you all were o.k. the only thing it is so hot here you can harley stand it.

I guess it is rather cold back there now isn't it, have you had any snow yet

Well Bessie it seems as if Gilbert and J. will never get thing straighten out dosen't it, did he ever get a divorce from her. I never knew if he did or not. I never ask or say anything at all about her in my letters to him

Yes Bessie I had a wonderful time in Australia and I got my fill of everything but I am now ready to go back there again, that is a nice place, as for my Babe down there I had it pretty bad for a while, what do you think? Should I bring her back to the states with me? No kitting [kidding] Bessie she was really a nice girld.

You asked me what kind of Thanksgiving I had well it was just another day, only we did have a very nice dinner.

Bessie between you and I, I think Paul H. is just a fool to ask for overseas duty, it won't take him long to get his fill of it. I be dam if I haven't got all of it I want you know I have been over here over two years and I Have no idea when I will.

No Bessie I haven't received any Xmas packages yet, but I guess I should be getting them in the near future.

Well Bessie there isn't much to wright this time so I hope to hear from you again in the near future, so I wish you all a happy Xmas, and I hope to be with you there for the next one, so the best of luck

Love Ernest

S/SGT GILBERT FRANKLIN 6619 PW ADM. CO. APO. 772. C/O PM NEW YORK, NY
Dec. 14 1944. France

Dear Bessie,

I received your letter today and I think I owe you two, I owe so many letters I don't know when I will catch up. I haven't had a minute for myself for over two weeks. I tell you we are really working now. I am so tide now I don't know what to do. Bessie I got four letters today but they were all over a month old. But I like to get any kind I got your Christmas card in seven day. Bessie I am glad you write and tell me anything because after all you are the only one knows. I got a nice long letter from Marg. Jimmie sister. She show do feel hurt. And she asked for your address said that she had lost it. They are running a Restaurant there where they live and doing good. So when I get back she said I wouldn't go hungry.

Bessie the grays pictures were taken here in France and the one with the flowers were in Italy. The House was where we stayed when we first come over. Not bad. I will have to wait to show you my girlfriend. I have a picture her that I might send you any way. I did hear from Cleo today. I haven't heard from Herman in a long time. But after so long a time I heard from Ernest and he is doing good Sgt. I hope he makes Master and that will kill Herman. I am like Ernest what in the world are they doing back there. If it wasn't for my people I just as soon stay over here. I show am glad Harvey got everything fixed up and wish we were there to finish every thing. Well I hope to be back next year this time but I wouldn't bet on it. Tell Paul I will trade places any day and pull K.P. three times a week.

Bessie Elizabeth wrote and told me that she had moved again I think she likes where she is now. Well everything you have sent me now is good and anything you do send will be good. I want to thank you. I just got two packages this week from Gladys and one of them was a fruit cake it look like a pan cake when I got it but it was good it was sent in Sept and I just got it. That is one of the best thing you can send over here. Now I am not asking for one—HA! Bessie you guessed right what I sent you perfume. I hope you like it. We can send that so easy. About the hose I don't get the time to go any where but I am sure they have them they have everything else. I just can't think what that is you are sending and why you said if I didn't like it you would never know. Well I guess the kids are all excited over Christmas I show would like to be there to get the train running. But I guess you are glad I wasn't there if I was going to do that—<u>HA</u>. Bessie I have been trying to send you some more money to put in the bank but I just haven't got to it I will though this week. Bessie I will try and write to Mrs Handbeck this week.

Tell the kids I will see them next Christmas I hope. Also tell Fred to have a big drink for me Christmas.

Love Gilbert

S/SGT GILBERT FRANKLIN 6619 PW ADM. CO. APO. 772. C/O PM NEW YORK, NY
Dec. 16, 1944 France

Dear Mother & Dad,

    I guess you think I have forgotten you. Well I have been so busy I haven't time to do any thing. I just received two letters from you and one from all the rest. You know I heard from Warren today and he was fine just had a pass and said he had a good time. Well it has been awful cold here but no snow. I heard from Ernest this week and he seem to be doing good. I show am glad he made Sgt. Mother I show do hope Poppa will get to finish the house and when we come back we will finish it. The package I have received have been in good shape and I liked them all. And I know I will like the sweater. Bessie wrote and told me she was sending me a sweater so I am going to be warm

    You asked me did I have any trouble with the Prisoners. No we don't. I have a good place to sleep and plenty to eat. Mother we show have been working awful hard but I am willing to do anything to get this thing over with. You know I wish Poppa wouldn't work so hard and take it easy. He aught to just go around and see all his people and rest up some because when we get back we are going to show him a time. Herman sent me some pictures where he had been fishing they were good. Mother I haven't gotten a chance to send that box yet but I will soon. Did Myrtle Haden ever get the V-mail letter I sent her. Tell all of them I will soon answer their letter.

Love Gilbert

Gilbert is a supply sergeant for the prisoner of war camp. It is the only letter we have that mentions it, yet it responds to his mother's question. Another reason why we believe some are missing.

The following letter is from Pete Conlon, Fred Conlon's nephew. He was the ship's cook on the aircraft carrier USS Hancock, CV-19. The ship was in a typhoon on December 17. On December 24, she put into Ulithi, an atoll in the Caroline Islands of the western Pacific, for six days. I included this letter because it is so similar to Uncle Ernest's Christmas letter of 1942.

P. J. CONLON SC USS HANCOCK CV19 5 DIV
FLEET C/O POST OFFICE SAN FRANCISCO,
CALIFORNIA
Dec. 25, 1944

Dear Bessie & Fred,

Thanks for your Christmas present. It just arrived this afternoon. Already the candy has practically disappeared, and the rest will not last long.

Though I cannot see where they will put anything else after the turkey dinner we had today.

All in all we had a pretty nice day with only the most urgent of duties being performed, while the rest of the ship went to shows, races, movies and boxing matches.

Sorry that I had no opportunity to get cards this year.

Hoping that your family had the best of Christmases and the happiness is carried out there the next year.

Sincerely
Pete
Peter J Conlon

ARTHUR L. JOHNSON

S/SGT GILBERT FRANKLIN 6619 PW ADM. CO. APO. 772. C/O PM NEW YORK, NY
Dec. 28, 1944. France

Dear Bessie,

    I think I owe you a letter and most everyone else. Well I just haven't had mutch time to write to no one. I am well and doing ok. I awful cold here and we had our first snow last week. How was Christmas I guess the kids had a nice time

    I wish I could have been there Christmas morning and seen Michael. I bet he had a time. Bessie, I have been working awful hard this last month. And look like we will for a while.

    I don't know whether I wrote and told you that I received the package with the cap in it. Well I want to thank you for it and all the rest of the things. I just got a package from Elizabeth today. I think I got all of mine but that one before Christmas. Mother sent me one with a fruit cake in it and that the best cake I believe I ever eat. I got a letter from Mother and she said that William Lampkin got kill and the Payne boy was back to the states. Well that just one of the thousands. I show do hope this thing will soon end.

    Bessie I wrote Mrs Hanback a V-mail did she ever get it. I received her Xmas card. Did you ever get the perfume I sent you? You guessed right when you said I was sending perfume. I don't know whether Elizabeth will ever get hers I sent it to her old address. I have some for mother but just don't get time to send it. This is good perfume. I got it at the factory and that place do smell good. Bessie was you talking about this paper when you said that you was sending me something that you would never know whether I would like it or not.

    Well did Fred get high Christmas and how was Paul? I had one little drink. I didn't work Christmas day, but

I worked most the night to get it off. We had the best dinner I ever eat. Well I will try and send you some money to put in the bank. I am trying to save all I can because I will want it when I get back.

Well I guess I had better eat.

Love Frank

CHAPTER 5

1945

JANUARY

American B29s drop bombs on Tokyo again. US troops land in Luzon, Philippines. Navy planes bomb Iwo Jima to prepare for invasion. In Europe, the Allies win the Battle of the Bulge. The Soviets advance toward Germany in the east.

Ernest is somewhere in the South Pacific. Gilbert is in southern France possibly near Nice.

S/SGT GILBERT FRANKLIN 6619 PW ADM. CO.
APO. 772. C/O PM NEW YORK, NY
Jan. 5, 1945 France

Dear Mother,

Now that I owe you two letters I will try and answer one of them. I have been so busy I just can't write like I use to. And I am not just telling you that to get out of it. We have been awful busy but caught up a little. Well what kind of a Christmas did you have a fine one, I hope.

I know you missed all of us but just wait we will be back with all of you and I hope soon. I just got a letter from Gladys and Elizabeth my mail has been good the last few weeks. I haven't heard from Bessie in a long time I guess she has been awful busy since the hollow days [holidays]. Mother you talk about cold well it has been awful cold here and when the wind blows it is awful.

It hasn't snowed but once since we been here. You be sure and get Poppa to finish the house and when Ernest and I get back we will do the rest. Mother don't you worry about me because we are getting the best to eat, and I have a good place to sleep. You tell Mrs Martin that Gorden was in a good outfit now. I don't know where he is, but he isn't very far from me. I will write to him when I get a chance. Did poppa get the letter I sent him. I never hear from Ernest I guess he would like to see some of this over here. Well I guess I had better close

Love Gilbert

S/SGT GILBERT FRANKLIN 6619 PW ADM. CO. APO. 772. C/O PM NEW YORK, NY
Jan. 7, 1945

Dear Bessie,

I just wrote to you yesterday, but I received the package with the sweater and cap in it. So I thought I would let you know I received it. I show was glad to get them and the cap was just the thing I really wanted. I really was proud of it all, and I want to thank you for the trouble you had getting the cap. I haven't heard from you way before Christmas but I know you have been busy. Bessie it is real cold here tonight it snowed yesterday but didn't last long. Have you had mutch snow there this time. I hate to see it snow there because it get so muddy. Well Bessie I am in hopes I will hear from you soon. I don't have mutch news so tell all hello. Thanks again for the things.

Love Gilbert Franklin

SGT ERNEST H. FRANKLIN 13TH TCS, 403RD TCG. APO 920 C/O PM SAN FRANCISCO, CALIFORNIA
Jan. 8, 1945

Dear Bessie,

    I had been some time now since I last heard from you, but I guess the mail has been built up over the holidays These few lines leaves me ok and I hope that it finds you all the same. Did you have a nice Xmas I hope that you did, mine was very quiet just another day.

    Bessie, I want to thank you very much for the package that I received from you, they were in pretty good condition the only thing some of the candy had melted. I have received quite a number of packages.

    When you wright, tell me what C.A. and Mickey got for Xmas. I guess Mickey had quite a time didn't he.

    Bessie that was some bad about William Lampkin being killed wasn't it, also about Lyne Payne, food being of no use to him now. I was sure sorry to hear about it.

    Bessie are you having much cold weather aback there now, it is still as hot as hell over here yet, and always is, I guess I would freeze if I got to any cold weather

    Bessie did Paul H. ever go overseas. If so I bet it won't take him long to get his fill of it.

    Well Bessie there just isn't any news this time so until I hear from you the best of luck. Tell all hello.

Love
Ernest F

ARTHUR L. JOHNSON

S/SGT GILBERT FRANKLIN 6619 PW ADM. CO. APO. 772. C/O PM NEW YORK, NY
Jan. 17, 1945. France

Dear Bessie,

    I just received your V-mail letter today the first I have heard from you since Nov. I did get all my package and I have written to you every time I received any thing. But I didn't write to any one in Dec. because I was so busy. We were so busy then I didn't have hardy time to eat. We are not working so hard now but we don't get any mail I just got these Christmas cards yesterday and your letter that about all I have gotten this month.

    Now don't you think I am mad with you because I don't write. You know I write to all of you when I have the chance. And I hope you get the money I sent you. You said that you liked the perfume I have some for mother and Herman both, but don't get the time to send It. Bessie we have had a big snow here but it is all gone now and has been warm the last few day but the wind has began to blow tonight. Bessie, I show do think a lot of my cap you sent me and all the thing I think I wrote and told you I received a Christmas card from Mrs Hanback tell her thanks.

    I got a letter from home and they were telling me Herman was there for Christmas I bet they was surprised I guess it has been 15 years since he been there for Christmas. Well I might be there in about two more. How is Paul doing and is he still at the same place. I never see anyone that I know most of them are in Germany. Well Bessie I don't have mutch news. Tell the kids I received the Christmas card and don't forget to write me a long letter and tell me all the news. I send Marg, J's sister, your address.

                                                    Love Gilbert

**S/SGT GILBERT FRANKLIN 6619 PW ADM. CO.
APO. 772. C/O PM NEW YORK, NY**
Jan. 24, 1945 France

Dear Mother,

I just received two letters from you and one from Elizabeth the first I have heard from Any one in over three weeks. I show was glad to hear from you. And believe it or not I got a letter from Ernest and I show was glad to get that one. He was well and doing ok Mother I haven't been writing so often because I didn't get any mail. When I don't hear from any of you, I just don't know what to write. You know I haven't heard from Bessie but once in over two months. She must be mad or something. I got a letter from Mrs Hanback who lives across the street from Bessie. Mother how did Ray Yates get kill? He hasn't been out the Army long had he? His mother show has had a hard time. Did poppa get the letter I sent him I try to write to each one of you as often as I can. Well we show are having some cold weather here now. It has been snowing a little and raining too. It's so muddy you can't hardly get around. Well Mother it is almost time for me to go to bed so I will write poppa a letter tomorrow.

Love Gilbert

**S/SGT GILBERT FRANKLIN 6619 PW ADM. CO.
APO. 772. C/O PM NEW YORK, NY**
Jan. 27, 1945 France

Dear Poppa,

I just receive your letter yesterday and show was glad to hear from you. I haven't been getting any mail. I received three letters today, one from Mother, Elizabeth, and Myrtle Haden. You tell Myrtle that I will answer her letter real soon. You know I show do like to get a letter from Elizabeth. She has so mutch to say. Poppa I don't know what the trouble with Bessie she use to write to me every week it has been two months since I heard from her. You write and find out the trouble. Well at last I heard from Ernest it looks like it is hard for us to get each other's mail. He seem to be getting on fine. Poppa Mother said in her letter that Warren had got wounded, I haven't heard from him but once. I hope it not bad.

I wrote to Gordon Martin but I haven't heard from him. Well I see where you are having a lot of rough weather back there. We are having some too. It show has been awful rough here and the wind show does blow. We haven't had so mutch snow. Poppa I sent you a paper the other day I hope you get it. You asked me whether I was doing the same kind of work yes I am we are not so busy now. We have been awful busy. Herman wrote me a letter and sent me a sketch of how he thought the house should be built and I thought it was good. So if you can try and get it started and when I get back we will finish it I have a good bit of money saved up. What happen to Syn Payne did he ever get to come home. I never see any one I know over here. Well sometime I think it won't be long before we will be coming home then again it looks the other way. We are getting the best to eat over here fresh egg every day and fresh meat too. Write me a long letter

Gilbert Franklin

S/SGT GILBERT FRANKLIN 6619 PW ADM. CO. APO. 772. C/O PM NEW YORK, NY
Jan. 28, 1945 France

Dear Bessie,

After so long a time I received your letter. The second letter I have had from you in two months you don't know how glad I was to get it. After all it seems like your letters mean more to me than anyone else. Well Bessie it show is cold here now and the wind blows all the time and everything is froze up not too mutch snow. I just received a lot of mail yesterday from Mother and the rest of them. And after all I got a letter from Ernest he is doing ok. Mother seemed to have had a nice Christmas as Herman being there he show has had it lucky. He is on a furlough now wonder whether he is going to take Cleo with him back.

Bessie from what we can hear over here they are taking a lot of fellows back there. It is good to know you are in 1A but I hope Fred don't have to leave you. You tell him it is nice over here but if I wasn't over here I would never come to find out. And you tell him he don't have to know how to speak "French" either. Bessie I would like to send you that picture but we can't send any kind now You know how it is sometimes you can send thing then again they won't let you send any thing. If I don't send any more pictures you will know why. You know I often think of the kids and how I would like to see them while they are small because I can have so mutch fun with them. I thought of the time I had with the train.

Well I hope I will be with all of you next Christmas. And Paul wrecked his car I guess Helen Was mad with him look like he is into something all the time. Elizabeth wrote and told me about James after all she shouldn't get mad because any one drink will get too mutch sometime. Bessie, in one of the package I got from home, it was a package of Standbeck. I have been keeping it thinking I would get on a big one. So far I haven't drank anything yet. I guess by this time you have gotten my letter letting you I had received the package with the sweater and caps. I show was pleased with the cap I have never used it yet I am going to wear it when I come back. HA. When I ask you to get me something I always know it is what I want. Bessie, I had a little flower painted on your cameo so you will always remember. I show do hope I will get to bring it back and soon too. You don't have to tell me what is going on back there because I guess we hear more about that than you do. And I know it will be a change when all of us get back. Well I guess you have heard enough so I will ask you did you get the money order I sent you I will try and send more next month.

Gilbert Franklin

S/SGT GILBERT FRANKLIN 6619 PW ADM. CO. APO. 772. C/O PM NEW YORK, NY
Jan. 30, 1945 France

Dear Mother,

I received two letters from you this week. My mail comes like yours all at one time. I received seven letters one day. It had been three week since I heard from any of you. Well I am working every day but not so hard now. I have a bad cold. The weather here would give any one a cold. We show are having some bad weather now what time the wind isn't blowing it is raining. Well after so long a time I heard from Bessie it show was a nice letter about fifteen pages. I had began to wonder what was the trouble. The kids seemed to have had a nice Christmas. You tell Myrtle Haden that I received her letter and I will answer it soon. She has been nice to write to me. I also got Fuller and his wife Christmas card. Mother, I wrote to Gordon but I haven't heard from him yet. Did he say whether he was in France. I will write to Warren but he can't tell me anymore then any one else. He can't write and tell how bad he is I heard from Ernest and he is doing ok. He said it was awful hot there. I would like to exchange some of the weather with him. Mother thing look good over here now I hope it won't be long before we will be coming back. Mother I met a fellow this week that use to be in the same co. Herman was in back in S.C. He said that he was with Herman about two months ago. You tell Poppa to hurry with the house because it won't be long before we will be back. HA. From what Elizabeth wrote me the [?Dass?] and [?Custards?] are still [ILLEGIBLE] [?traveling?]. Well I guess James Moon has tried every means to stay out the Army. It will do him good and for my part I hope he has to go.

Love Gilbert

FEBRUARY

Battles of Manila and Iwo Jima begin. The US bombs Prague.

SGT ERNEST H. FRANKLIN 13TH TCS, 403RD TCG. APO 920 C/O PM SAN FRANCISCO, CALIFORNIA
Feb. 7, 1945

Dear Bessie,

I received your letter yesterday and was indeed pleased to hear from you. I thought maybe you had forgotten me as it had been so long since I last heard from you. I was glad to learn that you all were ok, as for myself I am ok.

Well Bessie I guess I am pretty slow when it comes to writing myself so we will put it this way, when you have a letter from me, you answer it, and when I have one from you, I will answer it. In that way neither one of us will have any kick coming

Bessie we are not issued shorts over here, but I don't wear anything but my under shorts when I am working, I look just about like a negro man.

Yes Bessie this place was under enemy hands not so very long ago, in fact there is still a fear [few] around, yet.

You asked me if I was closer to civilization than I was before no I am farther away.

I am glad that you all had a nice Xmas, and that you liked the presents that I gave you. I thank you very much for the ones that you sent me. Bessie it was the carmel candy that was melted.

Well Bessie I am glad that Fred didn't haft to go into the army, but if he does I hope him the best of luck I understand that they are calling quite a few back there now. I just heard over the news that they were taking a lot of the boys returning from overseas in the air corps and putting them in the Infantry, that doesn't sound very good to me, it makes you wonder if you want to go back to the states after hearing that kind of news, I sure as hell don't want to get into the infantry

Bessie one of the boys just walked in with a bottle, so we just pulled the cork and are having a few short ones so if this letter sounds silly from now on, you will know the reason why. You know we can't get it very often and when we do it is really a treat

Bessie I think that is pretty dam low, of William Lampkin people making such a fuss over his insurance rather than his death, don't you, but its like you say money mean everything to some people, if I live to get back there I am going to make it a point to explane a few things to them.

Yes Bessie I had and could still make quiet a progress with my collection that I intended, but it is not allowed anymore, so I haven't any at the present, I intended on sending one home but I guess it is all off now

Well Bessie I guess I had better close for now so until I hear from you again the best of luck

Tell all hello.

Love Bro
Ernest F

S/SGT GILBERT FRANKLIN 6619 PW ADM. CO. APO. 772. C/O PM NEW YORK, NY
Feb. 14, 1945 France

Dear Bessie,

 I just received your letter and you don't know how glad I was to get it. Now it is not because of the money but I just haven't heard from you in a long time. I feel like your letters are more important than any of the others. Well I am ok except my sick has been giving me some trouble but don't let mother know it. I show am glad Fred doesn't have to go yet because I know what a time you would have. I was glad to get his letter and when I get a chance, I will write to him. We are having some wonderful weather here now it looks like spring. I think that winter is over with here now. You know I got two letters from Ernest this month and was I glad to hear from him. The way he wrote it show must be hot there. He also was telling me about the club they had. We have it nice here now a show three or four times a week and a dance once or twice a month. And do these girls here like to dance. We had a nice party last week good music (French) and plenty to drink and eat. I received a letter from Cleo and she was telling me about Herman being home and what a good time they had. I don't see why she don't go live with him I know if I was Herman, I would want her to. Bessie, I met a fellow that use to be in the same co. Herman is now. He hasn't been over here long he said that Herman had it made. Bessie, I wore the cap you sent me for the first time to the dance. I like it fine. Bessie, I show am trying hard to get that thousand dollars in the bank so I will be sending you some more soon. You know Poppa tells me in every letter to send my money to him and he would save it for me. But since I have started it where I have I don't want to change and then I want to surprise them. Bessie you tell C.A. I will try and write to her this week. And for her to write to me it has been a long time since I heard from her. Well I don't have mutch more.

Love Gilbert

FROM MOTHER FRANKLIN, GRETNA VA
(Feb. 27, 1945)

Dear Bessie,

Just a few lines to let you [know] I received the box you sent we sure do thank you a lot the cookies sure are good. I haven opened the candy yet we thank you a lot for it but you should not go to so mutch trouble to fix cookies for us but they sure come in handy.

Well I wish you was here now to see a real mess. Harry is fixing on the house and it has been raining the most of the day and they pulled down the sealing [ceiling] in the porch and all of that black mess is trampled all over the house. I really think it will be nice if we ever get it finished but I am afraid your daddy won't live to see if finished as it will cost a little more than he thought it would. He worries me to death I bet he don't even let Harry finish it what makes him that way I don't know. I really think money is his idle [idol].

Well Bessie I got a letter from Gilbert and Earnest both today but Gilberts was written Jan 30 he said he was well and not working very hard said it sure was rough weather he said he got a nice long letter from you he seemed to be real glad to hear from you Earnest said he was well and that it was still hot there he said sometimes things looked real good and then it was not good at all he said he thought it would be a long time before he got home and how I wish they all could come home.

Bessie you tell Cynthia Ann I got her letter and would answer real soon, and that I thought it was real nice in her to write to me.

Bessie I had planned to send you a piece of my fat meat last week but your daddy said he was coming up there and he said he would take it so he said he could not go now I don't know why but you know he has got to get the mood to go. Bessie, Wilson Doss is sending Gladys to Norfolk to a hospital for his baby to be borned and it will be for adoption so if you are going to adopt one try and not get that one.

Bessie I got the shorts and will make you some as soon as we get thru with that mess.

I will stay so write when you can lots of love to all,

Mother
thanks again for the nice box, I will try to get you a piece of meat this week.

The previous letter is to show the family concerns. I found this interesting to include as Bessie sent cookies down to her mother, and she wrote to thank Bessie. Ma and Pa lived on a small farm even though Pa also worked outside the farm in a factory.

Besides showing concern for the brothers, rationing was in effect since 1942, and the family takes care of each other. They were sending fat meat as Bessie has two children, and you were only allowed so much meat per person. Other commodities rationed were flour and sugar, to name a few. Yet they still send cakes and cookies to the brothers overseas. On another note, Gladys is not married.

MARCH

The US liberates Manila and fire-bombs Tokyo and Nagoya. American and British forces cross the Rhine as the Soviets approach Danzig (Gdansk), Poland, and also enter Austria.

ARTHUR L. JOHNSON

SGT ERNEST H. FRANKLIN 13TH TCS, 403RD
TCG. APO 920 C/O PM SAN FRANCISCO,
CALIFORNIA
March 1, 1945

Dear Bessie,

    I received your letter a few days ago and was indeed pleased to hear from you again, and to know that you all were getting along o.k. as for myself I am pretty well beat up but am still making it o.k.

    Bessie I sure wish that I had a piece of that pie you said that you had just baked, you asked me if we had good food over here, well just about all we get comes out of a can, and I have gotten so dam tired of that I can harley eat it, spam, Vienna sausages and corn beef is the main dish, but sometimes we have a good meal. I guess we are lucky to get what we do.

    Bessie, I had a letter from Gilbert not long ago and he seemed to be getting along o.k. You said he said that he thought it would be about two years before he got home, well from the looks of things I guess he and I will get back about the same time.

    No Bessie the picture you seen was not us, although they are sending a few boys back home on a thirty day leave, but Bessie I don't think I will sing [sign] up for it, because after the thirty days we haft to return and our overseas times starts all over again, so I think it best to stay an over here a while, and take a chance of staying there whenever I do get back although I would sure like to get home for a while, but don't you think this is the best idea. Don't say anything to mom and Dad about this because they might think I should take the leave, but Bessie I think you can see it my way.

    Bessie, if I were you I wouldn't let the cold shoulder from Guy and Ann worry me, because whenever I knew them, they were just out for whatever they could get out of anyone.

Bessie just between you and I what would you think if I should bring this girld back, you know it would be taking a long chance, and a guy would haft to do a lot of thinking before making a decision.

Bessie if ever I get back down to Australia it will be more than a pleasure to get you the thing you asked me to.

I planned on getting you all something the last time I was there. I was going to wait until the last day, but I got my orders to come back sooner than I excepted, and I didn't have time to get them, but if I see that I can't get back down, I will send to my girld to get them for me.

No Bessie I haven't any trouble getting cigarettes, we can get all we want now, but thanks for the offer.

Bessie I wish you would send me some of those crazy books that you was speaking off. Well I guess I have been on the end of this pen long enough, so until I hear from you again the best of luck. Tell all hello.

Love Bro Ernest F

SGT ERNEST H. FRANKLIN 13TH TCS, 403RD TCG. APO 920 C/O PM SAN FRANCISCO, CALIFORNIA
(March 10, 1945)

Dear Bessie,

I received your last letter and was indeed pleased to hear from you again so soon, and to know that you all were o.k. as for myself I am o.k.

Well it still is as hot as hell over here, but we have been having quite a bit of rain lately which makes it a little cooler.

I guess you should be having nice weather back there soon shouldn't you?

Bessie Gilbert never gave Jimmie a divorce did he, what did he ever say about, I never say anything to him about her. I bet he really raises hell with her when he gets back.

Bessie, I am like you I wish Mama & them would get rid of the cow and take it easy, but I have wrote and asked them quite a number of times, to take it easy, but it seems that it doesn't do any good, so if they are happy with all the work they do I guess that is best for them. I even offed them the money I sent back there but that didn't stop them.

Bessie, I guess the only way you can depend on Dad to come up, is when you see him at your door.

Bessie the last you saw of Mama & Dad did they look as if they had aged much. I sure would like to see them again, in fact I would like to see you all but I am afraid that it is going to be a hell of a long time yet.

Say Bessie, that was quite a bit of excitement you had up there, did they ever find the cause and who did it?

Bessie I am sending you a small folder of some of the picture of this Island I thought you might like it, but don't get to great of an impression of this place from the picture, well Bessie I guess I will knock off for this time so until I hear from you again the best of luck tell all hello

Love
Ernest F

S/SGT GILBERT FRANKLIN 6619 PW ADM. CO. APO. 772. C/O PM NEW YORK, NY
March 10, 1945 France

Dear Mother,

I have gotten a lot of mail this week. You don't know how glad I was to get it. Well I have been awful busy this week. I am doing the same kind of work so I guess you can see we are busy. Well at last I received a letter from Bessie what a time she has. I think she worry more than I do. I show would like to see that boy of hers. I bet I could have some time with him? I think I got a letter from all of you this week. Elizabeth show is good to write to me. I heard from Gordon Martin one time and I never did hear from Warren. I never see any one I know. Mother, Marg, Jimmie's sister, wrote me a long letter. They have sold their home and moving to Fla. She also sent me the fellow I use to room with, Herbert Fitzgerald's address. He is here in France some place. You tell Mr. Moon it would be a long time yet before I get back. But when I did just as soon as I hit land on that side everybody would know it. You tell Elizabeth to not worry about me over here when I get back is when she has to worry. Well I show am glad Herman is out again. Mother I would like to send you some more picture, but we can't. I guess I have gain weight, but I have had a cold and lost most of it. The weather here show is nice, but you can tell it is March the way the wind blows. I think I will like here this summer. I hope it don't get as hot like where Ernest is. I feel sorrow for those fellows. Well, have you done anything on the house yet? You better get it finished before I get back because I am going to bring one of those French girls back.

Love Gilbert

S/SGT GILBERT FRANKLIN 6619 PW ADM. CO. APO. 772. C/O PM NEW YORK, NY
March 17, 1945 France

Dear Bessie,

    I guess you think I have forgotten you. Well I haven't I have been trying to write all the week I got two letters from you one was written the 17 and the other the 23 of Feb but the one of 17 got here first. I show was glad to hear from you. I am well working every day. We are having some wonderful weather but awful dry. Bessie did you ever hear from Marg. Jimmie sister I got a long letter from her and she said that they had sold out everything and was going to Fla to live. They were to leave the first of March and was coming by to see you.

Bessie did dad come up to see you. He is always going someplace and never get there. I hear from him real often, but his letters are very short. I just got a package from Gladys, three rolls of films, nuts and writing paper, it was nice. You asked whether I got enough cigarettes yes, we get a package a day. That's one thing I can say we get plenty of everything. Our food is the best, I think. You know why because I'm the one that gets it <u>HA</u>! I draw all the ration for the camp. Bessie, I show do hope Dad get the house finished because it will mean so mutch more for them. Bessie my sick is a little better I just hope I won't have the trouble I have had.

Well someday this war will soon end. And I hope to come back but until it does end, I don't want to come back. I guess you know how I will feel when I do come back. I guess that one thing why I don't worry about coming back. Yes, we have plenty town near us and a pass every night. You asked whether the girls was nice to the boys? I think they are crazy about them most every boy in camp has a girl and they really like to dance. Bessie, I have often wondered why Cleo didn't go to see Herman. It's no reason why he can't get a place for her. Well I got a letter from "Sis" the other day tell me all her troubles I feel sorrow for her, but I guess she knows who did it. They just got a letter from Warren and he was fine. Bessie if you send me a package send me a necktie, I think I have written to everyone to send me one. And If you want to you can send me some cookies. Well I thought I was going to have time to get a money order to send to you to put in the bank, but I didn't. We have to have permission to send it home now. Tell the kids I show would like to be there Easter. Well I guess I had better close tell Fred if he do get in the army to come on over here there are plenty women and drinks too <u>HA!</u>

Gilbert Franklin

S/SGT GILBERT FRANKLIN 6619 PW ADM. CO. APO. 772. C/O PM NEW YORK, NY
March 20, 1945

Dear Mother,

Just received your letter today and show was glad to hear from you. Well I am ok and working every day. We are awful busy again and will be for a while. So, if you don't hear from me real often don't worry. I just got a letter from Gladys and one from Esther Monsen and I don't see how it ever got to me. I also got a package from Gladys. I never hear from Herman anymore. I guess he is too busy fishing. Mother the weather here is wonderful all the trees began to bloom, and the grass is all green. It's awful dry I don't think it has rained in over a month. Mother I would like for you to send me a fruitcake I think that's the best thing you can send over here. You said that you will soon have the house finish well I show do wish I was there to help. You know I see boys most every day going back, and I often wonder when I will get to go. Well you know how lucky I am. Sometime I think I am more safe here than I would be back there, because there is one thing that I have to do when I get back. It won't take long to do it. Mother I didn't know Tom Engream ever married, who did he marry? And what Dalton boy got killed? Mother I can say Gladys, Elizabeth and Bessie all have been nice to write and send me lots of thing and I hate to ask for anything after all we get plenty over here. It only something that we can get. You tell Elizabeth to not worry about me when she don't hear from me because I am ok. I think Ike Mayhew will be an old man when he get back he won't only have all his teeth out but be ball headed like I am. Mother, tell Sis I got her letter and I will answer it soon. It was a real nice letter I feel sorrow for her after all she know who did it. Tell Poppa to leave out everything until the list is set. I will write to him this week.

                                                  Love Gilbert Frank

S/SGT H. B. FRANKLIN, STATION HOSPITAL, MED PLATOON CPE, CHARLESTON, SC
(March 24 – Apr. 7,1945 based on postmark and that he said it took 10 days to write)

Dear Bessie & Gang,

    Dam it to hell don't fall over. But I am going and try and answer you most welcome letter. Which I received not long ago.

    Any way this leaves me in the best of health and I hope, this will you all the same.

    Bessie we are having the most beautiful weather you ever seen the temperature is around 85 degrees and all the flowers are in Bloom and the trees are so green. It is very beautiful down here in the spring, only wish you could see it.

    I had a long letter from Gilbert and Ernest this week and they are all ok. But would like to be home.

    Gilbert said that he was going to stay over there until it was all over. He sure did turn out to be a good soldier. You say that you never hear from his wife. Wonder where she is at. I'll bet Gilbert will raise hell when he comes back. He has never mentioned anything in any of his letters to me about his wife.

He has often said in his letters I am going to be a different person when he comes home. You can't blame him.

Bessie did they ever find out who was the woman that they found in the sewer.

Had a letter from Papa the other day, and he said that he has almost complete the extra room to his home. When we were all home, they had no room. Now no one is at home and they are building more room. Maybe they are expecting Earnest to bring a gal home, that would be something if he did that.

How is Cynthia Ann doing in school now. I'll bet she is a big gal and as smart as her mother when she went to school, I guess you can recall those days, or can you.

Bessie you tell Fred to get a bottle and have it handy because I am going to try and get me a three-day pass and come up there If I do where would be the best place to get off the train. In Alexandria or Washington Terminal

Bessie here I go again believe it or not I have been almost ten days writing you this letter.

I lose your address and I'll bet I spent two hours looking for it. But I found it. I knew it was Danville St but I could not remember the no. But I won't forget it anymore. Because it is almost like my army no. Mine is the last four 1024, and your no is 1023. Can't some people be stupid like me.

Yesterday was Easter and I knew you people had a nice time, as for myself, I spent the afternoon taking pictures and making a tour through Middleton Flower Gardens, and it was very beautiful. Wish you could have seen them.

What is Fred doing now. I guess he is still at the Army Camp. Wish I was near Washington so I could come and see you sometimes. But the way this war is going maybe I will soon be home.

Well it has rained here all this after noon and it is a little cool to-night. Most of the gardens has been planted down here, and they are up and looking very pretty. Do you and Fred have a garden this year I'll bet so

I guess you are tired of this mess, so I will sign off.

I won't tell you to write as I know you will some day.

I remain your Bro
Love to all
Herman

SGT ERNEST H. FRANKLIN 13TH TCS, 403RD TCG. APO 920 C/O PM SAN FRANCISCO, CALIFORNIA
March 25, 1945

Dear Bessie,

I don't know if I owe you a letter or not, but I know it has been quite sometime since I last wrote you, and I have been quite busy. I hope these few lines finds you all o.k. as for myself I am o.k.

Well I just had a letter from home, and they all seemed to be o.k. I think they have just a bout completed the house, from the way they talk it should be pretty nice. I think it was quite hard for them to get the material

Well Bessie I have been up in the Philippines quite a number of times, it is pretty nice up there, and some of them girls looks all right. I haven't been to any of the towns there yet, but I flew over one and it looked pretty nice of course you know that they have been damaged quite a bit, those Phillippinos sure like to see the Americans come in, they meet you and stay until we leave. I have got an invitation to a dinner and meet some of those girls when I get back up there if I have time, the most of them can speak good English or you know they used to go to school for it, but the schools have been closed down for about three years but they are opening them up again now.

Bessie mama wrote and told me about Ethel L. little girl being hit by an auto did you hear anything about it and how bad it was hurt, and are they still living in Richmond.

Bessie I received the birthday card, and also the [?lighter?] thanks, and I will be planning on getting a mixture of that drink when I get back there, as stuff like that is out of the question over here.

Bessie I had a letter from Herman and he sent me a picture of himself and over two hundred fish that they had caught the sure must have a good time back there.

Well Bessie there isn't much news so until I hear from you again the best of luck and tell all hello.

Love
Ernest F

APRIL

The Allies' offensive in Northern Italy starts anew. The US sinks the Japanese battleship Yamato north of Okinawa. On April 12, President Roosevelt dies suddenly, and Harry Truman becomes President. The Red Army pushes toward Berlin. On April 30, Hitler commits suicide.

S/SGT GILBERT FRANKLIN 6619 PW ADM. CO.
APO. 772. C/O PM NEW YORK, NY
April 1, 1945 France

Dear Bessie,

I guess you think I am not going to answer your letter. Well I will tell you I have been so busy I just haven't had the chance. And if you don't hear from me often you will know I don't have time to write. I received the long letter you sent and that the kind I like to get. It took me most the day to read it. I would read for a while and work a while. I guess you know we are busy from the papers. Look like it can't last mutch longer. You would have to see what we have here before you would believe it. Bessie I still haven't had a chance to get a money order I want to send some money for you to put in the bank I think I will get a chance this week sometime. Well we show are having some pretty wether here now and I think it's going to be a hot place here.

Well Bessie I started this letter two days ago so now I am trying to finish it. I just got a letter from Mother and one from Ernest. I guess it will be a week before I will get to answer them. Ernest said that he had just come back from the Philippines I think he liked there very much. He said that he had given up coming home. Mother didn't have mutch to say, all was well. It had been a cold spell there. Bessie, Paul shouldn't loose his head just because he is in the army. Look what I have gone through. But I don't know what I will do when I get back. I have in mine one thing the longer I stay over here the better off I am. Bessie I still have the long letter you sent me and I will answer it real soon.

Love Gilbert

SGT ERNEST H. FRANKLIN 13TH TCS, 403RD TCG. APO 920 C/O PM SAN FRANCISCO, CALIFORNIA
April 5, 1945

Dear Bessie,

I received your letter a few days ago and was indeed pleased to hear from you and to know that you all were o.k. as for myself I am o.k.

So, you have been having quite a bit of hot weather back there lately, but I guess it is about time you was having some hot weather. I sent it.

Bessie you said that you hadn't heard from Gilbert lately? Neither have I, but I guess he is kept to busy. I had a letter from home and mama said that she had heard from him, and that he had had a letter from Jimmie sister, and they had sold their home and were moving to Florida. I think Jimmie wanted them to take her mother with them. I guess Jimmie has really gone to hell don't you, I sure hate to think what Gilbert will do to her if he ever meets up with her again. Bessie, I started this letter but didn't get it finished, but since then I have heard from Gilbert, and he seemed to be o.k. I think he is having himself quite a time with those French girlds, he said that he didn't think he wanted to come home until after the war.

Bessie I guess it will be quite a while before I will get home, because I have started back flying, as things stand now it look like that is about the surest way of getting home, after I get my hours in I am eligible to go home, but on the ground, there dosen't seem like, any hope at all in getting back, and to, I will make more money, just don't say anything about this to Dad and Mama Bessie because I don't know if they want me to fly or not.

Bessie I was sure glad to learn that both Fred and James had gotten a deferment. I know it must have made both of you very happy.

Bessie is Fred still working at Bolling Field if so I know two boy up there. One is named Wicker and the other Vaughan, he might see them sometimes. They used to be over here with us. Bessie did Paul H. ever go overseas? I understand that they are sending a lot of the boy out of the states now.

Bessie, I received the greeting cablegram that you sent and thanks a lot. I hope that you all had a nice Easter, well Bessie there isn't much news this time so until I hear from you again the best of luck to you all tell all hello

Love
Ernest F

Ernest was a mechanic, not a pilot. What he meant by "started back flying" was that he could be the flight engineer. Ernest would fly with the plane to monitor its performance and fix or adjust as needed when the plane landed. He states earlier, in previous letters, that his mother did not like him flying, but that would give him more hours toward points to go home.

It is appropriate to mention the point system here as future letters will refer to it. As the end of the war became a reality, the Army began preparations for redeployment and end to hostilities. Those who had served the longest and fought the hardest would come home first. They devised a point system to determine the order. This system used the number of months in service, the number of months overseas, the battle campaigns, and the duties, infantry, medical, etc., to name a few. The war was weighing heavily on the men, so they began looking forward to going home. The system was not perfect, and the communication of how it worked was not always what happened. Future letters will show this. It only added to the frustration.

S/SGT GILBERT FRANKLIN 6619 PW ADM. CO.
APO. 772. C/O PM NEW YORK, NY
April 16, 1945 France

Dear Mother,

    I must owe you about three letters. Well I will answer them all at one time. I am ok and working awful hard and long hours but willing to do anything to get this thing over with. I have been getting a lot of mail. Look like when we are the busiest is the time we get a lot of mail. I just had two letters from Ernest and he was doing fine. Two from Herman and he even still fishing. He show has had it good but he still wants to come over here. If he knows what is good he would forget about it. Well self experience is the best. Mother we are having some nice weather here now I think its going to be awful hot here this summer. It's warm in the daytime but cool at night and morning. Mother I have some flower seeds I brought from Italy but didn't have time to plant them. I would like to send them to you but I can't. The poppies has began to bloom here and they show are pretty. I got a letter from C.A she wrote it while she was down to see you Easter. I guess she will be grown when I get back. I guess you have been awful busy since they have been working on the house. It's a good thing you have Elizabeth and James to help you, they show have been good to help you and Poppa. You know I haven't had time to answer Sis letter so you tell her I will soon. I don't see how this war can last mutch longer. You tell Bessie to not worry about me not writing to her because I will every chance I get. After all she has done enough for me that I could never forget. After all I get worried if I don't hear from her. Well tell Poppa I will write him next time.

Love Gilbert F

S/SGT GILBERT FRANKLIN 6619 PW ADM. CO. APO. 772. C/O PM NEW YORK, NY
April 17, 1945 France

Dear Bessie,

I received the telegrapher you sent me. When I got it I almost thought it was from you. It must taken a good while for it to get to me. When did you send it. Well I know you think I have forgotten you but I have been so busy I just haven't had time to write to anyone. I counted up the letters I owe and it was twenty-five. Now you know I have been busy I do try to write to mother every week. I guess you know we are busy from the news in the pappers. I have done more work this year than I ever did. It so long house I never go on a pass I really like to work so we can get this war over. I just don't see how it can last mutch longer.

You know I got two letters from Herman, but he forgot that he wrote to me. Well all he ever have to say is that he had been fishing. He still says that he would like to come over here. Bessie how did Ethel little girl get hurt and did she get hurt bad. Well we show are having some pretty weather, warm in the daytime but cool at night we haven't had any rain in a long time. I think it's going to be awful hot here this summer. Bessie, I got the letter you sent me with the clipping of Guy Welton death, and I just couldn't sleep that night I wouldn't have ever thought of him dying. What will Ann do well I guess she is as well off. Did they bring him back. I just received two letters from Ernest and he was fine and said look like he would be over there a long time. Well I have give up all hopes of coming for a long time. I guess I won't know the place when I get back. Mother said in her letter that they had almost finish the house. How do it look? It will be a lot of help to Mother. You know Elizabeth and James show has help mother and dad. Bessie I got C.A. letter that she wrote while she was down to Mother. I answered it yesterday only a V-mail. Bessie don't think hard of me if I don't write often because I just don't have the time. And I know you have a lot to do and don't get time to write to me. After all if you don't write you have done more than any of the rest for me. Now I want to ask for something will you send me another cap like the one you bought for me. We will wear that kind this summer. Bessie I will try and get you the salt and pepper shaker set for you. I have been trying to send you some money to put in the bank but just haven got to it yet. And I thought once I was going to the rest camp and I saved some for that but I don't know yet whether I will. I guess I had better close Tell Fred I said hello.

Love Gilbert

SGT ERNEST H. FRANKLIN 13TH TCS, 403RD
TCG. APO 920 C/O PM SAN FRANCISCO,
CALIFORNIA
April 23, 1945

Dear Bessie,

 I received your letter some time ago and would have written sooner but I just haven't had much time, when we go out on trip for three or four days and come back and pull inspection on our plane we don't have much time.
 I guess I told you that I had started back flying, another boy and myself flies with our plane, we have just about a new one, and boy it is a honey.
 We have a pin up girld painted on it, and named it the Patient Virgin, since I couldn't make cadets, and now that I have started back flying I am more satisfied that I have been since overseas and I always liked to fly.
 Bessie I am glad that you all had a nice time down home. Mama said that she was very surprised, but was indeed pleased to see you all, she said that your children sure was cute, I would sure love to see them, by the way Bessie I understand that I am going to be an uncle again. I just had a letter from Elizabeth and he said that she was excepting the big event to happen, she seemed very happy over it. I guess Herman is the next on the list isen't he, or do you mean he will ever have any kids, if he dosen't hurry up he will be to old won't he, but I don't guess you ever get to old and understand that Paul F is expecting another one.
 Bessie I guess you got the surprise of your life when you heard from Herman didn't you. I harley ever hear from him, not that it makes a dam to me, but I do think he should wright Mama & Dad more often, but I guess he is to busy having fun and fishing to wright
 You know I sometime feel as sorry as hell for some of those guys back there, as they are having it so hard,

to hear them talk, I would like to see some of them over here, then they would have room to bitch, as for myself I am dam lucky and have it nice to what some boys do over here, but I would just like to see them in my place for awhile.

Bessie I am sure glad to hear that Ethel kid is getting along o.k., and I hope that she will soon be well.

Well Bessie I guess I had better stop for this time so until I hear from you again the best of luck to you all.

Love
Bro Ernest F

S/SGT GILBERT FRANKLIN 6619 PW ADM. CO. APO. 772. C/O PM NEW YORK, NY
April 25, 1945 France

Dear Bessie,

I just received your letter and was glad to hear from you. I just wrote one to you the day before I got yours. I am like you I don't wait for any of you to write when I find time I just write. Well Bessie I just don't see how this war can last mutch longer. We show are doing our part now. I thought before I was doing a lot but now, I am doing twice as mutch. I have been awful sick with a cold but still keep going. Look like when I get a cold, I just can't get rid of it. Bessie thing show are pretty over here everything is green and all the poppies in bloom. The weather here is good it cool at night. You said you had a nice time down home. I will never forget the time we all went down. I often think of the good old times we all had. Well I wish sometimes I was back, but I think I will last longer over here than I would back there. Bessie you think Mother really made a big change in the house. I only wish we could have been there to help them. You said that you really got a long letter from Herman. Well I got two in one week. Now I know I won't hear from him for a long time I have been getting my mail good most of my mail come in ten day that not bad. The telegram you sent me it took ten day. Bessie when I get the time off I am going to get you the salt and pepper shakers. I won't come back until I get them so you can bet on them. So don't forget to send the film and cap. I will write again soon. Tell the kids I said hello.

Love Gilbert

S/SGT GILBERT FRANKLIN 6832 PW OVHD DET APO. 772. C/O PM NEW YORK, NY
April 29, 1945 France

Dear Poppa,

Just a few lines to let you know I am ok and working hard now. Well it won't be long before this is over. I guess you are still working hard Gladys wrote and told me that you had hurt your hip. I don't see why you don't quit working so hard. I have been awful sick with a cold I have had it all the year. The weather over here is good but it changes so mutch. It awful dry and the wind has been blowing all this month. I haven't heard from Ernest in a good while I guess he is ok. I got a long letter from Bessie and all was well. Well how do you like the house since you have finished it. I show do wish I was there. I guess I won't know the place. Tell Mother and Elizabet I will write to them this week. Take care of your self. I hope to be home sometime soon.

Gilbert

MAY

Germany surrenders on May 7, with the ceasefire one minute past midnight on May 8. The war continues in the Pacific, with continued fighting in New Guinea.

>POSTCARD (picture of coast from Nice to
>Cannes, France)
>S/SGT GILBERT FRANKLIN 6832 PW OVHD DET
>APO. 772. C/O PM NEW YORK, NY
>May 2, 1945)

Dear Poppa,

I guess you wonder why I haven written. Well I am now on a seven-day furlough. Having a good time.

Gilbert

>S/SGT GILBERT FRANKLIN 6832 PW OVHD DET
>APO. 772. C/O PM NEW YORK, NY
>May 5, 1945 France

Dear Bessie,

I haven't heard from you this week. But I did get the tie you sent me. It's so nice I think will keep it to wear it back. I began to think it may be rotten by that time. Well Bessie I am still sick with a cold I think I am going to be examined to see if I have the T.B. I just caught all the time. Well I got a nice long letter from Ernest and he was doing o.k. He told me he had started back flying again but not to let Mother know it. He also said when he got another thousand hours he would get to come home. I guess it was a crowded place there when the President died. I guess we heard it about the same time you did back there. Bessie I don't see how this war over here can last many more days. I know it will be at least a year or two before I will be back after it is over.

I got a letter from Elizabeth and she said that Mother was moving in the new home I bet she will be glad to get all settled. She said Poppa was mutch better. I wish he wouldn't work so hard, but you know how he is. You know James and Elizabeth show is a lot of help to Mother and Dad. Is your kids going down to stay with mother this summer. Look like we are going to have winter here again for the last week it has been awful cold. Bessie I haven't gotten your salt and pepper shakers yet but I will. I am hopping to go to the rest center in the near future then I will get them. That the reason why I didn't send any money. Bessie I have so many letters to write I will have to close. I want to thank you for the tie and all the rest you have done for me.

Love Gilbert Franklin

P.S. Bessie I had just finished this letter when I got yours so I will write to you again

SGT ERNEST H. FRANKLIN 13TH TCS, 403RD TCG. APO 920 C/O PM SAN FRANCISCO, CALIFORNIA
May 6, 1945

Dear Bessie,

Well it is Sunday here now, and at the present I am up flying it is very nice and cool up here to, as it was so hot on the ground.

Well Bessie I received your last letter, and was indeed pleased to hear from you, and to know that you all were o.k. as for myself I am o.k. Bessie I must say that is the first letter of that kind I have ever received, and it came in very handy as I hadn't had any of that kind in a long time and when I went to use it for what it was made for, I said to myself now this is just like being up town New York, and of course I had to let some of the boys use some of it to see what it was like again, HA. No Bessie I didn't use it for that purpose but I did get a big kick out of it.

Bessie you asked me what I did, no I don't fly a plane, we are known as Aerial Engineers as either crew chief, that is me fly with the plane all of the time, and fix anything that goes with the plane during a trip and see that it is landed and unloaded in the proper manner, and of course we draw flying pay which is half of our base pay and that comes in pretty good. I just got back a few days ago after a fine day trip in the Philippines, I had a pretty nice trip as I covered a lot of the Islands this time.

Bessie you said that Gilbert was very up set over the death of Guy, what Guy was this I don't think any one wrote me about this, and what was the matter with him.

Well Bessie the news on the other side really sounds good dosen't it, from the way it sounds it looks like Gilbert may be coming home soon dosen't it. I just had a letter from him not long ago and he seemed to be getting along o.k. but working rather hard. I haven't heard from Herman now in quite some time now.

Well Bessie I guess this is about all for this time so until I hear from you again the best of luck.

Love Bro
Ernest F

S/SGT GILBERT FRANKLIN 6832 PW OVHD DET APO. 772. C/O PM NEW YORK, NY
May 6, 1945 France

Dear Mother,

I just received your letter today and was glad to hear from you. Well I still have a bad cold look like I just can't get rid of it. Sometimes I think I have the T.B. I just received a long letter from Bessie and all seemed to be well. I guess it must have been a time there when the President died. We show was sorrow to hear it, he was a good man. Well Mother how do you like the new place since you have finished it. I guess we won't know it when we get back. Well, all I want is a good bed to sleep and no one to wake me up. I got a long letter from Ernest yesterday and he was fine. He seems to think it will be a long time before he will get back. Well if I get back in another year I will think I was lucky. Even though the war is over we will just be started. I guess I will get to see Ernest soon. Mother we have had some cool weather here the last few week but today it is nice and warm. I think the summer is late over here. How is Poppa hip I hope it better you tell him to not work so hard and keep in good shape till I get back and him and I will get on a big drunk. It's been three years since I been on one but I still think I can get on one yet. Well tell all I said hello.

Love Gilbert

S/SGT GILBERT FRANKLIN 6832 PW OVHD DET APO. 772. C/O PM NEW YORK, NY
May 14, 1945 France

Dear Mother,

I guess I owe you a letter although I haven't heard from you in over a week. Well I have been sick with a cold but mutch better now. I am still working pretty hard. Well I guess some of the people back there was glad to hear that the war over here was finished. Well I don't see how it could last mutch longer. I guess there will be a lot of boys coming back. It don't worry me. You know how my luck is I will be one of the last ones. So don't even think about me coming I might even go to the pacific which I hope I don't. I had a letter from Herman he wrote it while he was down to see you. Well he asked for it and I guess he got it. I hope he has done the right thing. I also got a long letter from Gladys she must come down to see you most every week. How is the new house since it has been finished? Is Bessie kids coming down this summer and sta [stay with] you. Well the weather here has begun to get hot now we haven't had any rain here in a long time. Mother don't worry about me now and I hope to be home sometime but it will be a good while yet.

Love Gilbert F

S/SGT GILBERT FRANKLIN 6832 PW OVHD DET
APO. 772. C/O PM NEW YORK, NY
May 25, 1945

Dear Mother,

I just got back from my furlough in Nice. I had seven days. What a time I had a nice bed with white sheets on and what a room. I took as many as three baths a day. I wasn't that dirty but it was just something new to me I haven't been in a bath tub in over two years. Well first of all when we got there they told us the town was ours and we really took it. We could wear anything we wanted to stay out till two o'clock. It was anything that you wanted there. I only drank eight beers all the time I was there. Now you can really say I have quit drinking. They served breakfast from 7 to 10. I really had a good time. Most all my time was spent sightseeing. Well now that I am back work again, I guess it will be two years before I get back, I had to stay over here two and a half years to get seven day. I don't see where our work has let up any. We had twelve men to leave our company going home they were over 42. If they make it 38, we will lose a lot more and it won't miss me far. I had a letter from Ernest, and he was well Just came back from the Philippines he show do get around. He says look like he would be over there a long time. If that point system would work right him and I both could come home I have about 90 and I know he must have that many. I also got a long letter from Bessie. I have been getting her mail good now. How is Poppa and is his hip better you tell him I will be older than he is before I get back. So don't look for me until the war is over in Japan. And I hope it is soon.

Love Gilbert

S/SGT GILBERT FRANKLIN 6832 PW OVHD DET APO. 772. C/O PM NEW YORK, NY
May 28, 1945

Dear Bessie,

 I guess you thought I had forgotten you well I have been awful busy. I just come back from a seven-day furlough and I have had so mutch work I Just haven't had time to write to anyone. I show did have a nice time while I was away. The army show do have everything fixed up there for the boys when we got there they told us the town was all ours and I mean we took it. You could wear any kind of cloths no MP to bother you stay out until two o'clock. Breakfast was from seven to ten. We were in the best of hotels, sleeping between white sheets the first two nights. I just couldn't sleep. The beds were too soft. Some of the fellow sleep on the floor. Bessie the place where we were in the wintertime the people go up on the mountains in the morning and ski, and in the evening go swimming. It's a wonderful place. Nice is the place. Did you get the folders I sent you? One is the hotel I stayed in. Well Bessie since the war is over with over here our work is just the same. The best part of it is I know we won't lose any more of our boys. The French over here show did celebrate for a week every town you went in had a street dance. I had a letter from Ernest, and he was well and doing ok. I had a letter from home and mother said Poppa James and Elizabeth were coming up to see you did they ever get up there. Well Bessie after so long a time I found you a salt and pepper shaker. Now they aren't very good, but I have been trying for the longest time they just don't have them. I hope you like them. I sent them to you last week. Bessie will you let me know where Herman is I don't know where to write to him. You know I got a fruit cake from Mother and I haven't even wrote and told her I received it. Well I don't know when I will ever come home I have enough points to get out. I want to come back, but it will never be the same I know I am going to get in trouble when I do. Well Bessie if you will send me Herman address I will write to him. I want to thank you a lot for all the things you have done.

Love Gilbert

(In the same envelope as above)

Dear Mickey,

You are a swell boy. I got the candy you sent me. And you be a good boy and when I get back you and I will have a big time. Tell CA I said hello.

Love Gilbert

JUST A FEW LINES

S/SGT GILBERT FRANKLIN 6832 PW OVHD DET
APO. 772. C/O PM NEW YORK, NY
May 30, 1945 France

Dear Poppa,

Just a few lines to let you know I am thinking of all you. Well I am back working after my seven day furlough. I have a lot of work now I am doing the same kind of work and plenty of it. We have a lot of P.W. here now and still getting more. I had a long letter from Ernest and he was well and doing good. Poppa the wether here is awful cool but when I was up to Nice France it was awful hot. I don't think I even told you but I am here clost to Marseille France if Herman ever came over sea he will come here first. There are a lot of our fellows going back home thirteen of them have gone but they were 42 years of age. I have enough points but I don't know when I will ever get back. All I hope is I don't go to the pacific but you can't never tell. Poppa you tell Mother I got the cake and it was in good shape and I mean it is good every night I eat a piece of it tell her I said thanks. Everything over here looks quiet since the war is over. Poppa I have been over here so long I don't know what I would do if I should get out. You know I have been in the Army over three years twenty six months over sea. I have five battle stars that not so bad I think I have done my part. You wouldn't know it but I been through a lot to still be here. Well I always said I would get back after I was treated like I was. I think the good lord saved me to come back and straighten things up back there.

Love Gilbert

JUNE

Japanese airfields on Kyushu are bombed. Australia takes Brunel. Osaka, Japan is heavily bombed.

>S/SGT GILBERT FRANKLIN 6832 PW OVHD DET
>APO. 772. C/O PM NEW YORK, NY
>June 4, 1945

Dear Mother,

Just got your letter yesterday ever glad to hear from you. Air mail hasn't been coming so good the last few weeks. Well I am ok working every day. We still have a lot of work. I think I am getting like Herman now I went fishing Sunday, the first time I went out the camp since I came back off my furlough. I just don't care to go anywhere. I had rather stay around the camp. We can go out every night if we want to, we have trucks going to two different towns every night until twelve o'clock. What kind of a time did Poppa have up to Bessie, and did he get any rest? I just got a long letter from Elizabeth and she was telling me about them going up to see Bessie. She also said that Warren was on his way home. Well I show do hope he don't have to go to the pacific which I think he will. From all I know I don't think I will have to go but they can do anything with you now. Sometime I begun to think I will never get back I get so disgusted I don't know what to do. I don't never want to come home unless I can get out the Army.

Mother I wrote to papa and told him I got the cake and I think I wrote to you too. Well it was in the best of shape and so good that's about the only sweet thing I eat over here. I neve eat any candy I am going to try and send a box of a lot of junk in it I have had it for a long time. I just sent Bessie a salt and pepper shaker. It took me about six months to find then they are cheap but the best I could find. Well we are having some nice weather here now still cold at night. Mother if I have to stay over here for Army at occupation I am going to ask to go to Nice, France where I spent my furlough. The weather there is nice the year around. And most of the people speak english. I haven't hear from Ernest in a good while I show do hope he will soon be coming back. Well I know it will be at least a year before I will get back so don't look for me. I have to write so many letters I guess I had better close.

Love Gilbert

S/SGT GILBERT FRANKLIN 6832 PW OVHD DET APO. 772. C/O PM NEW YORK, NY
June 5, 1945

Dear Bessie,

    I think I have answered your last letter but I have a few minutes and I will drop you a few lines. Well I am ok working pretty hard now. I have began to get over my furlough I show did have a good time. If I have to stay over here for Army Occupation I am going to ask to be station there. I know it will be a year or more before I get back you know how lucky I am. All I ask is don't send me to the pacific but they can do anything now.
    I just got a letter from Mother and Elizabeth and they were telling me about Poppa, Elizabeth and James being up there. They seem to have had a good time. I don't see how you kept Poppa up there. How do Poppa look is he began to look old he show has done a lot of hard work I don't see how he has stood it. Bessie I haven't received the package yet but all our mail is awful slow now. Bessie I just bought me a 35mm camera it's a French one it is suppose to be a good one it sells for about $200 but I didn't give that mutch it's so you can buy some films over here I

just took nine rolls in town today to get developed They were some I taken while I was on my furlough. Bessie I thought one time I would get to come home when they were talking about letting the ones 38 to 40 but it didn't go through. I have enough points but it seems like they don't do any good. Well Bessie I don't have mutch new I am sending a money order so you can put it in the bank.

Tell the kids and Fred hello.

Love to all Gilbert

Ernest is a Staff Sergeant now.

S/SGT ERNEST H. FRANKLIN 13TH TCS, 403RD TCG. APO 920 C/O PM SAN FRANCISCO, CALIFORNIA
June 13, 1945

Dear Bessie,

I received your letter a few days ago and was indeed pleased to hear from you as it had been quite a while since I last heard from you I hope these few lines finds you all o.k. as for myself I am o.k.

Bessie I was up in Manila a few week ago and had a very nice time. That city sure must have been a beautiful place before the war, but I guess you can imagine what it is like now, as for the girlds up there they are all right. I was out out with one and we had a lot of fun, they can speak pretty good English, but it is broken

Bessie there sure is an inflation up there, everything is so light you can harley get any thing. I started to buy a pair of sandals and asked the price of them and they were fifty pesos which is twenty five dollars in our money, and a small dish of chicken cost three dollars but it is so hard for them to get anything I guess they haft to charge that kind of prices.

Bessie as for the girld in Australia I thought it taking to much of a chance so I called it off, but we are still good friends and wright to each other.

Yes Bessie I think my points still means just as much to me, especially when I get back, as it stands now I have two ways of getting back, by point system and through air crew rotation. I am in hopes of being back there within four months, but I am not building my hopes up two hight as you can never tell what will happen. I think Gilbert should be coming home soon don't you? I hope he does.

Bessie I think Dad, Elizabeth and James enjoyed their trip very much up there.

Well Bessie I am up with Herman & Gilbert now, as I made another stripe this last month, and I was very pleased to get it.

Well Bessie there isen't much more to wright this time so until I hear from you again the best of luck to you all, tell all I said hello.

Bro Ernest F

S/SGT GILBERT FRANKLIN 6832 PW OVHD DET APO. 772. C/O PM NEW YORK, NY
June 15, 1945 France

Dear Bessie,

This is the third letter I have written to you since I received any from you. I haven't gotten but two letters in over a month and one was from Gladys and one from Elizabeth. We just don't get any mail at all. And when I don't get any I just can't write. Well I received your package today and it was fine. All the boys said Frankie your people show do know what to send you. I was tickle to death with all the things. The cap just fit and the cigarettes came in good. I haven't had a Chesterfield in over two weeks. We don't always get what kind we smoke. Bessie I think I wrote and told you I have bought me another camera it's real nice but I don't have a case for it. Bessie I was up to the perfume factory and bought Cleo a bottle of perfume and it was nice so I was going to get it ready to send and I broke it. It almost broke my heart. I still smell yet from it. Well I managed to get her some more so I sent it to her. I hope she like it. I don't guess you have received the package I sent you. It's nothing mutch in it but just something for remember. I just sent a package to Mother and one to Herman. I am going to write to Herman tonight I just got his address I hope he get it.

Bessie there are a lot of fellows that are leaving our co going home there were seven left today going by plane I gave one of them your address and he was going to call you up when he got there. He is from Strasberg Va. Bessie I have began to want to come home. I often wonder what going to happen when I get back. I show do hope Ernest can come home soon. Well how is Paul making out and is he still clost by home. How is his kid. Tell Mickey when I come back I am going to take him with me down home. How is Fred getting along and do he get mutch to drink. You know it so I just can't stand to drink any thin even beer. We get all the beer we want now. Well Bessie I want to thank you for the package but don't send any more until I ask for it because it [?so hard for?] them to come through now. Did you get the letter with the money order.

Love Gilbert

S/SGT GILBERT FRANKLIN 6832 PW OVHD DET APO. 772. C/O PM NEW YORK, NY

June 21, 1945 France

Dear Mother,

Just a few lines to let you know I got your letter today. the first I have heard from you in a month. I have gotten three letter this month. We just aren't getting any mail. I got a letter from Ernest today and he was well and doing great he show do get around a lot. Well I am doing ok working pretty hard now. I don't see where our work has stopped at all since the fall of Germany. Mother you don't know how bad I want to come back so I can sleep between the sheets. That one thing I do miss. You know the picture I sent with the old woman and I? Well you see it was taken in a cemetery. Well that old lady takes care of that cemetery. She was there all the time I don't care when you would go by there she was ever there. She put fresh flower on the graves every day. She asked me to take a picture with her. Well we are having some hot weather here now awful dry. Mother don't have too mutch plumbing done to the house until I get back because I want to have a good job done when I do get there. Mother Elizabeth shouldn't worry about me now because we are as safe as any on can be now. Mother I have two or three packages on the way. It's a lot of junk but something to remember. So, don't send any more thing to me until I ask for them because they are so long gettin here. I might send some of my clothes that belong to me sutch as Cap ties and under wear they don't want us to have them. I will let you know when I do send them. Tell Poppa to be show to send me something to drink I will get home sometime I will write to him next time. Tell Elizabeth and Gladys I will write soon

Love Gilbert

Uncle Gill and the woman who takes care of the cemetery.

S/SGT GILBERT FRANKLIN 6832 PW OVHD DET
APO. 772. C/O PM NEW YORK, NY
June 27, 1945 France

Dear Poppa,

I guess all of you think I have forgotten you. Well I haven't. You know I haven't got but three letters from any of you in over a month. Now I know all of you are writing but it is holt up some place. But I get disgusted I just don't know what to write. I just got a letter from Elizabeth today and I show was glad to get it. All the boys over here feel down and out. No mail and no one going home. We hear about a lot getting back to the states but they show are not coming from over here. We had seven to leave about three weeks ago and I be dam if they wasn't over here to see us and said they didn't know when they would ever go. A lot of this stuff is a bunch of ----. Well they say a good soldier will bitch and I guess I am one of them. Poppa it's awful hot and dry over here. I don't see where our work is any diference and I don't think it will be. We will be here for a long time we are an Army of occupation. I show do hope Ernest get to come home. I know it will be a long time befor I will. Poppa did any of you get any picture post cards I sent you while I was on my furlough. I also sent two or three packages. did you get these? Write and let me know. I also sent you a enlarge picture of Mt. Civious [Vesuvius] in Italy. I was up there the night it was taken. Tell Mother in those boxes I sent are some flour [flower] seeds that came out my garden in Italy but they are all alike. Tell Mother I will write to her next time.

Love Gilbert Franklin

This was taken in March 1944 but was not talked about until now.

(Bad handwriting shows "Jan" for January, but return address and postmark confirm "June.")
S/SGT GILBERT FRANKLIN 6832 PW OVHD DET APO. 772. C/O PM NEW YORK, NY
June 28, 1945 France

Dear Bessie,

    Just a few lines to let you know I haven't yet received a letter from you. I received the three rolls of films and show was glad to get them. That's two packages I have gotten from you and no letters. You know I got the films in seven days. We just don't get any mail at all. All the fellows over here are awful blue. They claim that so many of us was going back to the states, but it seems like now no one is going. I think I have gotten three letters in a month. Now I know all of you are writing but the mail just don't get here. I got a letter from Elizabeth today and everyone there seems to be ok. Bessie the weather over here is awful hot now and awful dry. I don't remember when it did rain. Bessie did you ever get the package I sent you. I also sent a money order but I am not worried now don't get [me] wrong.

    Bessie how is the kids and are they going down to stay with Mother this summer? I think it would be a lot of help to you and be a lot of company to Mother. I show do wish I could come home before the summer were over but you know how lucky I am? Well the longer I stay over here the safety I am. No telling what I will do when I get back there. All I say is that bitch better hide when I get back. I have seen thousands over here in shape she ought to be in. Well Bessie I show do hope I hear from you and the rest of them. And I want to thank you for the two package you sent me. But don't send anything else until I write write because we don't get our mail so good.

Love Gilbert Franklin

JULY

MacArthur announces that the Philippines are liberated. Attacks on Tokyo continue.

S/SGT GILBERT FRANKLIN 6832 PW OVHD DET
APO. 772. C/O PM NEW YORK, NY
July 3, 1945 France

Dear Mother,

    Just got your letter yesterday and was glad to hear from you. Well I have heard from all of you in the last week except Herman and Ernest. I got a long letter from Bessie today. Well it hasn't been so hot here in the last week but the wind look like will blow the place away and it is a cloud of dust all the time you can't hardly breath Mother we have plenty of work over here and look like we will for a time to come. I don't think thing will be closed up over here in ten years. It is a mess we don't get half enough to eat now. but it won't be long before we will get plenty to eat over here when some of the men are shipped out. Well one time I thought I might get back this year, but things change so often. I guess it will be at least twelve to eighteen months yet. But don't worry because I am sure to be back and how happy will I be. I just live to see the day when I can get back. I guess it won't be long before Warren will be coming back. Mother don't believe anything that's in the paper because we have plenty of men here in two companies that have way over 100 points and some as high as 147 and they are still here. We have never heard anything about 75 points.
    Ernest had made S/Sgt [staff sergeant] well that was one of the best news I have heard. That has showed that all three of us has a little since [sense]. I was up for another rating, but I had over 85 points and I couldn't get it. Well one thing there are some fellows that I came in with that

doesn't have anything yet. Well Mother don't you and Dad worry about us because we will all be together soon. And I will do my best to help both of you when I do get back. First of all I am going to have us a flour garden. It sounds silly but I think thats all I can do.

Love Gilbert

The previous letter was the first mention of Ernest's promotion to Staff Sergeant. The following is from nine-year-old Cynthia Ann to her mother, Bessie. Cynthia just arrived at her grandmother's in Gretna, Virginia, where she will spend the rest of the summer. The rosary that she mentions was sent to her from Uncle Gilbert when he was in Italy. The rosary is significant to her, and she still has it.

FROM CYNTHIA ANN TO HER MOTHER BESSIE
July 8, 1945

Dear Mother,

Will you send my rosary? I went off and left it. Send it right away. I got home alright tell Mickey hello

Love
Cynthia Ann Conlon

S/SGT GILBERT FRANKLIN 6832 PW OVHD DET APO. 772. C/O PM NEW YORK, NY
July 8, 1945 France

Dear Mother,

I got six letters yesterday and you don't know how glad I was I just don't get any mail. Well this week it has been hot. We have sutch funny weather here one week it is cool and the next is hot. Mother it won't be any one there we get back the way they are dying. We lost a good man when Mr. Adams died what will they do now. I got a long letter from Ernest and he was well and hope to be home soon. I show was glad he got another stripe, he must be a good man. Well I can say I don't think any of us three has done so bad. I also got a letter from Herman the first I have hear from him since he left his old Co. I think he has begun to learn what the Army life is. I just hope he don't have to go over sea. And I don't think he will now. Mother look like they aren't sending any one from over here home. This country is full of soldiers. I guess you have hear about the staging area over here well we are set up clost to it. And I wish you could see that place I guess it is ten or fifteen miles around it. It's seven miles around our camp. Mother Gladys sent me some picture and they show was good the old place made me homesick it's quite a change in the house I just wish I could get back to help finish it up. Did you ever get the enlarged picture of Mt Civious [Vesuvius]. I also sent two package I guess you will soon be getting them. Well tell Poppa I will write to him in a day or so.

Love Gilbert Franklin

As the men came from the battlefields, they were sent to one of several staging areas to await transportation home. As the wait could be several days or weeks, the frustrated men could get a little rowdy.

S/SGT GILBERT FRANKLIN 6832 PW OVHD DET
APO. 772. C/O PM NEW YORK, NY
July 12, 1945 France

Dear Bessie,

Received your letter the other day I had just written to you when I got yours. I also got six letters that day. It had been a long time since I got any mail and was I glad to get them all. Well this leaves me well but working awful hard. I don't see where our work lets up any if we ship out any prisoners that many more come in so you see our work is just the same. I did take off last Sunday but I did two day work that Saturday I sleep most all day. I am so tired when the days work is done I don't do anything but lay down and rest I will be so glad when we can come home I don't know what to do. From the way thing look it will be a long time before we will ever get back. We have had six men to leave from here to go home since the war was over and they stade in the standing area for month and yet I don't know whether they went home. Now it's a bunch of -- if they say that a lot of men are coming home on the point system we have a lot of men with a 100 and up to 110 here now. Well Bessie I am glad you got the package and it was in good shape. Those other things in the package was from German prisoners. When I get the chance I have a few things I want to send Mickey it nothing mutch but he won't know the difference.

    Bessie I will try and send another money order the last of the month. I got a letter from Herman and from what he had to say he must have just began to learn what the army life is. Well he don't have to come over seas and look like he could take anything back there. Bessie I show am glad Poppa had a good time up there. Gladys sent me some pictures of all them and they show was good. I hope mother comes up there and she has just as good of a time I know she will. Well Bessie if I do ever get back I will come by your house first because I will come through Fort Mead M.D. Bessie I show was glad Ernest made another stripe and it shows that he is a good man. I don't think any of us have done so bad. Well Bessie tell the kids I received both letters and will answer them soon.

    Love Gilbert

JUST A FEW LINES

S/SGT GILBERT FRANKLIN 6832 PW OVHD DET
APO. 772. C/O PM NEW YORK, NY
July 14, 1945 France

Dear Mother,

Just a few lines to let you know I got your letter Well my mail isn't coming too good but I do get a letter once in a while. I just got a letter from Ernest today and he was ok. He said that he had 102 points but didn't know whether it would help him to get back. I show do hope they will. It looks like the points system isn't getting so many back. It will be a long time before I get back I don't think I will get back this year. I have give up all hopes Mother I guess the time we get back all the old people we know will be dead. I guess by the time you get this letter you will be back from Bessie I hope you had a good time and I know you did. I got a long letter from Bessie and I still have to answer it. I also got a letter from Herman the first I got from him since he left S.C. I don't think he likes what he is doing. Mother you asked me to send you some [?Banners?]. Well you know I haven't see one since I left the states but if I do you show will get them. Mother I sent two more package home and in one of them is some films and you put them away in a dark place and keep them for me. The other box is some things from prisoners. Did you get the big box I sent I had a lot of thing in there some perfume for you and two little box for the other kids one scarf for you two blankets those blankest are hand made. Arabs make them in Africa. Well from what Elizabeth said I guess the home was all fixed up when you got back.

Love Gilbert

ARTHUR L. JOHNSON

S/SGT GILBERT FRANKLIN 6832 PW OVHD DET APO. 772. C/O PM NEW YORK, NY
July 17, 1945 France

Dear Poppa,

    I have been trying to write to you all the week. Well I am working every day haven't been feeling so good for the last few weeks it might be that I am homesick. I just heard from Ernest and he was fine he show do get around a lot don't he. Well Poppa I show will be glad when I can come back home, I have got enough over here. Poppa don't forget to save me a good drink you know I never touch a drop over here and it so many men over here now, it's not safe to get out the camp. If they don't send them soon where I don't know what will happen. Poppa it will be a good while before I will get back. So there is one thing I want to tell you I want to see all of you. And you are too old to do hard work now you take it easy and <u>don't</u> you do any kind of cement work. I can't do the thing I use to but when I get back I know I can make enough we can live on. Now don't forget what I ask you.

Love Gilbert

S/SGT ERNEST H. FRANKLIN 13TH TCS, 403RD TCG. APO 920 C/O PM SAN FRANCISCO, CALIFORNIA
July 30, 1945

Dear Bessie,

    I was beginning to think that I wasn't going to hear from you anymore. I would have written sooner but as you know I told you when I received a letter from you I would write.

I hope these few lines finds you all o.k. as for myself I am o.k.

Well Bessie I have had quite a number of letters from Gilbert lately and he seems to be getting along o.k. but didn't think he would be coming home for some time yet. Bessie I also wrote him on the subject of Jimmie, and in my reply I think he is going to consider the matter when he gets back before he does anything that he will be sorry of. I know it is as hard as hell on him, but I think he will do the right thing when he gets back.

Well Bessie I had a letter from Mama and I think she enjoyed very much being up there. I also had a note from C.A. and I think she is enjoying being down home. Mama seems very pleased to have her, as she said that she was quite a lot of help to her.

Bessie do you ever hear from Herman I haven't heard from him since he left S.C. but the last letter I got from home they said that he had been assigned to a new company as a [?Palagraphia?]. I guess he should do all right as I think that is what he likes.

Bessie I had a letter from Russell F. not long ago and he is over this way, and on my last trip I was only about fifteen miles from him, but I didn't get to see him, but I hope to the next trip. It won't be long before I will have a new APO number then I should get to see him just after. I sure hope that we can get together.

Bessie tell Mickey that I received his letter and will answer it in the near future. Well Bessie there dosen't seem like there is much to wright this time so until I hear from you again the best of luck

Love
Ernest F

AUGUST

The first and second atomic bombs drop on Hiroshima and Nagasaki, Japan. Japan surrenders.

> S/SGT GILBERT FRANKLIN 6832 PW OVHD DET
> APO. 772. C/O PM NEW YORK, NY
> Aug. 1, 1945 France

Dear Mother,

    I think I owe you two letters, but I have been so busy I just haven't had time to write to anyone. Look like we have more work now than we ever did. It been so hot here and it hasn't rain here for over six months and the wind and dust is so bad. I don't think I have ever seen a storm over here. I don't see how the people raise anything here. Well Mother I am glad you got the package I have forgotten what I had in it but those two blankets I got those in Africa they were made by the Arabic hand made. The wooden soldier was made by a prisoner and gave to me. When I come back I will tell you all about the thing I still have another package, beside the films I have an old long watch and a compas tell Poppa the watch is for him if he want it. Did you ever get the picture I had drawn of Ernest? One of the prisoners did it and I thought it was good. Well there are a lot of beautiful places over here but just let me get back there I have seen all I want since I been over here. Mother those flour seeds are all the same kind but when I get a chance I will get some more and send you. I would like to send a lot of thing but I just don't have the time to do any thin. One of the fellows that work for me so long he left for home this week he is over 40 years. I show do miss him he was a good man. That the only ones that they are sending home. I see some papers from back there where they say that all the men with 85 points and up was either home or on their way.

Well that's a lie. All our Co has from 85 to 109 points now and all of us are here yet. Well I just hope I will get home sometime.

Love Gilbert

The results of Gilbert's Fishing trip.

ARTHUR L. JOHNSON

S/SGT GILBERT FRANKLIN 6832 PW OVHD DET
APO. 772. C/O PM NEW YORK, NY
Aug. 25, 1945 France

Dear Poppa,

    I guess you think I will never write to you Well I have been very busy. I just got three letters today one from Mother, Gladys and Elizabeth and show was glad to get them. Well the fall of the year has begun here it's cool here now and the days are shot and it has begun to rain. I see where Herman is getting another breech going to NY.
    Poppa what did you think of the war being over in the pacific we were tickled to death I show do hope Ernest will soon be coming home. Look like I will never get back. Well I guess it won't be too long now before I get back if the 38 age go through. I will be able to get out Poppa I have you a knife not too good but the best I could get. It's an American case. I will send it to you when I get a chance. I have a few thing I want to send home and I will send it then. Poppa when I think I am coming I want you to get my car fixed up and in shape to run. I will let you know you might have to spend a bit of money but I have it. I will let you know when I will come. I think this coming month will be the biggest that ever went back We have twelve leaving the first of Sept. I show do hope I will get there by Christmas. Poppa did the films I sent home ever get there. And was there a hunting knife and a compas in one of the package I sent. I would like to send everything I have because they won't let you bring anything back any more. We have a time to even send a package any more. Poppa don't buy too mutch for the bath room wait until I get back because we want to put the right kind of thing in. If you get a chance you can get thing fixed for the [?cest?] pool.

Gilbert Franklin

The following photos are from Gilbert's collection. I believe he is the photographer. They appear to be the men heading home.

Heading to the ships.

Several ships ready for departure.

On board the ship heading home.

On board the ship heading home.

Arriving in New York harbor.

SEPTEMBER

Japanese instrument of surrender is signed on board the USS Missouri, September 2, 1945.

> S/SGT H. B. FRANKLIN, DISPOSITION AREA 8,
> CAMP KILMER, NJ
> (September 23, 1945)

Hello Bess & Fred,

I know will be surprise to hear from me. I am in Fort Bliss. Was over in Old Mexico yesterday. I had a nice time. Will leave here tonight for the East.

Love to all
Herman

There are no letters from Uncle Gil to either my grandmother Bessie or to his parents since August 25; however, a telegram was sent to both on October 8, 1945. Here is the one to my grandmother:

```
Western Union Telegram
Oct 8, 1945
Mrs F J Conlon=
NA 789 FT15= AREA SEVEN CAMP SHA NKS NY 7 Mrs
F J Conlon=
North Danvilles St Arlington Vir=

BACK AT LAST FEELING OK HOPE TO SEE YOU
SOON LOVE.

GILBERT.
```

The next letter is from an Oscar Smith, a friend of Uncle Ernest. He returned before Ernest, and by the time the letter arrived in the South Pacific,

Ernest was on his way home or even home already. I included it because it describes the trip and what the boys went through to get back.

M. OSCAR E. SMITH
Abbeville S.C.

S/Sgt Earnest H. Franklin ~~13th Troop Carrier SpA 403d Troop Carrier G.P. HPO. 74 ℅ P.M. San Francisco, Cal.~~
Ret to U.S.A. Box XX Gretna Virginia
M O.E. Smith

Oct. 20, 1945

Hello Frank,

    I know you think I was never going to write to you. You know how it is. I have been taking my honeymoon and doing a lot of work. You know the kind I'm talking about. I haven't caught up with it yet either.

    I'm writing this letter to you but you may be on your way home. I sure hope you are. I see by the news that all the old veterans will be home by June. The news stated this morning that five thousands were flying back from the 13th air force and the [ILLEGIBLE].

    Let me tell you about that wonderful boat ride I had coming home. We had swell it at room. Down in a hole with about 200 other guys. One good thing though I didn't get sick as when I went over. Had to sweat on a boat for ten days and it took us 11 days to cross the Pacific. Six days to cross the States and six days to get a discharge. Some ride I can tell you. I lost ten pounds on that ride but I have gained most of that back with good food and a lot of <u>sleep</u>. (HA HA).

    Tony Delors had all of his money taken from him two nights out of San Francisco. You can bet I got my hands on mine.

I haven't did any work as yet. I don't know when I will. For I don't know what I'm going to do. I have an application into to air lines for a job. Don't know what they will do about it as yet. I sure safe to get one there for they pay good wages.

You know what I told you when I left there. Well she have been looking at that [?culing?] quite often I can tell you. You can't make up for lost time so don't try. I have been giving it [?my all?] but it has about got the best of me instead. How is the fellows back there in the squad. if they are still there I sure hope a [?some?] of you [?travel?] come to the States. I know of one that is already here. Well Price is at home. I havn't seen him as yet. I would like to talk with him to find out how many came with him. You know he is from the town.

Tell [?Vallely?] hello and that I hope he is holding down that C-46. I would write him but I don't have his serial number. If you fellows are still there send me his number will you.

Boy this civilian life sure is the stuff I am telling you. There is nothing like it. I sure will be glad when you get back to it.

I didn't have any trouble getting a discharge. The first thing they ask me. Do I want a discharge and boy you should have heard me saying yes sir.

As I told you before I lost ten pounds coming home but I have gained six or more of those back. That boat was so hot down in that hole and they wouldn't let us sleep on deck. Then when I hit the States I had one of the worse cold I have ever had. I thought I was going to die. Cold too. I thought I was going to freeze.

A lot of things are pretty hard to get back here. Car tires are the hardest to get. Civilian clothes are not too plentiful. One thing though you can get all the gas you want to use if your tires will take the driving.

I will close for now. Hope you can read this writing. If you are not in the States or on your way I sure hope you are soon. Tell all hello. Keep them flying.

Your Pal
Oscar E. Smith

GILBERT C FRANKLIN
Gretna Va
Nov. 27, 1945

Dear Bessie,

I am like you I just can't seem to get any writing done. I guess I got this night. Bessie I don't know any one by the name Jonnie I don't see who it could be. Well we haven't done anything to the back room. I have tried to get some tools but just can't. And it has been so mutch company here you can't to do anything and the hunting season is just come in. Look like J. is having a time of her life. Well I can say one thing if she is having any more than I am she is going some. Bessie I won't write mutch because I might be up here last of this week or around the first of next

I am helping Poppa and I am so tide I thought I would have to lay down to write.

Uncle Gilbert must have been tired as he did not sign the letter, and it stopped about half way on the page, so I know a page is not missing. But all are home now.

CHAPTER 6

CLOSING THE BOX OF LETTERS

I had a long talk with my mother, Cynthia Ann, about the letters and what she remembers.

She told me about an October afternoon, walking home from school. Mom noticed her mother and someone else walking from the commuter train station. She recognized it was Uncle Gill, and went running to meet them. My mother was nine, going on ten. Uncle Gill stayed with them for a few days, then went on to Gretna, Virginia. He would eventually move back up to Northern Virginia and have a job working in Fort Belvoir as a steamfitter plumber.

Uncle Ernest transitioned out of the Army at Fort Meade, Maryland. From there, he traveled straight home to Gretna, not stopping at his sister Bessie's house as Gill did. Mom remembers being in Gretna at a family gathering after all were back. She said she remembers Uncle Ernest crying about all the bodies. He was with the planes as they flew the bodies back. That is what he is speaking of in the letter dated Aug. 23, 1944, when he said he needed "to forget some of this mess over here." Ernest eventually married Clara Scruggs.

When do we see the first signs of trouble from Jimmie? It is hard to tell, as she would write every day or at least every other day. You then have the mail stopping and starting as the troops move around, and delivery needs to catch up.

But in 1943, Jimmie took a new job, and much to the disapproval of Gilbert, went on a business trip to New York. She wrote a letter to Gilbert saying that she always thought he would be the first to take her there. Shortly after, the letters slow down in frequency. Did something happen in New York? In the Thanksgiving letter from Jimmie to her in-laws, it sounds as if everything is just fine.

The letters are arranged as written, not necessarily as when received. It could take one to six weeks to get a letter between the South Pacific and Virginia, depending on troop movements and battles. When the system is working, it takes as little as eight days.

In the letter from Ernest on January 25, 1944, he responds to one from Bessie in which she confides in Ernest about something she saw or heard. I guess Bessie was hoping she was wrong about what she saw and asked Ernest not to say anything about it to Gilbert. In his response, he states an incident that happened earlier and sounds to be of a similar nature.

On January 26, 1944, Gilbert showed concern for Jimmie because she said she was going home for Christmas but did not. On February 6, 1944, he wrote that the letters have stopped coming from Jimmie. On February 9, he wrote that she must not have liked the Christmas presents he sent to her.

By February 15, Bessie's letter to Ernest reached him. He responded that he was "sure sorry that Jimmie is acting like she is, as she thought so much of Gilbert," and mentioned she should go and try to talk with Jimmie. The letter would have arrived in Arlington, Virginia, around the 22nd, and would have then set into motion the events leading to the cablegrams and Bessie's letter on February 24, 1944.

The whole of March is comprised of letters getting delayed, adding miscommunication and frustration that they cannot handle the issue with speed because of the war.

In Jimmie's letter on February 23, 1944, she states that she had not felt the same since they last saw each other in February 1943. The Thanksgiving letter makes it sound as if all is fine. Was that a letter of guilt, or trying to rekindle a lost marriage?

I simply do not have all the facts on Jimmie.

The last envelope from my mother contained a letter from lawyers stating the items my grandmother and Jimmie were to hand over to one another to complete the divorce. The letter was dated 1948.

I found the divorce document online. It stated Jimmie's name as Mary Elizabeth and the marriage date as November 1942. I can only assume the marriage referred to in Ernest's letter of May 6, 1942 was not recognized by the army, and they had a civil wedding in Rockville, Maryland, in November when Gill was home on leave.

There were some letters in a box of pictures from Gill, dated 1953. One was from a woman named Eloise and was written as if they were dating. In the letter it mentioned troubles with Jimmie again, as if it was not yet all over. Gill never remarried.

If I ever met Gill, I do not remember. I was born in 1960, and he died in 1963, at the age of 56, from a brain hemorrhage.

I remember meeting Uncle Herman and Aunt Cleo. One summer, we were vacationing in Pennsylvania, and we stopped by for the day. I remember them as kind and gentle folk, always smiling. They had a small house with a big yard that was all vegetable garden. I guess that was a holdover from the depression and growing up on a farm.

I never met Uncle Ernest. I went down to Gretna only once as a child, and Uncle Ernest, who lived in Roanoke at the time, could not make it the weekend we were there. He died in May, 1992. Uncle Herman died one month later.

In 1949, Joseph Campbell wrote his book, *The Hero with a Thousand Faces*, where he analyzed the narrative of myths like *The Iliad* and *The Odyssey*, to name a few. In the book, he describes a storytelling structure called the hero's journey, which explains how the hero in most stories goes through seventeen stages. In *The Writers' Journey*, Christopher Vogler changes it to twelve levels.

These stages apply to the three uncles, as they likely do to most soldiers (heroes) of the war.

The "Ordinary World" would be the first letter, traveling home from Thanksgiving in 1940.

Their "Call to Adventure" would be the bombing of Pearl Harbor.

Next we have the "Refusal of the Call." Some men joined the Army within a few days of the attack, while others waited for the draft notice to arrive. Refusal here would mean jail.

"Meeting with the Mentor" is basic training.

"Crossing the First Threshold" is traveling, to the South Pacific for Uncle Ernest and to Tunisia for Gilbert.

"Tests, Allies, and Enemies" include the first separation from home, then moving camps as the battles move.

"Approach to the Inmost Cave" and "The Ordeal" include changing duties, news from home, and losing loved ones—both at home and friends on the field.

There was a "Reward." We won, but at what cost?

And the journey is still not over. "The Road Back" is full of waiting.

"The Resurrection," in the myths, includes when the hero dies and comes back changed from the land of the dead—sometimes physically, and other times spiritually or emotionally. Here, all the men who survived the war are all changed in some capacity. None were ever the same.

"Return with the Elixir" is not a magic potion in this case, but what each person learned about themselves.

Is life imitating art or the other way around? After reading the letters, I wondered if the great epics are just embellishments of events that happened. My uncles may not be Achilles or Odysseus, but they certainly underwent the journey of a hero.

PHOTOS

My mother also gave me a box of photos and an envelope of negatives. After reviewing them, I came to the conclusion that these were Uncle Gill's photos, but most were not labeled, so unfortunately I do not know when or where they were taken. Some were mentioned in the letters, but others I can only guess at. Some seem like they were taken right after battles, but most are clearly after the war has ended. In all, there are well over 250 pictures. I have included only a few here.

The pictures start with training camps at Camp Blanding and at Camp Edwards. After he deployed, Uncle Gill was the supply sergeant for the allied POW camps. After the war ended, while waiting for his turn home, he took pictures in the surrounding areas.

There are also a few photos sent home or to Gilbert of Ernest and Herman.

Herman Franklin (right) with a friend.

On the back, this picture is entitled, "Three Drunks." It is Herman Franklin (left), his first mess sergeant, and another mess sergeant.

A C-47 transport crew. The type Ernest flew on.

Soldier in barracks.

Uncle Gilbert on leave.

Nice, France?

Nice, France?

POWs that helped at the POW camp.

Maj. Gen. Reckard and Lt. Col. Rosma.

Maj. Gen. Reckard and Lt. Col. Rosma.

Lt. Gen. Sommerville and Lt Gen. Lee.

Lt.e Gen. Sommerville, Lt. Gen. Lee, Brig. Gen. Ratoy.

The perfume factory in Grasse, France.

JUST A FEW LINES

ARTHUR L. JOHNSON

JUST A FEW LINES

Gilbert, Herman and Ernest Franklin at home in Gretna, Virginia, sometime after October, 1945.

AUTHOR'S NOTE

I want to thank you, the reader, for your time. This book is reality without television. When I was first reading the letters back in 1997, I felt this story needed telling. Movies show strategy, tactics, and planning. These show what real soldiers were going through. I thought it could help others who have served, as well as those serving and their families. They are not alone, no matter how isolated they feel sometimes. For those who love history and World War II in particular, the letters could give insight into what the soldiers were going through.

I started to scan and transcribe all the letters in 2015, which took longer than anticipated. I found a service to help with the transcriptions. Reviewing the returned documents showed problems with the scans, and a few needed rescanning and transcribing. Some of the letters were not in an envelope, or the letter dated 1945 in an envelope postmarked 1943. Over the years, readers would not be careful in putting the letters back correctly.

In Chapter One, I mention that all the letters are at the Library of Congress. They were to be there before publishing the book, and it is still the goal to get them there. However, due to the COVID-19 pandemic, the Library is closed to the public. As soon as they reopen and start accepting donations, I will bring them the letters. It would be interesting to see if researchers can analyze the handwriting and the phrasing to get a picture of the mental state and stress the men were going through. I would have loved to include that information, but I am not qualified. I do believe the letters here still show the stress and loneliness.

Along with the letters, there were journals written by family members around the same time. I took a break from this project, and I published one of the journals in 2019 as *On The Eve of War: Three American Sisters Travel to Europe July to August 1939*. I issued that journal first to get an idea for the process of writing and publishing. It could also serve as a prequel to the letters.

I want to thank my uncles for their service during the war. And all who have served, no matter which engagement. Thank you, be safe to those currently serving, and know that you are not forgotten or alone.

Finally, it would help if you would be so kind as to leave a review. As an author, this helps to get the word out to the intended audience and others that will find the underlying story of interest.

www.ingramcontent.com/pod-product-compliance
Lightning Source LLC
Chambersburg PA
CBHW071229070526
44583CB00017B/2109